Rebound 1991

POETRY AND BELIEF
IN THE WORK OF
T. S. ELIOT

BY

KRISTIAN SMIDT

Skrifter utgitt av Det Norske Videnskaps-Akademi i Oslo
II. Hist.-Filos. Klasse. 1949. No. 1

OSLO
I KOMMISJON HOS JACOB DYBWAD
1949

Fremlagt i fellesmøte den 25. mars 1949 av Winsnes

A. W. BRØGGERS BOKTRYKKERI A/S

Preface.

There are many ways of making the acquaintance of a poet. I must confess that what I first found intriguing about T. S. Eliot was not the power of his art, but the knowledge that he was both a radically "modern" poet and a devout church-goer. This interesting and seemingly anomalous combination set me off in a pursuit of his ideas, aims and methods, a pursuit of which the present book is the outcome. I was fresh from immersion in the works of James Joyce, in which I had found form and private faith to be closely inter-related, and I was curious and eager to approach a writer in whose development a positive and traditional faith had come uppermost. It was in the course of the ensuing studies that I came to appreciate and admire Mr. Eliot's poetry for its own sake.

Now I agree with those who think that poetry should be primarily enjoyed and that the main task of criticism is to heighten enjoyment. But criticism has other tasks, too, which cannot be ignored on the ground that they are of secondary importance, and which may even be of the first importance when regarded from other points of view than that of aesthetics: philosophy, the history of ideas, cultural history, sociology, ethics and linguistics may all claim legitimate interests in literature. And it is possible to approach literature from a viewpoint which belongs to several of them at once, as well as to aesthetics. Such a composite approach is what I have attempted in the case of T. S. Eliot.

Undoubtedly the majority of Mr. Eliot's critics have occupied themselves with interpretation, and I presume that most of them have had enjoyment as their ultimate aim. Others have been urged by sheer analytic curiosity. The purpose of the present study is neither to *interpret* Mr. Eliot's individual poems, or even his poetry as a whole, nor to *analyse* them in detail. It would be presumptuous, in any case, to attempt an exhaustive interpretation, as many critics have already declared. Poetry cannot be altogether rationalised or be adequately expressed in any other terms than its own. And any exposition of its ideas must leave a residue that cannot be expounded. Nor is it of great avail to list and classify its ideas in order to understand it as poetry. James Johnson Sweeney, Louis L. Martz and others have detected many literary and philosophical echoes in their elucidations of Eliot's works. Such discoveries are helpful, but individual references to philosophers are not our present concern, unless they actually indicate more or less permanent views of the poet's. We are in search of Mr. Eliot's basic views and attitudes, not just the relatively valid ideas of the separate poems. I wish to determine the character of Eliot's poetry from a point of view which is not the purely artistic one, and as something that touches us in the ultimate questions of life and death. So we shall examine this poetry not only in terms of sensibility, or of poetic conventions, old and modern, as Professor Matthiessen, Mr. Raymond Preston and others have done, but in relation to Life in a very comprehensive sense. In one way my effort is parallel and complementary to that of Professor Matthiessen, though I would not claim the latter's insight and competence. Matthiessen stresses technique where I shall stress ideas. My point of view will be both ontological, ideological and aesthetic. About Mr. Eliot's poems as poems, I have accordingly little to say, save for possible stray remarks or occasional pronouncements where they are relevant to the matter in hand.

A further statement of my aims and terms of reference will be found in the Introductory chapter.

The need of a study of this kind has been well stated by Mr. R. P. Blackmur in the chapter from one of his works which is given in Leonard Unger's *T. S. Eliot: A Selected Critique*. There is a class of readers and critics, says Mr. Blackmur, "the members of which unfortunately cannot stop short on the level of their unconscious appreciation but necessarily go on, risking any sort of error and ultimate mistake, until they are satisfied as to what a poem means". This class "includes that very small sub-class of readers of 'greater sensitiveness and understanding' for whom the meaning of a poem reveals itself gradually". And it is this class which "confronted by a sensibility so powerful and so foreign as Mr. Eliot's, is determined to get at the means as well as the meaning". It is this class to which we think we belong by the need which we feel to clarify the writer's poetic views, and to which we are ambitious of belonging by the qualifications of sensitiveness and understanding.

Mr. Blackmur has actually handled the same subject as myself; but he has restricted his investigations to the Christian sphere of ideas and has hardly gone beyond an essayistic treatment of the subject. Nor have I come across any other more systematic treatment of the problems here approached.

It is in the nature of my subject that some slight overlapping is inevitable here and there. Thus no absolute dividing line can be fixed between the treatment of the material aspect (philosophy) and the treatment of the psychological aspect (belief) of the meaning of poetry. I trust, however, that the overlapping has been restricted to a minimum. In cases where the same quotations are used in different contexts, I have endeavoured to avoid stretching their meanings to make them answer different requirements.

A certain difficulty in obtaining books in these post-war days may have led to lacunae and cases of lopsidedness in my study which might otherwise have been avoided. Also I obtained Mr. Unger's *Selected Critique* too late to derive much real benefit from the bibliography attached to it, and the book of homage to the poet compiled by Richard March and Tambimuttu I did not manage to obtain till I had practically finished writing. I should like to recommend the essays by Luciano Anceschi and Brother George Every in the latter book as being both penetrating and particularly germane to my subject. They contain in condensed form much of what I have tried to elaborate, such matters as the basis of Eliot's poetic vision in physical perception, the conception of the unity of the soul, and the question of the relation of poetry and philosophy.

I regret not having known René Wellek's and Austin Warren's *Theory of Literature* while I was still writing. This excellent work would no doubt have helped to clarify some of my views and to confirm me in the integral view of poetry which I have been trying to suggest.

My thanks are due to Mr. Eliot for granting me personal interviews in which he very kindly and patiently answered the questions I put to him. He is of course not responsible for any of my opinions or my interpretations of his statements. I am also obliged to Mr. Eliot for permission to print quotations from *The Criterion* and from his address *On Poetry;* to Mr. Eliot and Faber & Faber for quotations from *Murder in the Cathedral, Four Quartets, The Use of Poetry and the Use of Criticism, Selected Essays* and minor quotations from other sources; to Mr. Eliot and the Editor for quotations from the *New English Weekly;* and to Mr. Eliot and the Editor for quotations from *The Listener*.

Oslo, June 1949.

Kristian Smidt.

Contents.

— "I am not eager to rehearse
My thought and theory which you have forgotten.
These things have served their purpose: let them be."
                              ("Little Gidding".)

The various attempts to find the fundamental axioms behind both good literature and good life are among the
most interesting "experiments" of criticism in our time.
                              ("Experiment in Criticism".)

The restless demon in us drives us also to "interpret"
whether we will or not.
                    (Introduction to *The Wheel of Fire.*)

I.

Introductory.

The Poet and the Critic.

In certain lights the faculties of criticism and poetic creativeness may appear thoroughly incompatible: one seems destructive, the other constructive, one dull and earth-bound, the drudging Caliban of literature, the other gay and heaven-aspiring, its skylarking Ariel. But a more penetrating light easily reveals the intimate relationship between the two, and shows us that they are simultaneously creatures and inhabitants both of the poet's mind and of the critic's.

To begin with, a good critic must not only possess a sympathetic understanding of the creative processes by which poetry is brought into being; he must also be able on occasion, if his criticism is to be positive and not merely fault-finding, to imagine other or more perfect discharges of the creative genius than those to be found in the works which he examines. And his own work of criticism should itself be a species of artistic creation.

As for the poet, he would never be able to exercise his creative gifts unless his critical faculty helped him to sort out and select what was valuable in the multitudinous impressions, fancies and ideas which came begging to form the material of his poetry. And by critical faculty I do not necessarily mean a conscious and ratiocinative faculty, but rather a quality of the sensibility itself which makes it act as a kind of filter to anything that impinges upon it.

Criticism may therefore rightly be said to be an integral part of creation.

A good poet must have a highly developed critical sensibility. But that is not to say that every poet must be a critic in the occupational sense, though, as T. S. Eliot points out in his wary way, "it is to be expected that the critic and the creative artist should frequently be the same person".[1] In point of fact, the poet-critic is a very common figure in the history of English literature, from Sir Philip Sidney to Robert Bridges. And as for the contemporary scene, there hardly seems to be a poet who does not also write works of critical appreciation or aesthetic theory: Herbert Read, Day Lewis, MacNeice, Spender, Edith Sitwell, Henry Treece, John Lehmann and many more are at least as prolific as critics as they are as poets.

---

[1] "The Perfect Critic", SW p. 16.

In the case of T. S. Eliot, it is hard to decide whether the poet or the critic should take precedence, so equally is his literary personality divided between the two. Measured by bulk alone, of course, his criticism would easily outweigh his poetry, but that would be an inappropriate way of assessing the importance of either. There would have been little need to determine the question of precedence if his critical writings had been more or less a logical projection of the critical activity that went to the composition of his poetry, for then the two forms of writing would have been obviously complementary. But as it is, he writes relatively little of his own experiences as a poet and still less does he philosophise in general terms about aesthetics. His prose writings therefore appear as a thing apart from his verse, dealing as they do mainly with his impressions of other poets. And when he does enter the field of general ideas it is frequently — or so at least it appears — to trample the ground from which his lyrical flowers are culled. Paul Elmer More found his poetry chaotic and out of keeping with the classicist views expressed in his prose, and similar objections have been voiced by many others. Eliot is generally recognised as a great poet and an important critic, but his reputation is clearly divided between these two component capacities.

There is sufficient evidence to show that Eliot himself regards his critical work as of some importance. In saying this, I am not imputing to him any arrogance in regard to his achievement, which would be foreign to his nature, but merely indicating his conception of the sort of task he has been engaged in for about thirty-five years.

As early as 1917, in "Tradition and the Individual Talent", he enunciated his view that the whole past order of literature was continually being altered, not only by the shifting outlook of every new age, but by the very fact that new works were constantly being added to the total pattern of literature. And on a later occasion he stated that "every hundred years or so, it is desirable that some critic shall appear to review the past of our literature, and set the poets and the poems in a new order".[1] Such major critics were Dryden, Johnson and Arnold. When Eliot himself began to write, he felt acutely that a new work of adjustment, a revaluation of past poetry for the benefit of the twentieth century, was needed; and whether or not he imagined at that time that he might join the succession of major critics, it is obvious that he set himself to perform this task for his own age. It is largely due to Eliot that the poets of the seventeenth century have become as prominent as they have in the mind of our generation.

Another early tenet of Eliot's was that poetry must be directly nourished from contemporary speech. And because poetic diction always tends to petrify after a certain time, continual efforts must be made to keep the life

---

[1] UPC p. 108.

stream of language open. This duty, of course, it is particularly incumbent on the poets to perform, and Shakespeare, Dryden and Wordsworth had in turn performed it in earlier periods.[1] But such a task obviously calls upon the critic in a poet, and it was first and foremost as a critic that Eliot realised the necessity of "another revolution in idiom" shortly after the beginning of the present century, and planned, with Ezra Pound and others, to effect the revolution in a new style of poetry.

We need only add Eliot's unusually high regard for the critical labour involved in the work of creation [2] to understand what importance he attaches to the critical side of his activity. As for his real achievements in the field of criticism, they have been praised by numerous authorities. Ezra Pound, in his *Polite Essays,* pays a glowing tribute to Eliot's integrity and acumen. Eliot's paragraphs, he says, are "as clear, and deep, as incisive and as subtle as the delicate incision of a great surgeon".[3] Professor Allardyce Nicoll, who knows the Elizabethan and Stuart periods as well as anybody, is an admirer of Eliot's scholarship and judgment. And in a well-reasoned and valuable book by John Crowe Ransom we find the estimate that "Eliot is a critical scholar on the order of Dryden, or Doctor Johnson. — — It is likely that we have had no better critic than Eliot".[4]

Mr. Ransom finds Eliot the critic at loggerheads with Eliot the poet: they are a Jekyll and Hyde, and Ransom does not seem to care much for the Hyde. However, in spite of Mr. Ransom and all the other eminent men and women who have extolled Eliot-Jekyll the critic, and even, as it may appear, in spite of Eliot's own conception of his high calling as a critic, it seems to me that the poet is his more considerable character. For this preference, too, authoritative support may be found. Thus both Edmund Wilson and B. Ifor Evans apparently hold a higher opinion of Eliot's verse than of his critical writings.[5] I certainly think the poetry is *intrinsically* much more important, although the criticism, largely because of its timeliness and the way in which it was accepted and interpreted, has had a very great influence. As a matter of fact T. S. Eliot's influence in this respect is to a great extent that of earlier critics exerted at second hand through his own restatements, and much of the credit that has gone to him, is due in the first place to such people as Matthew Arnold, Arthur Symons, Ezra Pound, Rémy de Gourmont and T. E. Hulme.

I have no wish to detract from Eliot's reputation as a critic. I have a high admiration of his prose works and the greatest respect for his scholarship and discernment and originality. Thus it is only on the assumption that these things can stand some reduction in the common estimation without

---

[1] Cf. *Milton,* especially p. 18.   [2] Cf. "Function of Criticism", esp. SE p. 30.
[3] Op.cit. p. 102.   [4] RAN p. 139.   [5] Cf. AC, and Evans: *Eng. Lit. between the Wars.*

losing their significance, that I venture to insist a little on their limitations and on one or two weaknesses by which they are marred. My purpose is to establish, within the framework of this study, the superiority of Eliot's poetry over his criticism, and so justify a concentration of attention on the former.

T. S. Eliot himself repeatedly asserts that he has no capacity for abstruse thinking,[1] and in his own opinion he does not altogether deserve the reputation for learning which he acquired in his younger days.[2] Those who attempt to enthrone him as a literary dictator would do well to mark these statements. They are the words of a modest man, but they cannot be put down to mere modesty. A lack of definiteness is a frequent feature of his statements in prose, and he rarely hazards excursions into the lands of general theory or abstract speculation. When his climbing is at all steep, he likes to tie a rope round some jutting quotation or detail of style and work around from that to the end of his tether, being content with the general view of the landscape which he may obtain in this way. His treatment of poets is comparative rather than dogmatic, and this, though it gives him great freedom of movement within a given area, very much limits his horizon. J. C. Ransom finds him to be "a practitioner of Arnold's 'touchstone' method of judging poetry, though with infinite refinements; he cites, not the same handful of resounding lines for every purpose, but lines similar to the given lines, with an easy perception of which lines are best. No critic proceeds so regularly by the technique of comparative quotation".[3] Eliot's description of Swinburne as an appreciator rather than a critic,[4] might well be applied to himself.

In spite of his appeal to tradition, he more often conforms in his appreciation of literature to Gourmont's rule: "Eriger en lois ses impressions personelles." Accordingly we find no explicit code or system of opinion in his prose writings, and though something like a body of opinion may be compounded from his scattered pronouncements, the view of Eliot as a literary legislator owes more to his interpreters than to himself. True, in his youthful enthusiasm he did write a programmatic article of general scope, "Tradition and the Individual Talent", but this probably worked up an expectation for more of the same sort, which in turn fostered the illusion that Eliot actually was providing more of the same sort. He has given us such lectures as *The Use of Poetry*, "Religion and Literature" and *What is a Classic?* but no comprehensive or fundamental treatise. One often finds a sweeping interpretation of such phrases of his as "objective correlative" and "direct sensuous apprehension of thought", which may deserve a wide application, but which were not originally coined for general currency. There is also

---

[1] E. g. *Milton*, p. 6; CRI, Jan. 1932, p. 274. He certainly invalidates the statement somewhat by coupling himself with F. H. Bradley in this respect. [2] Cf. *Classics & Man of Letters*, p. 5. [3] RAN p. 146. [4] SW p. 19.

a mistaken notion that T. S. Eliot uniformly exalts the minor Elizabethans and the Metaphysicals as if on general principle, though his praise and blame of them are apportioned with great nicety.

Are we absolutely wrong in expecting a poet to have, or to elaborate for himself, some system of aesthetics? I think not, though no one can demand that he should present the public with any such system. Now Eliot professes to be incapable of remembering prosodic rules and distinctions,[1] to be uninterested in aesthetic theory[2] and even to believe that the study of aesthetics may be harmful to the creative ability of a poet.[3] He obviously has good reason to profess these things, but one sometimes feels that he is simply burking crucial problems, such as the problem of the use of poetry (art for art's sake or art for life's sake) or the problem of poetic inspiration. Instead he takes refuge in aesthetic opportunism.

That, of course, is putting an unfavourable construction upon his reticence. To see the matter in a more favourable light, we may remark that Eliot is keenly aware of the dangers of dogmatising and strives very earnestly to avoid them. He may have inherited from Santayana a distrust of "treating artificial problems in a grammatical spirit".[4] Writing about Machiavelli, Eliot says that the Florentine's thoughts form no system but that this merely shows Machiavelli's exactness of vision, "for a system almost inevitably requires slight distortions and omissions".[5] On one occasion Eliot suggests that he is by nature "trop disposé à mesurer toutes choses selon les règles d'une conception dogmatique qui tendrait de plus en plus à devenir rigide et formelle",[6] and that he must consequently train his mind to a more pliable treatment of literary matters.

Be this as it may, it is certainly true that Eliot does well to avoid abstract and general discussions, for those of his essays and studies which have a more prominently dogmatic character than the majority are relatively vague and poor. He often finds it hard to substantiate his general claims. Thus in the essay "Donne in Our Time",[7] and in *John Dryden, the Poet, the Dramatist, the Critic,* the author gives occasional concrete examples to illustrate his arguments, but the examples do not seem very relevant to his conclusions, which are based on a general appreciation (I am not saying, of course, that this makes them wrong). Eliot trusts that what he points out will be more or less immediately evident to his readers, but he sometimes takes too much for granted. In the lecture on *The Music of Poetry,* he never really specifies what is meant by "the music of poetry", whilst in the essay on *Milton* he gives insufficient evidence to prove his statements that "in Milton there is always the maximal, never the minimal, alteration of ordinary language" and that it is above all the paragraph that is the *musical* unit

---

[1] MUS p. 9.   [2] SFP.   [3] E. g. in UPC p. 150.   [4] Santayana: *Reason in Art.*   [5] *For L. Andrewes,* p. 58.   [6] "Rencontre", *Nouvelle revue fr.,* avril 1925.   [7] *A Garland for J. Donne.*

of Milton's verse.[1] A Swedish critic recently found *After Strange Gods* a typical instance of Eliot's inability to propound and develop an argument.[2] And the sociological study, *The Idea of a Christian Society,* is immediately exposed as superficial and ineffectual if any comparison is made with Maritain's *Humanisme Intégral,* which helped to inspire it.

That there should be inconsistencies and self-contradictions in a critic who has no coherent aesthetic theory is no more than is to be expected. Eliot himself admits them[3] and thus takes the edge off any complaints that we may make. He might have done well to have worked out an aesthetic for himself, if only to avoid inconsistency in his generalisations. Still, the trend of his criticism is usually clearer and less ambiguous than Yvor Winters, for instance, would have it.[4] It is more disappointing to find a certain prevalence of prejudice, which leads the author to treat men like Gilbert Murray and Matthew Arnold in a somewhat captious way.[5] In many cases Eliot has had to change or modify his view of a writer because he began by being too intolerant. But it certainly does him credit that he should have publicly expressed regret at his depreciatory treatment of, for instance, Arnold, Whitman and Milton.[6] At an early time Eliot took a stand against individualism in poetry. He has later been driven to accept individualism, even eccentricity, as in the cases of Milton and Kipling. He is somewhat specious in doing so, but manages to contradict himself with a fairly good grace.

It is part of Eliot's conception of criticism that the criticism and understanding of poetry can never be final, but must change with the times.[7] Thus he has some theoretical justification for the fluctuations in his own opinions of poets and their works. But it is hard to avoid discovering a measure of uncertainty in his views, as though he were unsure of his judgments. After an early period in which he found it exciting to pull down the mighty from their seats and exalt those of low degree, he developed a tendency to extol whatever personality he happened to be writing about — Pascal, Tennyson, Kipling — no matter how uncongenial an impartial observer might think they must be to Eliot. Thus his personal judgment is partly suspended when he is carried away by a subject. There is nothing unusual in all this, and it may be only comforting to see that Eliot is fallible like the rest of us. But there appears to be a deep-rooted diffidence in his nature which is one of his peculiar and characteristic features. He is seized at times by a logical fury, which makes him disdain to avail himself of any arguments that he himself can gainsay. But such stringency is in one of its aspects only another form of diffidence; it springs from a profound distrust of whatever is not entirely irrefutable.

---

[1] *Milton,* pp. 9, 12.   [2] C. Schaar in *Bonniers Litterära Magasin,* mars 1948. [3] MUS p. 8.   [4] Cf. SELCR.   [5] He censures Arnold for inconsistency in his essay on Bradley (cf. SE p. 414).   [6] Cf. SW p. XI; "Ezra Pound", NEW, Nov. 7, 1946; *Milton.*   [7] Cf. "Shakespearian Criticism from Dryden to Coleridge", *Companion to Shakesp. Studies.*

Eliot tells us that F. H. Bradley always assumed "an attitude of extreme diffidence about his own work".[1] The same might be said of Eliot. But he is not only modest about his work as a whole. Within this work his opinions are usually given with the utmost wariness and fenced about with qualifications:

> And his conversation, so nicely
> Restricted to What Precisely
> And If and Perhaps and But.

Diffidence seeps into his very style. It does not make it "unpleasant to meet Mr. Eliot", but at times his constant circumspection may be just a little irritating.

Miss M. C. Bradbrook has written an excellent appreciation of "Eliot's Critical Method". She is of the opinion that "the influence of Mr. Eliot as a critic must surely be noted rather in the history of taste than in the history of ideas",[2] and, further, that "Mr. Eliot employs criticism not to the communication of truths but to the co-operative delineation of the poetic experience".[3] I think Miss Bradbrook is perfectly right. The limitations and weaknesses that we have noted in T. S. Eliot's critical works have probably prevented him from becoming a theoretician of his art or a critic of the philosophical or purely scholarly type. He does not really belong to the fraternity of Croce, Curtius, More, Fernandez. But his limitations have perhaps made him all the greater as a connoisseur of poetry. His freedom from dogmatism, his attention to detail, his ability to change his ground and his mind, and his careful precision when formulating an opinion combine to make him one of the best arbiters of taste of our generation. It is extraordinarily enriching to have the beauties of Dante or Lancelot Andrewes pointed out by so discerning a judge. Eliot's power of relating the concrete and particular to the abstract and general may not be impressive; his capacity for close reasoning may be limited; his loyalties and prejudices may be fortuitous in origin and subject to change; but his sensibility may be counted on; and his prose style, though sometimes hesitant, has a remarkable finesse which has enabled him more than once to invent memorable phrases for subtle relationships. I must also point out that my negative remarks about Eliot as a critic do not touch him as an essayist pure and simple. As such he has few equals.

But all this means that Eliot's best qualities as a critic are precisely those which make him a poet, and which would, indeed, have made a poet of a lesser man than he. Sensibility and mastery of style may even be said to be attributes of the poetical *rather* than of the critical mind. And, on the other hand, the limitations which make themselves felt in Eliot's criticism

---

[1] SE p. 406.   [2] F3 p. 119.   [3] F3 p. 123.

impose no restrictions, or much less noticeable ones, on his verse. The "incapacity for abstruse thought" does not matter so much in poetry, where truth may be attained by a language different from that of reason. Logical inconsistencies, if rightly managed, often lend depth to poetic speech. And as the poet is freed from the anxieties of rational argument, his diffidence disappears at least in so far as expression is concerned (though he may write *about* the uncertainty that he feels, e. g. with regard to religion).

In poetry Eliot has made a virtue of the unsystematic and fragmentary form of composition. And it may be argued that his later poetry in particular is made all the more captivating by the latitude of dogma which it presupposes. Now a man who can give full scope to his positive qualities and at the same time turn his limitations to advantage only in poetry must surely be a poet primarily and anything else only in a secondary character. And in any case it is certain that Eliot makes a far stronger appeal to me as a poet than as a prose writer.

Nevertheless, the poet, as I have said, cannot in the last resort be separated from the critic. The value of Eliot's poetry is partly dependent on the extent to which it either illustrates the practicability of his critical views (e. g. the necessity of drawing on the style of modern speech), or, on the contrary, contradicts his theories. Nor can the verse be fully appreciated without reference to the views expressed in the prose. And the views expressed in the prose writings may legitimately be looked for in the poetic works.

Apart from that, the value of the poetry is largely a matter of taste and circumstance — of individual readers and of the generations to which they belong. Few people would be as unappreciative as the London bookseller who, on being asked for a book called *The Achievement of T. S. Eliot,* indignantly demanded, "What achievement?" And not everybody would rapturously compare Eliot's work with the Grand Canyon in Colorado, as does the author of *T. S. Eliot and the Lay Reader.* But between these extremes there is still room for many gradations, from admiration through indifference or bewilderment to vexation. And again, among the many admirers of Eliot's poetry, some will be found who admire it for this reason and some for that. It has assumed importance in our generation because it appeared at a time when a bold lead in a new direction was badly needed. But T. S. Eliot would be the first to recognise how differently his works may be treated in the future. Our children, if they read *The Waste Land* and *Four Quartets,* will almost certainly find other values in them than those which recommend them to us.

Yet we must assume that a genuine work of art has qualities of permanent value, whatever the occasion which produced it, or the circumstances in which it first appeared. And Eliot's poetry has now been with us so long that it should be possible to approach it from a fairly objective point of view. It has also reached a stage of development and maturity which enables us to compare its different parts and phases with each other and so disengage its distinctive artistic features from the temporary and fortuitous elements of which it is also composed.

The Aim of This Book.

Any attempt at a thorough appreciation of Eliot's poetry encounters a number of serious problems. There is first the problem of what the poet is saying, and of the feeling, tone and intention (to use I. A. Richards's concepts) with which he says it. To grasp his meaning fully it is necessary to have some acquaintance with his philosophy of life and to see how this philosophy has informed his poetry.

I do not aim at a line by line elucidation of Eliot's poems. This is a task which has already been often and skilfully performed in respect of most of the poems. The concrete and individual contents of his works I assume to be accessible to any intelligent reader who takes the trouble to look for them. But the general background of attitudes, beliefs and ideas from which the works have sprung is far too often ignored, though it determines the trend of much of the poetry, and continually affects us more subtly than we may be aware. Eliot's philosophy of life (using this term in a very wide sense) as it is evinced in his poetry, and as distinct from his merely aesthetic ideas, is a field which has not been properly explored. For it is not enough simply to find, as many people do, a message of despair in his early poetry, and a Christian message in his later poetry. Philip Wheelwright's essay on "Eliot's Philosophical Themes", included in Mr. Rajan's symposium, is unsatisfactory. R. P. Blackmur, from the standpoint of a sympathetic outsider, has written an interesting and stimulating study of the relation between Eliot's poetry and his religion,[1] but it remains somewhat sketchy. James Johnson Sweeney traces a number of philosophical connections in his reading of "East Coker",[2] and several other writers, including such eminent critics as Edmund Wilson and F. O. Matthiessen, have given us aspects of Eliot's philosophical attitudes. But few, it seems, have attempted to correlate the different aspects or to study their real significance in the whole scale of values proper to Eliot the poet.

One of our first aims, then, must be to investigate Eliot's philosophical assumptions. It may seem presumptuous for one who is neither a philosopher nor a theologian to enter upon a labour of this kind, especially when we consider that the object of this enquiry devoted himself wholeheartedly for several years to the study of numerous and diverse philosophies. But the very magnitude of the task may serve as my excuse: for since it is manifestly impossible to trace all the ideas and beliefs which have gone to the

---

[1] Cf. SELCR.　　[2] Ibid.

making of Eliot's poetry, it would seem to be the most useful thing to point out only the main streams of thought and their inter-relations, leaving aside both the detailed exploration of these streams, and of the minor rivulets of belief and speculation which appear here and there. In this endeavour we shall be comforted by the knowledge that when literary criticism ventures into the fields of theology, politics, the natural sciences, etc., it is doing its duty to literature, and not posing as an expert in these fields. Nor can expert knowledge be legitimately demanded of it, so long as it contents itself with general principles. Literary criticism has to do with technique. But it also has to do with thought.

To a critical mind, the clarification of the philosophy of a poet is not only a work of appreciation; it also helps enjoyment. Possibly Eliot has a number of readers who are able to enjoy his poetry without puzzling over it in the least — a happy brotherhood indeed. But probably the majority of his readers find that their pleasure in his work increases in proportion to their patient study of it. And such readers will hardly stop short at Eliot's technique and concrete "plots" and declare that they have understood enough. It is a very powerful curiosity that impels one to discover the genesis and sources of a poem that pleases one. Whether this curiosity is legitimate from an aesthetic point of view is another question. But at least discovery of this sort satisfies one kind of need as much as the direct impact of the poem satisfies another (or the same) need.

Personally I think intellectual understanding, if it is not carried to the extreme at which it becomes merely disintegrating analysis, may be a powerful aid to the enjoyment of such poetry as Eliot's. Nevertheless, it is not my *aim* in this study to further the enjoyment of his poetry, at least not directly.

I wish rather to determine the relation of the poet's thought to the philosophical directions of our time, to examine his pattern of ideas and estimate its cultural significance. In this connection it will be apposite to enquire whether Eliot is fundamentally an individualist or a traditionalist, his position being somewhat ambiguous on this point. "Pour Rémy de Gourmont, le symbolisme était avant tout le culte de l'individualisme en littérature",[1] says M. Taupin. Eliot no doubt shared de Gourmont's view, but at the same time strongly urged the necessity of an objective tradition.

An important problem will be the extent to which the poet is concerned with *what* he says, and the extent to which he is concerned with *how* he says it. This is the old rivalry between form and matter, which is given added actuality by the fact that both these categories seem to clamour so pointedly for attention in Eliot's poems, and by the fact that his critical writings contain interesting remarks on poetry and belief. Do these remarks show a definite attitude, and, if so, can they be applied *ohne Weiteres* to the

---

[1] *L'Influence du Symb. Fr.,* p. 43.

poetry? Do the categories of form and matter make an integral whole in Eliot's work, or must they be viewed separately?

These are questions which it is part of the purpose of this study to answer. But in turn they raise questions of principle, which can very conveniently be dealt with in connection with Eliot's poetry. Because the poet in his later phase is a professing Christian and uses religious themes for his works, we have to ask ourselves whether any aesthetic view of poetry as an autonomous field of human activity can be reconciled with the demand of Christianity to be all in all. We shall have to decide, in the case of Eliot, whether or not he has confused issues by using matters of belief as mere material for his poetry. And it will be interesting to see whether he fits into Henri Brémond's description of the poet as a kind of mystic, or Mr. Montgomery Belgion's conception of him as an "irresponsible propagandist".

It will be seen that the question of faith and imagination is a crucial one. Accordingly this study will be chiefly a critical examination of the import, ideological, aesthetic and cultural, of Eliot's work, with especial reference to the relation between poetry and belief, or poetry and meaning, (in theory and practice). In determining the ideas that are incorporated in the poems, it will of course be necessary to compare the poems with the essays. Thus Eliot's ideas on art give us his own conception of his work. This may not be right in all respects: we must always remember the distinction between the intention of the poet and the final effect of the poetry. But the poet's conception of his work is in any case an important clue to his meaning.

The poems can and must be deciphered in philosophical terms. But it is unnecessary for our present purpose, even if it were possible, to decipher them in terms of personal experiences. Eliot derides this kind of deciphering.[1] It is undeniable that the poetry may have its most significant sources in private experiences, and that we are curious to know these experiences. But since we must renounce knowing them out of respect for the poet's privacy, it is comforting that the poetry itself gives us the terms of reference that we need to enable us to examine its outward and public significance. In principle, then, we are not concerned with the poet's private life, nor is it our business to try to analyse and reconstruct his psychological make-up. Yet the private citizen cannot be entirely separated from the poet or the critic, for they all dwell together in one person, and, unless we are prepared to plunge into dark profundities of argument, we may take it that they *are* one person. A man does not simply arrive at his opinions by logical deductions from accepted premises, nor does he write poetry by a process of mechanical gestation of impersonal matter. Therefore the life of a writer always concerns us up to a point — the point at which we know enough to understand what he really wishes to convey and to avoid being held up in our enjoyment by his peculiarities and particularities.

---

[1] Cf. *Nation & Athenaeum* Feb. 12, 1927.

Thus, especially if we wish to estimate the cognitive nature of T. S. Eliot's poetry, it is necessary that we should know something about his life: his geographical and cultural environments in successive periods, his main activities and interests, salient events in his career, and the people with whom he has most closely associated. Eliot has always been reticent with regard to his personal history, and apparently there exists no biography of him of any length. Many things must remain obscure. But there still remains enough, I think, to give an adequate background to our study. Much, of course, can be inferred in a general way from our knowledge of the places and people that Eliot has known.

Biographical Sketch.

There is one advantage in being dependent for biographical information mainly on the occasional and fragmentary remarks of the author. Though he obviously has not made mention of everything of importance in his life, at least we may assume that most of the things he *has* mentioned have struck him as being of some importance. And so we are spared the labour — impossible to carry out perfectly in any case — of sifting the great from the small.

In the development of every man it is probably the first thirty years or so that count most. Knowledge and experience come to him with the greatest novelty in those years, his interests become clear to him and his profession is chosen or forced upon him. His opinions, tastes and attitudes have usually solidified in their main outlines by the time he is thirty. Afterwards comes a slower accretion of knowledge and experience, and, though sudden illumination and sudden changes occur, the rest is normally adaptation and modification on the existing basis, as well as the gradual strengthening or the gradual crumbling of that basis itself.

In T. S. Eliot's case it seems that growth and development were protracted over a somewhat longer period than usual. He was still allowing himself to be guided quite extensively by the opinions of others when he was well over thirty, as is evident from his submission to Ezra Pound in the drafting of *The Waste Land*. His period of acknowledged Christianity did not begin till he was almost forty, and the process of freeing himself from the tutelage of others and from old prejudices can be traced to quite recent years. It may be asserted with some plausibility that Eliot only found himself in middle age. Nevertheless, the impressions and events of his early life have doubtless been of great significance,[1] and accordingly a relatively large space will be given to them in the following brief review of his development.

---

[1] "The primary channel of transmission of culture is the family: no man wholly escapes from the kind, or wholly surpasses the degree, of culture which he acquired from his early environment." — NDC p. 43.

I shall omit, however, much of the factual information that may be found in such works as Kunitz and Haycraft: *Twentieth Century Authors.*

America and England may now vie with each other for the honour of Eliot's literary nationality, but in any case his beginnings were American, and his descent, moreover, American of the first water.

Eliot spent the first eighteen years of his life mostly in St. Louis; and it may be considered surprising, in view of the relatively short time that he spent in and near Boston, that his New England background should be so frequently and so strongly stressed.[1] But we must accept the fact that the old roots of Yankee families clung with particular tenacity to their ancient soil when transplanted to the loose sands of mid-western and western communities. It is credible enough that even the children should have imbibed in their home something of the atmosphere of Massachusetts, where their mother had grown up, whence sprang their ancestors on both sides, and where the family had its strongest connections.

Probably some of the glory of New England lingered with the family and was imparted to the children. But at the time of "Tom" Eliot's birth in 1888, New England culture was declining, and the Yankee spirit was not what it had been. "The Boston Mind", says Mr. Van Wyck Brooks, "once so cheerful, was full of the sense of last things, as if it hoped for no resuscitation".[2] The literary tradition was exhausted, and the religious tradition, dissolving before the progress of Roman Catholicism, Jewry and Christian Science, was also in an advanced state of decay.[3] The fatigue may have communicated itself to some extent to the Bostonians settled in St. Louis, and if this is so, it would not be idle to suppose that some of the seeds of the pessimism which flourished in Eliot's early poetry were sown in his childhood. His closer contact with New England life in his youth would tend, at any rate, to water the weeds of despondency among the sunflowers of his education.

The family background included the extreme development of Protestant rationalism known as Unitarianism, and the philosophies of Schleiermacher, Emerson, Channing and Herbert Spencer [4] were held in high regard. Unitarianism to Eliot seems intimately connected with what he calls "the Boston doubt: a scepticism which is difficult to explain to those who are not born to it. This scepticism", he goes on, "is — — — not destructive, but it is dissolvent".[5] In another context, however, he speaks of "the best aspect of Unitarianism, a kind of emotional reserve and intellectual integrity".[6] It is clear that in maturity he found much in this teaching that appealed to his temper, whether or not the temper itself had been gradually formed by the teaching. But a child must have been chiefly struck by the austerity of Uni-

---

[1] E.g. by Edmund Wilson; cf. AC p. 102.   [2] *New Eng.: Indian Summer*, p. 409. [3] Ibid. p. 414.   [4] Cf. Introd. to *Savonarola* by Charlotte Eliot.   [5] "A Sceptical Patrician", Athenaeum, May 1919.   [6] Book review, CRI, May 1927.

tarianism. It lacked the picturesque elements of most Christian doctrines. In
fact it excluded itself from Christianity proper: "I was brought up outside
the Christian Fold, in Unitarianism; and in the form of Unitarianism in which
I was instructed, things were either black or white. The Son and the Holy
Ghost were not believed in, certainly; but they were entitled to respect as
entities in which many other people believed".[1] This stern enlightenment
must have been salutary in many respects. But children need at least
as much nourishment for their senses and emotions as for their intellects. And
they take it where they can find it, irrespective of creed, as may be shown by
a piece of information that Mr. Eliot gave me in a private conversation in
1948. The reading of *Ash-Wednesday* had reminded me very vividly of
Murillo's beautiful picture of the Immaculate Conception, with the Virgin,
in white and blue, standing upon a crescent moon. On my question as to
whether he had ever been struck by this picture, Mr. Eliot said it was curious
I should mention this, because now he remembered that there had been
a steel engraving of Murillo's Immaculate Conception hanging in his
father's house.

Tom's father was in business, and the morality of the Puritan business
man pervaded his home. T. S. Eliot wrote in later life that in the Puritan
morality that he remembered, it was tacitly assumed that if one was thrifty,
enterprising, intelligent, practical and prudent in not violating social conventions, success was assured.[2] He has come to see this morality as a
"secular heresy", but it is not improbable that his own adherence to it contributed to his fair success in wordly affairs.

We have Eliot's words to the effect that Missouri and the Mississippi
have made a deeper impression on him than any other part of the world.
"I feel", he wrote to a St. Louis paper, "that there is something in having
passed one's childhood beside the big river, which is incommunicable to those
who have not."[3] However, the scenery of Massachusetts has entered into
his poems as much as that of Missouri. He tells us in one of his prefaces [4]
that his family "guarded jealously its connexions with New England; but it
was not until years of maturity that I perceived that I myself had always
been a New Englander in the South West, and a South Westerner in New
England — —. In New England I missed the long dark river, the ailanthus
trees, the flaming cardinal birds, the high limestone bluffs where we searched
for fossil shellfish; in Missouri I missed the fir trees, the bay and goldenrod,
the song-sparrows, the red granite and the blue sea of Massachusetts". The
river and the sea, associated in the poet's mind with two such different places,
become symbols of two planes of existence, as in the first section of "The
Dry Salvages". There, the river is "a strong brown god" —

---

[1] Book review, CRI, July 1931.   [2] Book review, CRI, April 1937.   [3] Quoted
by Matthiessen, ATSE p. 186.   [4] Mowrer: *This American World*.

> His rhythm was present in the nursery bedroom,
> In the rank ailanthus of the April dooryard,
> In the smell of grapes on the autumn table,
> And the evening circle in the winter gaslight.

And the sea has its

> beaches where it tosses
> Its hints of earlier and other creation:
> The starfish, the horseshoe crab, the whale's backbone;
> The pools where it offers to our curiosity
> The more delicate algae and the sea anemone.

These are boyhood observations put to a use undreamt-of when they were first treasured up.

It is possible that feelings of ecstatic happiness are remembered in connection with some of these observations. Sensitive children may be almost overpowered by unaccustomed impressions of colour and pattern such as they may gain from flowers. A friend of mine has told me of his sense of mysterious exaltation on entering a greenhouse for the first time as a boy. And Eliot speaks of "the experience of a child of ten, a small boy peering through sea-water in a rock-pool, and finding a sea-anemone for the first time." It may be a simple experience, he says, but is "not so simple, for an exceptional child, as it looks".[1]

There was enough for the eye in the landscapes in which Eliot grew up, and enough that called upon the activity of a youngster.

What is clearly a memory from childhood which frequently occurs in his poems, is the image of children climbing in an apple-tree in an orchard. It has become a symbol of innocent bliss, and is an instance of the poet's continual insistence on childhood as the period of happiness. One becomes aware that he feels quite strongly on this subject, and his childhood happiness fits well into our general picture of his development. This development is sketched — impersonally, but necessarily with much personal matter — in "Animula", where the child, in its first contacts with the world, takes pleasure

> In the fragrant brilliance of the Christmas tree,
> Pleasure in the wind, the sunlight and the sea;
> Studies the sunlit pattern on the floor
> And running stags around a silver tray;
> Confounds the actual and the fanciful,
> Content with playing-cards and kings and queens,
> What the fairies do and what the servants say.

But this serenity did not last:

> The heavy burden of the growing soul
> Perplexes and offends more, day by day;
> Week by week, offends and perplexes more

---

[1] UPC p. 78.

With the imperatives of "is and seems"
And may and may not, desire and control.
The pain of living and the drug of dreams
Curl up the small soul in the window seat
Behind the *Encyclopaedia Britannica*.

It seems that Tom Eliot, like most others, had not got it in him to submit passively to tradition and authority. And the way of ·knowledge was a thorny one to the young child. Perhaps "the drug of dreams", too, has a personal application, for as boyhood turned into youth it looks as if real happiness dwindled. "I am quite well aware", said the poet in a broadcast talk, "how unpleasant early youth can be or how few sensitive men were happy in it".[1] That young Eliot was more than usually sensitive we need not doubt, and since he was intelligent as well, his experiences came to him in double guise. "It is probable", he wrote when he was thirty, "that men ripen best through experiences which are at once sensuous and intellectual; certainly many men will admit that their keenest ideas have come to them with the quality of a sense-perception; and that their keenest sensuous experience has been 'as if the body thought' ".[2] It is possible that Eliot's later reticence and reserve were due to a delicate sensibility, which, too often hurt in an insensitive world, sought refuge in aloofness. Edmund Wilson suggests that Eliot, like Henry James and several other New England writers, spent much of his maturity "regretting an emotionally undernourished youth", the main cause of which was the Puritanism of his environment and upbringing.[3] Probably Mr. Wilson is unduly prejudiced against Puritanism, but there may be some justice in his words. As for the "situations unexplored" and the "passions inhibited" that Mr. Wilson darkly suggests, they must, if real, be left to the poet's privacy. We may speculate upon, but we must not infer too much from, what the poet himself has given us: namely the frequently recurring episode of an ecstasy of love broken and frustrated, in some vague period of childhood and youth, a scene in an arbour during a shower of rain, a girl with brown hair holding flowers in her arms. The scene is glimpsed in a great number of poems, in "La Figlia Che Piange", "Dans le Restaurant", *The Waste Land, Ash-Wednesday, The Family Reunion,* to mention the most conspicuous cases; and almost everywhere it is used as a symbol of frustration. However, the scene may have only a general application to the poet's feelings, itself being entirely imaginary, or it may have been suggested by Dante and others — so we would do well to refrain from biographical guesswork.

We do not know how school life agreed with Tom Eliot. But at Smith Academy he wrote, in his last year, his first published poems, which were printed in the school magazine. He refers to them himself as "verses in the

---

[1] LIS, April 6, 1932.   [2] "A Sceptical Patrician", *Athenaeum*, May 1919.
[3] AC pp. 102, 105.

manner of *Don Juan,* tinged with that disillusion and cynicism only possible at the age of sixteen".[1]

Up to now, his interest in literature had, by his own accounts, been sporadic. As a boy he had "a liking for martial and sanguinary poetry" such as *Horatius, The Burial of Sir John Moore, Bannockburn,* Tennyson's *Revenge.* But Shakespeare left him cold. Then, he says, "my early liking for the sort of verse that small boys do like vanished at about the age of twelve, leaving me for a couple of years with no sort of interest in poetry at all. I can recall clearly enough the moment when, at the age of fourteen or so, I happened to pick up a copy of Fitzgerald's *Omar* which was lying about, and the almost overwhelming introduction to a new world of feeling which this poem was the occasion of giving me. It was like a sudden conversion; the world appeared anew, painted with bright, delicious and painful colours. Thereupon I took the usual adolescent course with Byron, Shelley, Keats, Rossetti, Swinburne". This period he takes to have persisted until about his twenty-second year, and while it lasted his consciousness was from time to time completely under the sway of different poets, so that what mattered was not so much the actual poetry that he read as the "new and delightful feelings" in which he was absorbed. The frequent result was "an outburst of scribbling which we may call imitation, so long as we are aware of the meaning of the word 'imitation' which we employ. It is not deliberate choice of a poet to mimic, but writing under a kind of daemonic possession by one poet".[2] At school the boy was introduced also to the classic poets of Greece and Rome. He enjoyed very much reciting Homer or Virgil, he says, but in his own fashion, which meant that he ignored the metrical rules.[3] As for contemporary writers, or American writers, there were apparently none that made any impression whatsoever upon him. And this continued to be so after he had entered Harvard. Here are his own words:

Whatever may have been the literary scene in America between the beginning of the century and the year 1914, it remains in my mind a complete blank. I cannot remember the name of a single poet of that period whose work I read: it was only in 1915, after I came to England, that I heard the name of Robert Frost. Undergraduates at Harvard in my time read the English poets of the nineties, who were dead: that was as near as we could get to any living tradition. Certainly I cannot remember any English poet then alive who contributed to my own education. Yeats was well-known, of course; but to me, at least, Yeats did not appear, until after 1917, to be anything but a minor survivor of the nineties. (After that date I saw him very differently. — —) — — there was no poet, in either country, who could have been of use to a beginner in 1908. The only recourse was to poetry of another age and to poetry of another language. Browning was more of a hindrance than a help, for he had gone some way, but not far enough, in discovering a contemporary idiom. And at that stage, Poe and Whitman

---

[1] "Byron". *From Anne to Victoria,* p. 602.   [2] UPC p. 33—.   [3] MUS p. 9.

had to be seen through French eyes. The question was still: Where do we go from Swinburne? and the answer appeared to be, nowhere.[1]

About 1906 Eliot first read John Donne,[2] but it was his discovery of the French Symbolists that really launched him on his career. In 1908 he read Arthur Symons's *The Symbolist Movement in Literature,* which came to him "as an introduction to wholly new feelings, as a revelation".[3] "But for having read his book", he says, "I should not, in the year 1908, have heard of Laforgue or Rimbaud; I should probably not have begun to read Verlaine; and but for reading Verlaine I should not have heard of Corbière. So the Symons book is one of those which have affected the course of my life".[4]

How deeply it affected the course of his life only appears if we read it. One feels that Eliot may have modelled himself, simultaneously or in turn, on each and all of the writers presented by Symons, *as* presented by Symons. Of Huysmans, for instance, Symons says: "From the first he has been a man 'for whom the visible world existed', indeed, but as the scene of a slow martyrdom. The world has always appeared to him to be a profoundly uncomfortable, unpleasant and ridiculous place; and it has been a necessity of his temperament to examine it minutely with all the patience of disgust —." [5] And then, of course, we are introduced to the fastidious Laforgue, to Maeterlinck the mystic, and a number of others whose dominant traits may also be discovered in Eliot.

It was in the French Symbolists that Eliot found a hope for poetry, having failed to find it in what was being written in his own language. And it was chiefly to Jules Laforgue that he went for guidance. Laforgue was a poet of spleen and profound pessimism, and this may have attracted the young man, still in the grip of his Byronic cynicism. But above all he was intrigued by Laforgue's idiom and technique. Laforgue brought the modern world and its language into poetry, and he experimented with a great diversity of lines and broken sequences. Eliot was searching for some criterion of formal beauty which would enable him to master English verse technique. He had read the classics, but had never had a mind for the rules of prosody or even been "able to retain the names of feet and metres". So, he tells us, "when it came to applying rules of scansion to English verse, with its very different stresses and variable syllabic values, I wanted to know why one line was good and another bad; and this, scansion could not tell me. The only way to learn to manipulate English verse seemed to be by assimilation and imitation, by becoming so engrossed in the work of a particular poet that one could produce a recognisable derivative".[6] It is something like an irony of fate that Eliot should have learnt English verse

[1] "Ezra Pound", NEW, 31 Oct. 1946. Cp. also CRICOM, April 1934.   [2] Cf. "Donne in Our Time", *Garland for J. Donne.*   [3] SW p. 5.   [4] Book review, CRI, 1930.   [5] Op. cit. p. 138.   [6] MUS p. 9.

technique from a French poet, but the fact that he did learn from a Frenchman obviously helped to liberate him from the manners that had been exhausted by the Victorian poets, and enabled him to introduce a new sense of rhythm into English verse. He now actually made a "deliberate choice of a poet to mimic", and one of the nine poems which he published in the *Harvard Advocate* in the years 1907—1910 was "Humouresque. (After J. Laforgue)". Even one or two of the poems in his first printed collection, especially "Conversation Galante", are clearly imitations of Laforgue. Laforgue's *vers libre* he found to be analogous to the free verse of the later Shakespeare, and of Webster, Tourneur and other English dramatists of the same period, whom he also studied at this time.[1]

Presumably Eliot in his Harvard years did not seriously contemplate giving himself up to poetry. For one thing, there was nobody of standing in the literary world to encourage him. He declares that "at a time which may be symbolised by the figures 1910, there was literally no one to whom one would have dreamt of applying. One learnt something, no doubt, from Henry James, and might have learnt more. But Henry James was a novelist — —." As for such people as Shaw and Wells, "they lived in another world altogether. One did not read them".[2]

To-day we may find cause for congratulation in the fact that Eliot continued his academic studies, and did not fall into any temptation to do otherwise that he may have felt.

Books apart, far and away the most important influence in his Harvard days seems to have been that of Professor Irving Babbit. He knew him first in 1909, when Babbitt was instructor in French and when, as Eliot says, "his reputation was only amongst a few. — — his outspoken contempt for methods of teaching in vogue had given him a reputation for unpopularity which attracted to him some discerning graduates and undergraduates at Harvard University. — — The lectures which I attended were, I believe, concerned with French Literary Criticism; but they had a great deal to do with Aristotle, Longinus and Dionysius of Halicarnassus; they touched frequently upon Buddhism, Confucius, Rousseau, and contemporary political and religious movements. Somehow or other one read a number of books, Aristotle's *Politics* or Lafontaine's *Fables,* just because Babbitt assumed that any educated man had already read them." Eliot was also struck by "the frankness with which he discussed the things which he disliked, and which his pupils came to dislike too".[3] He found in Babbitt not merely a tutor, "but a man who directed my interests, at a particular moment, in such a way that the marks of that direction are still evident". He was to retain his affection for and admiration of the older man, though his views came to differ from Babbitt's. He paid a tribute of gratitude to his master when

---

[1] Cf. Introd. to Pound's *Selected Poems*, p. viii.   [2] NEW, 12 Sept. 1935.
[3] CRICOM, Oct. 1933.

he wrote in an article on Paul Elmer More: "These [Babbitt and More] seem to me the two *wisest* men that I have known".[1]

Babbitt was an authoritarian, in politics, in ethics, in education and in literature. An anti-romanticist, he believed in classicism and tradition, in the suppression of sentiment and the control of emotion. He promulgated his opinions with a fierce conviction, and allowed them to colour whatever subject he spoke upon. He would have been a movement all by himself, even apart from his friend Paul Elmer More and the discerning students who gathered around him. T. S. Eliot, at an age when he was making up his mind about things, was evidently fascinated by a man who did not hesitate to erect signposts, and for better or for worse his opinions remained stamped by most of the teachings of Babbitt. If Eliot had had leanings towards authoritarianism and anti-romanticism before, they were confirmed by Babbitt, and what the young man lacked in the way of dogma was supplied by his instructor. The main subject on which the disciple was later to differ from the master, was that of humanism. Babbitt, for all his abhorrence of eccentric individualism or sloppy enthusiasms, was an idealistic believer in human nature, its power to keep itself under an "inner check" and the possibility of creating a sound society by rational discipline. Eliot may have absorbed these views at first, but he later found them incompatible with Christian orthodoxy. He underwent a similar revulsion with regard to Babbitt's interest in Primitive Buddhism. Writing about Babbitt in 1937, he declared: "One of the reasons why Buddhism appeals to him is apparently his hostility to Platonic ideas, and his dislike of the Platonic influence upon Christian theology".[2] Nevertheless, Buddhism was an interest which Babbitt imparted to his disciple enduringly.

A contemporary of Babbitt's was George Santayana, who, then in middle age, taught in the philosophical department of Harvard University. But he was very unlike Babbitt in many respects. One has the impression of a very modest and unassuming personality. His philosophy, based on disillusion, was primarily that of an aesthete. His stoic religion, which he called naturalism, assumed that life had no meaning or metaphysical import, but that there was a unity in nature to which man belonged and that a relative purpose could be achieved by means of gratuitous good. "There is no opposition in my mind", he wrote, "between materialism and a Platonic or even Indian discipline of the spirit". He saw in his own philosophy a kind of pragmatism, though he could not stomach the William James of the later years, who gave himself up to "romantic metaphysics".[3]

Surprisingly enough, Santayana did accept "a pure and radical transcendentalism", which recognised no facts (these being in a different sphere of

---

[1] *Princeton Alumni Weekly,* 5 Feb. 1937.   [2] *Revelation,* I, p. 16.
[3] "Brief Hist. of My Opinions", *Philos. of Santayana,* pp. 12, 14.

perception), but only "essences", corresponding to the Platonic ideas. The realm of essences was an eternal and infinite one, to be penetrated by a species of thinking akin to poetry. "Many ideas", he declared, "may be convergent as poetry which would be divergent as dogmas".[1]

It is hard to find consistency in some of Santayana's ideas on art, best expounded in *Reason in Art* (1905). He seems to have believed both in supernatural inspiration and in the human intelligence each as the only source of art.[2] But it clearly emerges that he was a classicist, who had no use for speculative aesthetics; he believed "that imitation is a fundamental principle in art" and that "the specific values of art are technical values". Art, he thought, should aim at universality, by rendering universal and primary experiences and by expressing ultimate truths. It must be incorporated in the life of reason, and recognised for what it is: a servant with a useful function in our lives. "Romanticism, ritualism, aestheticism, symbolism" are names of diseases which tend to degrade art from its useful function. Santayana praises Virgil and Dante as classic poets,[3] and in a later work, *Three Philosophical Poets* (1910), he declares that the poet is never greater than when he grasps and expresses the philosophic vision of his universe, as Lucretius, Dante and Goethe did for successive ages.[4]

Many of Santayana's ideas would naturally appeal to Eliot. The philosophy of naturalism and disillusion might well attract a sophisticated young man who was immersing himself in the French Symbolists. The defence of classicism in its various aspects chimed with what Babbitt was teaching, and no doubt fell on good ground. Virgil, Lucretius and Dante were poets whom Eliot was to admire highly, though he was more critical of Goethe.

Another of Eliot's masters at Harvard was "that extraordinary philosopher Josiah Royce".[5] Royce was one of the leading monists and post-Kantian idealists. He held the whole universe to be contained in an all-comprehensive Mind, the Logos, or the Absolute; and to be differentiated within this Mind into individuals, both human, organic and "inanimate". The successive moments in the life of an individual were held together by a common memory in a larger self. But a richer life could be attained by the self, according to "the law of mediation", if it lost itself in devotion to other individuals and to common causes. In the ethical corollaries of Royce's philosophy, order and security were supreme goods, as with Babbitt. And loyalty was the greatest virtue of the individual, taking him beyond himself, and thus redeeming him for the complete life of reality. Royce's philosophy was voluntaristic in that it stressed the ability of the individual to work out his salvation by an effort of the will. But this effort was only made efficacious by the grace afforded by the Community.

---

[1] Ibid. p. 18. [2] Ibid. pp. 220, 250. [3] *Reason in Art, Philos. of Santayana,* pp. 231, 236—7, 241, 244, 247. [4] Op. cit., *Philos of Santayana,* p. 342. [5] Introd. to *Savonarola,* p. viii.

I think we may assume that it was Royce who led Eliot to take an interest in F. H. Bradley.

In the field of philosophy, F. H. Bradley was incomparably the most important literary influence on T. S. Eliot. He made a thorough study of Bradley's works, *Ethical Studies* (1876), *Principles of Logic* (1883) and *Appearance and Reality* (1893), and wrote his doctoral dissertation on Bradley and Meinong. Bradley, who was partly inspired by Hegel and Lotze, was an exponent of the new idealism, an opponent of the Utilitarian philosophy of Bentham and J. S. Mill and a critic of the somewhat mechanistic psychology of Bain and others. The *Principles of Logic* is a closely-reasoned attempt at establishing the paramount importance of universal notions over particular perceptions in various modes of thinking. Again we have something that reminds us of Plato's ideas. In *Appearance and Reality* Bradley endeavours first to prove, by a penetrating epistemological criticism, that all our knowledge is mere illusion and appearance. He then goes on to argue that even appearance exists in some sense, and must therefore form *part* of Reality. It only needs to be completed in a transcendent pattern to become fully real. Even pain and evil have their place in this pattern: being transcended, they are submerged in good. Bradley is less of a voluntarist and more of an intellectualist than Royce. He does not believe in individual immortality, but thinks that individuality is only a passing phase of the final Reality, or the Absolute, as he calls it. During this life of Appearance, however, we are isolated each in his own mind. Bradley develops a theory of "finite centres", according to which all consciousness is contained in closed units complete in themselves and yet united in the Absolute.

In his admirable essay on F. H. Bradley, Eliot describes the philosopher in words which would be very applicable to Eliot himself,[1] and which reveal a strong congeniality between the two. He praises Bradley's style, for which he has still a great admiration, and which certainly is extremely smooth. Eliot was probably captivated at an early date by this excellent and persuasive prose, but he was also struck by Bradley's wariness of extreme positions and by the "catholic, civilized, and universal" qualities of his philosophy compared with the "crude and raw and provincial" philosophy of the Benthamites. Bradley, he writes in his essay, had a large share of wisdom; "wisdom consists largely of scepticism and uncynical disillusion; and of these Bradley had a large share. And scepticism and disillusion are a useful equipment for religious understanding; and of that Bradley had a share too".[2]

In his University days, Eliot was completely in sympathy with the ideas of Bradley. But he soon adopted a more critical attitude. In an essay in *The Monist*[3] he demonstrated the similarity between Leibniz's theory of

---

[1] SE pp. 406—7.   [2] SE pp. 411—2.   [3] *Monist*, 1916.

monads and Bradley's theory of finite centres and found a weakness in both philosophies in that they had to have recourse to "divine intervention" to explain the connection that subsisted between the subjective units, or atomic universes. And Eliot's conversion to Anglicanism would naturally estrange him further from Bradley. But as we shall see in this book, the idealistic philosophies of Royce and Bradley never lost their hold on him.

Even in 1912, however, the Idealists did not hold the ground un-challenged. Their claims were disputed by the Realists, who apparently exercised a certain counter-attraction on Eliot, since he could later write of them as follows:

The Six Realists whose co-operative work, "The New Realism", made a considerable stir in the philosophical department of American universities in that year [1912] — — were animated by a missionary zeal against the Hegelian Idealism which was the orthodox doctrine of the philosophical departments of American universities at the time, and which had begun to turn manifestly mouldy. This Idealism was an inheritance from the times in which philosophy was generally taught by retired non-conformist ministers — — who accepted the Ethics of Kant and the mysticism of Schleiermacher. It is handled with tender reverence — — by George Santayana in his essay on "The Genteel Tradition in American Philosophy". The Six Realists were un-Teutonised, and on the whole anti-religious, which was refreshing; they were ascetically, even gloomily, scientific; and they professed consider-able respect for Mr. Bertrand Russell and his Cambridge friends. All this was to the good; but it must be admitted that the New Realism, like most pre-War philosophies, seems now as demoded as ladies' hats of the same period.[1]

It is no exaggeration to say that Eliot was completely absorbed in his philosophical studies. He has said in conversation that they *were* him at the time. During his visit to Paris in 1910—11, he listened to Bergson's lectures at the Sorbonne, and wrote an essay criticising his *durée réelle* as "simply not final".[2] Back at Harvard, he applied himself to the ancient philosophy of India, reading Sanskrit and Pali under the guidance of Charles Lanman and studying Patanjali's metaphysics under James Wood. The philosophical gain from these latter studies was meagre, he has admitted. He was left "in a state of enlightened mystification".[3] But *affectively* he was deeply impressed. And he is well aware that his poetry "shows the influence of Indian thought and sensibility".[4]

Anthropology and psychology were subsidiary interests. Eliot shows familiarity with the works of Durkheim, Lévy-Bruhl, Frazer, etc. He wrote a paper for Royce on "The Interpretation of Primitive Ritual". Royce was also interested in psychological experiments and experiences, such as the use of ether to produce an "anesthetic revelation" of metaphysical truth.[5] William James's theories of mental associations were dominant at Harvard.

---

[1] "Views & Reviews", NEW, 6 June 1935.   [2] ATSE p. 183.   [3] ASG p. 40.
[4] NDC p. 113.   [5] Morgan & Wohlstetter in HA, Dec. 1938, p. 29.

Vid.-Akad. Skr. II. H.-F. Kl. 1949. No. 1.

3

And at the time when Eliot wrote "The Love Song of J. Alfred Prufrock", the nature of schizophrenia was being investigated by Morton Prince and the "Boston School" of psychologists.[1]

After his short stay in Germany in 1914, Eliot went to Merton College, Oxford. He chose this college because of its associations with Bradley, (whom, incidentally, he never met), and because there he would sit under Professor Harold Joachim, who was not only a great authority on Aristotle, but also a disciple of Bradley's. Together with Bradley's Idealism, he continued his studies of the German Phenomenologists Meinong and Husserl. But above all he devoted himself to Aristotle and deepened a familiarity with and an admiration of that philosopher which could not fail to colour his general outlook.

His finished doctoral dissertation is dated 1916. But neither that, nor anything else by Eliot, was published during the years from 1910 to 1915. The philosopher in him lingered on, as we can tell by the essays in *The Monist* and a number of reviews in the *International Journal of Ethics* of 1916 and 1917. But he was soon swallowed up by the poet and the literary critic. We may, however, discern many of the features of the philosopher in the physiognomy of the poet, and these we will endeavour to describe in subsequent chapters.

During his years of study he kept up his interest in poetry, and wrote a number of pieces, some of which were to be included in his first printed collection. His Paris year must have been the realisation of a cherished dream fostered by his reading of the French Symbolists. It may have been the poet in him which chiefly profited by the stay. He perfected his French so successfully that he was able to write French verse of some merit. And he made friends among French poets. Many years later, in a *Criterion* Commentary, Eliot wrote of the Paris he knew in his youth. "I am willing to admit", he said, "that my own retrospect is touched by a sentimental sunset, the memory of a friend coming across the Luxembourg Gardens in the late afternoon, waving a branch of lilac, a friend who was later (so far as I could find out) to be mixed with the mud of Gallipoli".[2] This friend must be the poet Jean Verdenal, to whom Eliot inscribed his first volume of poems. He may even, with his branch of lilac, have entered into the composition of Eliot's favourite frustation image.

Another vivid impression of Paris was provided by the reading of Philippe's *Bubu of Montparnasse,* the story of sordid vanities and squalid loves, of deceitfulness and genuine emotions among the panders and prostitutes of the French metropolis. In his Preface to an English translation of this book, Eliot said that he first read it in 1910, when he first came to Paris. "Read at an impressionable age, and under the impressive conditions, the book has always been for me — — a symbol of the Paris of that time."

---

[1] Ibid. p. 28.   [2] CRICOM, April 1934.

After 1911 there seems to have been a lull in Eliot's poetic production. Philosophy engulfed him, and the need to make a career. He may not have thought that he had a future ahead of him as a poet. And anyhow he could not, and probably would not, make his living from poetry. But his poetic interests were no doubt instrumental in deciding him to settle more or less permanently in England.

The notion of settling there was not strange to him. As early as 1909, recognising "the failure of American life at present", he wrote in a book review of the class of "Americans retained to their native country by business relations or socialities or by a sense of duty — the last reason implying a real sacrifice — while their hearts are always in Europe".[1] Henry James was a Londoner, and was soon to become a British citizen. Pound, J. G. Fletcher, Aiken, H. D. and Robert Frost all lived in England in the years preceding and during the Great War. And Mr. Tinckom-Fernandez tells us that while at college he and Eliot discussed the idea of emigrating to a milieu more congenial to a writer, as Ezra Pound had done.[2] When Tinckom-Fernandez did go to Europe, Eliot saw him off. And in the following year he took ship himself. As it happened, his departure had something of finality about it. Eliot was not to see his childhood home again in the lifetime of his parents. Nor was he to see America again for eighteen years, by which time he was a British citizen.

The war-time London in which he settled must have been a very unpleasant place in many respects. But one doubtless had the feeling there that things were happening, and that, with courage and perseverance, much might be achieved. Eliot, at any rate, grew to like the huge, rambling town, in spite of many things that he detested, perhaps in part *because* of the things that he detested, for they gave him an outlet for the spleen that he was nursing and which craved an aesthetic release. He feels that he expressed great affection for the city in *The Waste Land*, and it is true that one finds a kind of paternal fondness for the ugly medley of streets, pubs, gashouses and barges that is visualised there. Eliot, having always been a town-dweller, confesses to ingrown urban habits,[3] and London has (or had) characteristics which make it, to him, "preferable to any other metropolis in the world" that he knows: "it is still to a great extent, a collection of villages the borders of which touch, each retaining a local character of its own". He does not need to be told, he says, that a number of the London villages he has in mind are scandalously filthy and ought to be torn down; he knows that quite well, and is not simply indulging a taste for the picturesque slum. But there is something he abhors, and perhaps rightly, more than the slum, and that is the "endless line of houses along a ribbon road over which passes a ceaseless stream of cars".[4]

[1] HA, 7 May 1909.　　[2] HA, Dec. 1938, pp. 47—8.　　[3] Cf. CRICOM, April 1938.　　[4] LIS, 30 March 1932.

The most momentous event during his first years in London, was no doubt his meeting with Ezra Pound. But again we will let Eliot speak for himself:

"I was introduced to *Personae* and *Exultations* in 1910, while still an undergraduate at Harvard. The poems did not then excite me, any more than did the poetry of Yeats: I was too much engrossed in working out the implications of Laforgue. I considered them, however, the only interesting poems by a contemporary that I had found. My indebtedness to Pound is of two kinds: first, in my literary criticism; and second, in his criticism of my poetry in our talk, and his indications of desirable territories to explore. This indebtedness extends from 1915 to 1922, after which period Mr. Pound left England, and our meetings became infrequent".[1]

"I had kept my early poems (including *Prufrock* and others eventually published) in my desk from 1911 to 1915 — with the exception of a period when Conrad Aiken endeavoured, without success, to peddle them for me in London. In 1915 (and through Aiken) I met Pound. The result was that *Prufrock* appeared in *Poetry* in the summer of that year; and through Pound's efforts, my first volume was published by the Egoist Press in 1917."

Pound was rather eccentric, but very kind if he became interested in anybody. "He was so passionately concerned about the works of art which he expected his protegés to produce, that he sometimes tended to regard the latter almost impersonally, as art or literature machines to be carefully tended and oiled, for the sake of their potential output."

"Whether the name and principles of imagism were Pound's invention or Hulme's, I do not know, and I am not very much interested. Imagism produced a few good poems — notably those of H. D. — but it was quickly absorbed into more comprehensive influences, including Pound's. Then, with *The Catholic Anthology, The Egoist, The Little Review,* Pound accomplished more than any other man could have done with anthologies and periodicals of such limited circulation. — — Pound did not create the poets: but he created a situation in which, for the first time, there was a "modern movement in poetry" in which English and American poets collaborated, knew each other's works, and influenced each other."[2]

Writing in 1946, Eliot still considered Pound's critical writing "to be almost the only contemporary writing on the Art of Poetry, that a young poet can study with profit".

"I think that Pound was original in insisting that poetry was an art, an art which demands the most arduous application and study; and in seeing that in our time it had to be a highly conscious art. He also saw that a poet who knows only the poetry of his own language is as poorly equipped as the painter or musician who knows only the painting or music of his own

---

[1] "On a Recent Piece of Criticism", *Purpose,* Apr./June 1938.   [2] "Ezra Pound" I, NEW, 31 Oct. 1946.

country. — — Pound's great contribution to the work of other poets — — is his insistence upon the immensity of the amount of *conscious* labour to be performed by the poet." [1]

Pound was learned. The literatures of Italy, of Provence, of China and Japan were well known to him; and he extended the interests and educated the tastes of those who gathered about him. In poetry he favoured a hard, unsentimental precision of statement, and an expression so clipped as to become enigmatic. He taught the necessity of taking contemporary speech as a model of style, of choosing for subject-matter and imagery "topics and objects related to the life of a modern man or woman" and of seeking material that in itself was non-poetic. [2] The results called down a good deal of abuse upon the heads of the innovators, [3] but they were undismayed.

Pound it was who made Eliot see W. B. Yeats in a new light, [4] who induced him to study Gautier [5] and who confirmed him in his admiration of Dante.

It was only after some difficulty that Eliot arrived at an acceptance of the *Divine Comedy* in its entirety. He was held back, he says, by two prejudices: "one against Pre-Raphaelite imagery, which was natural to one of my generation" and the other against "cheerfulness, optimism, and hopefulness", words which "stood for a great deal of what one hated in the nineteenth century". [6] But when he did accept Dante, it was with enthusiasm. I can imagine no other poet of whom he can have been thinking when, in 1919, he wrote the following words: "There is a kind of stimulus for a writer which is more important than the stimulus of admiring another writer. Admiration leads most often to imitation" which, with awareness of it, easily turns into hatred; but the other relation "is a feeling of profound kinship, or rather of a peculiar kind of intimacy, with another, probably a dead author. It may overcome us suddenly, on first or after long acquaintance; it is certainly a crisis; and when a young writer is seized with his first passion of this sort he may be changed, metamorphosed almost, within a few weeks even, from a bundle of second-hand sentiments into a person. The imperative intimacy arouses for the first time a real, an unshakeable confidence. — — we have not borrowed, we have been quickened, and we become bearers of a tradition". [7]

I imagine that some of the confidence of which Eliot speaks is present in his manifesto of 1917, "Tradition and the Individual Talent". But if the credit is Dante's it is certainly also Ezra Pound's. One can almost hear Pound's whisper in the words of the young Eliot that tradition is necessary and must be obtained by great labour, and that it involves "the historical

---

[1] "Ezra Pound" II, NEW, 7 Nov. 1946. [2] *Milton*, pp. 18—9. [3] "Drunken helots", I believe, was one of the epithets that were used. [4] Cf. "Ezra Pound" I, NEW, 31 Oct. 1946. [5] Cf. "Ezra Pound" II, NEW, 7 Nov. 1946. [6] "Dante" SE p. 262. [7] "Reflections on Contemp. Poetry", *Egoist*, July 1919.

sense, which we may call nearly indispensable to anyone who would continue to be a poet beyond his twenty-fifth year".[1]

The Imagist movement, of which Eliot made passing mention in a passage we quoted above, may not have been very important as a school. But its determined onslaught on the Georgians, and the general principles it enunciated were extremely favourable to the creation of a new style of poetry, and have been potent factors in the development of most poets for the last few decades. The movement, which included poets on both sides of the Atlantic, originated about 1912, and aimed at restoring to poetry its direct appeal to the senses, chiefly to the sense of sight by the precise use of visual images. A poem was to be a presentation rather than a description, moods were to be inferred from situations rendered in concrete terms, unnecessary words, especially adjectives, were to be shorn away, etc. A model was found in the handful of poems written by T. E. Hulme.

Eliot never met Hulme. The latter enlisted at the beginning of the Great War, went to France in 1915, and was killed in 1917. But he had long been the centre of a group of philosophers, writers and artists, and his spirit and ideas lived on in the literary circles of London when Eliot came to the capital. Many of his views coincided with those of Irving Babbitt. He was a disciplinarian and a classicist, and withal a believer in dogma. But unlike Babbitt, Hulme distrusted humanism and held only "the religious conception of ultimate values to be right".[2] He believed strongly in the reality of Original Sin and the inability of man to attain perfection by any human effort. His religious attitude was to mean something to Eliot later, especially after his *Speculations* were published in 1924. But at first it was only his literary ideas that mattered.

A schism occurred in the Imagist group when Ezra Pound and some of the other members seceded to Vorticism, a movement which Mr. Wyndham Lewis started in 1913, and which he is now trying to disinter from historical oblivion.[3] To all intents and purposes, Vorticism in poetry was the same as Imagism. The concrete image was to serve as the form, or the "VORTEX, from which, and through which, and into which, ideas are constantly rushing".[4] Eliot was drawn into this Vorticist-Imagist group, and it may have meant something to him to have been associated, in the beginning of his career, with such daring, not to say eccentric, experimenters as Wyndham Lewis. It is curious now to reflect that Eliot, like Joyce somewhat earlier, earned his living in the prosaic capacity of a bank clerk while engaged in what many people deemed to be literary anarchy, and that he was commended for his weekly digests of foreign trade reports and his articles on foreign trade movements in the *Lloyd's Bank Economic Review* while "Prufrock" and "Mr. Apollinax" were shocking the public.

---

[1] SE p. 14.   [2] Cf. SE p. 452.   [3] Cf. letter to the Editor, TLS. 28 Aug. 1948.   [4] Pound: "Vorticism", *Fortnightly Review,* 1 Sept. 1914, p. 469.

While Eliot was assistant editor of the progressive review called the *Egoist,* he also contributed a great number of articles, mostly reviews of books, to other periodicals. In 1919, which was a year of considerable output, and in 1920, he wrote especially for the *Athenaeum,* then being edited in its last, brilliant phase by Mr. Middleton Murry, Katherine Mansfield's husband and the intimate friend of D. H. Lawrence. Mr. Murry, like Eliot, was struggling to find a foothold in philosophy or faith, and for a time, it seems, they were able to harmonise their views and aspirations, though in the years to come they were to drift far apart. Eliot informs us that some of his essays of this early period were written directly at the suggestion of Mr. Murry.[1]

However, a stronger ascendancy than Middleton Murry's was exercised by the critical writings of Rémy de Gourmont, whose influence Eliot gratefully acknowledges in the 1928 Preface to *The Sacred Wood.* Gourmont, who died in 1915, was one of the first critics to do justice to the French Symbolists, particularly Mallarmé. He has been described as "antireligieux, antirationaliste, amoraliste, sceptique, en un mot anarchiste, puisant dans son tempérament, voluptueux, sensuel et artiste, la loi même de ses curiosités, s'il est vrai, comme l'a remarqué son frère, que 'rien ne soit entré dans son intelligence que caressé par sa sensibilité' ".[2] Gourmont would hardly be an acceptable guide for a young man in search of anything but a hedonistic philosophy. But he realised the need of a cultural tradition in Europe transcending the boundaries of the nations; he also had a fine perception in matters of literary style, and it was in such matters that Eliot, stimulated by Gourmont, was principally interested at the time. What gives coherence to the essays of *The Sacred Wood,* says Eliot, "is the problem of the integrity of poetry, with the repeated assertion that when we are considering poetry we must consider it primarily as poetry and not another thing".[3] From Gourmont's writings Eliot takes his title quotations for his essay on "The Perfect Critic":

"Eriger en lois ses impressions personelles, c'est le grand effort d'un homme s'il est sincère." — *Lettres à l'Amazone.*
"L'écrivain de style abstrait est presque toujours un sentimental, du moins un sensitif. L'écrivain artiste n'est presque jamais un sentimental, et très rarement un sensitif." — *Le Problème du Style.*[4]

These may be taken as examples of the maxims and observations of Rémy de Gourmont which gave Eliot many of his impulses in these early years of his career as a critic.

By 1920 a number of Eliot's poems had been printed in three or four separate collections. The modernist poets were advancing, but they had not

[1] Cf. Preface to SW 1938, p. viii.   [2] Lanson et Tuffrau: *Manuel Ill. D'Histoire de la Litt. Fr.,* p. 751.   [3] SW p. viii.   [4] SW pp. 1, 8.

yet established their position. Writing about this time, Aldous Huxley complained: "We to-day are metaphysicals without our Donne. Theoretically we are free to make poetry of everything in the universe; in practtice we are kept within the old limits, for the simple reason that no great man has appeared to show us how we can use our freedom. A certain amount of the life of the twentieth century is to be found in our poetry, but precious little of its mind. — — — The twentieth century still awaits its Lucretius, awaits its own philosophical Dante, its new Goethe, its Donne, even its up-to-date Laforgue. Will they appear?" [1] Many people hailed the appearance of the poet of the age, when *The Waste Land* was published in 1922. But it is noteworthy that many of the admirers of the poem were not guided by genuine appreciation. If Pound is to be trusted, "the bearing of this poem was not over-estimated, nevertheless the immediate reception of it even by second-rate reviewers was due to the purely fortuitous publication of the notes, and not to the text itself. Liveright wanted a longer volume and the notes were the only available unpublished matter".[2]

In the actual shaping of *The Waste Land* Pound played a significant part. And as usual Eliot acknowledges his debt. "It was in 1922", he says, "that I placed before him [Pound] in Paris the manuscript of a sprawling chaotic poem called *The Waste Land* which left his hands, reduced to about half its size, in the form in which it appears in print. I should like to think that the manuscript, with the suppressed passages, had disappeared irrecoverably: yet, on the other hand, I should wish the blue pencilling on it to be preserved as irrefutable evidence of Pound's critical genius".[3] The history of *The Waste Land* is unromantic. It is nevertheless a masterpiece, and we need not grudge Pound some of the credit. Pound had at an earlier time induced Eliot to destroy some verses which he did not consider to be original enough, and Eliot subsequently, it seems, came to regret the destruction. But we may assume that the pruning of *The Waste Land* was all to the good.

The poem first appeared in the *Criterion* (without the notes). Eliot had only recently launched this review, which was to attain to such eminence, and thus the year 1922 was a very important one in his life.

His regular contributions to the *Criterion* consisted in the Commentaries, in which he ranged over a great number of subjects of topical interest: literary and artistic, philosophical, educational, economic, political, etc. He achieved excellence in many of these Commentaries, and enriched the discussions of the day with well-founded views and careful criticism. But the review was equally important in bringing together many of the best brains and pens not only of England, but of the whole of Europe, and of America too. About 1929 the editor was able to state with pride that the

---

[1] "Subject-Matter of Poetry", *On the Margin*.   [2] Cf. Gallup: *Bibliographical Check-List*, p. 13.   [3] "Ezra Pound" I, NEW, 31 Oct. 1946.

Criterion "had been the first periodical in England to print the work of such writers as Marcel Proust, Paul Valéry, Jacques Rivière, Charles Maurras, Henri Massis, Wilhelm Worringer, Max Scheler, E. R. Curtius".[1] Thus the *Criterion* was strongly instrumental in creating that sense of the unity of European culture which the editor always thought so important, but which, unfortunately, was to be shattered by the impact of the Second World War and the events leading up to it.

Eliot never earned a living as editor or poet. For "eight very satisfactory years",[2] he continued working in Lloyd's Bank, then he joined the staff of the publishing firm of Faber and Faber (then Faber and Gwyer), where he is at present a Director. But the years spent with the *Criterion* were formative and fruitful. Not least important, of course, were the many contacts that were made and the friendships that were sealed. Thus about 1927 Eliot became personally acquainted with Paul Valéry.

Gradually a change of interests, or perhaps rather an expansion of interests took place. Possibly the year 1926 marks the beginning of a spiritual awakening and a growth of independence. "Only from about the year 1926", says Eliot, "did the features of the post-war world begin clearly to emerge. From about that date one began slowly to realize that the intellectual and artistic output of the previous seven years had been rather the last efforts of an old world than the first struggles of a new".[3]

Eliot was attracted to "a larger and more difficult subject" than that of the integrity and autonomy of poetry. He passed on to the problem "of the relation of poetry to the spiritual and social life of its time and of other times".[4] And this again was part of a larger movement of his mind which resulted in his entering the Anglo-Catholic communion about the same time as he became a British citizen in 1927. In his preface to *For Lancelot Andrewes,* he defined his position at the time (1928) as "Anglo-Catholic in religion, — classicist in literature, and — royalist in politics". The definition gave rise to a certain amount of misunderstanding, but it certainly mirrors a determined choice of allegiances. Since the late twenties Eliot has followed religious and ecclesiastical affairs very closely, as witness his *Thoughts after Lambeth* and his collaboration in the report on *Catholicity. The Rock* and *Murder in the Cathedral* have about them something of the convert's missionary zeal.

His conversion was not sudden. In a talk on "Christianity or Communism" he gave the following testimony:

Towards any profound conviction one is borne gradually, perhaps insensibly over a long period of time, by what Newman called "powerful and concurrent reasons". — — — At some moment or other, a kind of crystallisation occurs, in which appears an element of *faith*. — —. In my

---

[1] Cf. "Last Words", CRI, Jan. 1939, p. 271.   [2] *Poetry,* p. 7.   [3] "Last Words", CRI, Jan. 1939.   [4] SW 1928, p. viii.

own case, I believe that one of the reasons was that the Christian scheme seemed to me the only one which would work. I hasten to add that this is not a reason for believing; it is a tenable hypothesis to maintain that there is *no* scheme which will work. That was simply the removal of any reason for believing in anything else, the erasure of a prejudice, the arrival at the scepticism which is the preface to conversion. And when I say "work", I am quite aware that I had my own notion of what the "working" of a scheme comprehends. Among other things, the Christian scheme seemed the only possible scheme which found a place for values which I must maintain or perish (and belief comes first and practice second), the belief, for instance, in holy living and holy dying, in sanctity, chastity, humility, austerity. And it is in favour of the Christian scheme, from the Christian point of view, that it never has, and never will, work perfectly. No perfect scheme can work perfectly with imperfect men.[1]

Eliot's declaration of faith became a subject of controversy in literary circles, especially when it became apparent that Christian themes were more and more invading his poetry. Some people thought that he had suddenly and deplorably arrested his progress,[2] others were confident that the new inspiration would possess him of his full powers. Time has shown that there was no drying-up of the sources of poetry, whatever we may think of the philosophical value of the later poems compared with the early ones. But in the field of criticism it seems the artistic interests suffered. Thus it became impossible for Eliot, with his own changed and changing outlook, and with the background of political developments in Europe, to continue editing the *Criterion*. In January 1939 he wrote his "Last Words". The "European mind" which he had championed, had disappeared from view, he said, in the political turmoils of the thirties. He had introduced young British writers to replace the absentees from the Continent. But even so he found it impossible, in the long run, to continue:

For myself, a right political philosophy came more and more to imply a right theology — and right economics to depend upon right ethics: leading to emphases which somewhat stretched the original framework of a literary review. — — —

I have wondered whether it would not have been more profitable, instead of trying to maintain literary standards increasingly repudiated in the modern world, to have endeavoured to rally intellectual effort to affirm those principles of life and policy from the lack of which we are suffering disastrous consequences. But such a task, again, would be outside the scope of *The Criterion,* would require the whole of the editor's time, and probably a more competent editor: this is perhaps another indication that *The Criterion* has served its purpose. — — —

In the present state of public affairs — which has induced in myself a depression of spirits so different from any other experience of fifty years

---

[1] LIS, March 1932.   [2] Cf. SE p. 358.

as to be a new emotion — I no longer feel the enthusiasm necessary to make a literary review what it should be. This is not to suggest that I consider literature to be at this time, or at any time, a matter of indifference.[1]

Eliot reluctantly came to the conclusion that the writer must take a direct interest in politics; and one of the signs of this new attitude was his book on *The Idea of a Christian Society*. Only a few years earlier, when the civil war in Spain was calling upon the enthusiasms of so many young British poets and authors, Eliot declared, "While I am naturally sympathetic, I still feel convinced that it is best that at least a few men of letters should remain isolated, and take no part in these collective activities".[2] Such pronouncements were liable to stamp him as a fascist and reactionary, but they were rather the signs of his persistent loyalty to the disinterestedness of the poet. Unlike some others, he did not leave England during the nightmare of 1939—1945, except for lecture tours, under the auspices of the British Council, to Sweden and elsewhere. And he contributed to the war effort in his way, by labouring to keep alive the sense of perennial cultural values.

Eliot is a hard-working man, who attempts to throw no glamour over his poetic career, which, on one occasion, he referred to as "a mug's game".[3] "An artist", he says, "needs to live a commonplace life if he is to get his work done — a life far more of routine, and indeed less 'inextricably strange' than that of a politician or a stockbroker".[4] And elsewhere he declares that "the compensations for being a poet are grossly exaggerated; and they dwindle as one becomes older, and the shadows lengthen, and the solitude becomes harder to endure".[5] We have seen him accepting Pound's insistence on the amount of conscious labour to be performed by the poet. But he finds the labour of composition painful rather than pleasant.[6] He admits that he is too sceptical of his own abilities to be able to make a whole-time job of writing poetry, even if he had the means.[7] He would rather have no career than pander to a debased taste for "commercial literature". In all this there is a certain aloofness, a sense of loneliness in which the poet is imprisoned. His scepticism of his own abilities might also be interpreted as an exaggerated self-conciousness or as being due to inhibitions which bar the way against his natural urge for self-expression. Only "once in every five or ten years" does inspiration flood the barriers. The rest is practice and patience.[8]

Eliot's dislike of facile optimism is very characteristic. He speaks somewhere of "the Catholic philosophy of disillusion",[9] and this is clearly the philosophy that he has embraced. One of the things it teaches is "to look

---

[1] CRI, Jan. 1939, pp. 271—4.　　[2] *Authors Take Sides.*　　[3] UPC p. 154. [4] *Revelation*, p. 30.　　[5] Monro: *Coll. Poems*, "Critical Note", p. xvi.　　[6] Private conversation; cf. also UPC pp. 144—5.　　[7] CRICOM, Jan. 1932.　　[8] Cf. Introd. to Pound: *Sel Poems*, p. xviii.　　[9] SE p. 275.

to *death* for what life cannot give".[1] "We fight", he says, "rather to keep something alive than in the expectation that anything will triumph".[2] Accordingly he regards it as the highest stage that civilised man can attain "to unite the profoundest scepticism with the deepest faith".[3] In this latter statement we see that there are dimensions in his perspective of life: he is not the peevish recluse that some of his statements might be twisted to suggest. But he does go through life with an acute sense of its troubles and discomforts.

Of how it feels to be a great and famous poet, he has himself given a description, which I cannot resist quoting at some length, because it throws such a flood of light on his character:

> I have always been haunted by one or the other of two doubts. The first is, that nothing I have written is really of permanent value: and that makes it hard to believe in what one wants to do next. Neither one's inner feelings, nor public approval, is satisfactory assurance: for some men have been enthusiastic about their own poetry, and nobody has agreed with them; and other men have been acclaimed as great poets, and ridiculed by a later generation. But the second doubt is still more distressing. I sometimes feel that some, at least, of what I have written, is very good, but that I shall never again write anything good. Some imp always whispers to me, as I am struggling to get down to any new piece of work, that this is going to be lamentably bad, and that I won't know it. At least three times during my life, and for periods of some duration, I have been convinced that I shall never again be able to write anything worth reading. And perhaps this time it is true. Certainly ambition, or the desire to do something of permanent value, is of no help, but rather a hindrance. And the more you get success, that is to say the more your work is praised and talked about in the magazines, the more difficult it becomes to write the next thing so that it shall be the thing you have it in you to write, instead of the thing that you know people expect of you to do.
>
> Whether this is true for all artists I cannot say: but I am sure that for a poet humility is the most essential virtue. That means, not to be influenced by the desire for applause, not to be influenced by the desire to excel anybody else, not to be influenced by what your readers expect of you, not to write something merely because it is high time you wrote something, but to wait patiently, not caring how you compare with other poets, for the impulse which you cannot resist — or to accept the outside invitation just as a job to be done without worrying whether it is to be poetry or not. I wrote "The Waste Land" simply to relieve my own feelings; I wrote "Murder in the Cathedral" because I was asked to provide a play for a festival at Canterbury Cathedral, under certain conditions and by a certain date.[4]

No one who has met T. S. Eliot in private life or has looked into the hundreds of articles of diverse kinds that he has written, can doubt that he has gone a very long way in perfecting himself in accordance with his high

---

[1] Ibid.   [2] SE p. 411.   [2] LIS, 9 Jan. 1947.   [4] *Poetry*, pp. 8—10. This pamphlet is a printed recording of an address to a girls' school.

ideals and aspirations. But his practice of humility, instead of making him irresolute and weak, seems to have kindled in him a peculiar graciousness. Above all he is eminently sincere, and the conviction of his sincerity is of capital importance in judging his poetry.

His Christianity, which in his prose writings may seem lacking in enthusiasm, a matter of the head rather than of the heart, a matter of Church membership even, is probably suspect to many people. But he never wraps it up in stock phrases to which he cannot give personal assent, nor does he affirm more than he safely may. On the contrary, one often feels that he understates his religious views, and is over-scrupulous in revealing the limitations of his religious sensibility. That he sometimes makes rather extravagant claims on behalf of the Church is another matter.

From Eliot's own point of view it is possible that the peaks of what seems a fairly humdrum life have been the "kind of unexplainable experiences which many of us have had, once or twice in our lives, and been unable to put into words".[1] To a mind naturally inclined towards the metaphysical, any mystical experience which seems to put him within reach of another plane of essence or existence must be something to treasure up. Eliot has no faith in dreams, and finds his "night-mind" "quite uninteresting".[2] But with memories there is some mystery at work.

Why, — he asks — for all of us, out of all that we have heard, seen, felt, in a lifetime, do certain images recur, charged with emotion, rather than others? The song of one bird, the leap of one fish, at a particular place and time, the scent of one flower, an old woman on a German mountain path, six ruffians seen through an open window playing cards at night at a small French railway junction where there was a watermill: such memories may have symbolic value, but of what we cannot tell, for they come to represent the depths of feeling into which we cannot peer. We might just as well ask why, when we try to recall visually some period in the past, we find in our memory just the few meagre arbitrarily chosen set of snapshots that we do find there, the faded poor souvenirs of passionate moments.[3]

There is more in memory, however, than meets the eye of consciousness. Of all that happens to us, nothing is wholly lost, and this is particularly true of shy and reticent people, who are often peculiarly sensitive to impressions. And intellectually impressionable people like Eliot store up a great mass of ideas which do not necessarily enter into or even agree with the opinions that they express in public. Those whom they have once listened to attentively, or whose works they have read with interest, continue to speak to them. "No voice is wholly lost". So the poet sings with more voices than one.

---

[1] LIS, 19 Dec. 1946, p. 895.   [2] *Transition* Spring 1938.   [3] UPC p. 148.

II.

The Views of the Critic.

Being a survey of Eliot's views on the Art of Poetry, as collected from his prose writings, with reflections on the subject of a Christian aesthetic.

The year 1921, when the three essays later collected in the volume *Homage to John Dryden* were first published, may be said to close a distinct period in Eliot's criticism, the period of the eager young firebrand, intent on making the *bourgeoisie* sit up and take notice that a new era of poetry was at hand — only of course his fire was frosty, and his blood was passionately cool.

The attitude of the intellectual is marked in this early criticism, and we are not surprised to find, as one of its characteristic features, an insistence on the important role of the intellect in the processes of poetry. Eliot favoured the idea of the intellect merging, so to speak, with the senses of the poet. The intellectual poets (as distinct from the reflective poets like Tennyson and Browning) were able to "feel their thought as immediately as the odour of a rose".[1] Such poets were Jonson, Chapman and Donne. They were capable of a "direct sensuous apprehension of thought, or a recreation of thought into feeling",[2] to quote one of Eliot's now famous phrases.

Mr. J. C. Ransom fails to find this peculiar combination of thought and feeling in the seventeenth century poets, and inclines to think that there was nothing of the sort there.[3] And indeed it is hard to see exactly what Eliot refers to, unless it be the imagery of these poets, so loaded with personal emotions and yet so seeming-cool and so sustained. I have already quoted Eliot's statement that the keenest ideas come to us "with the quality of a sense-perception" (p. 26): it may have been his private intuition of some such fusion between idea and sensation which he projected on to the Metaphysicals.

His advocacy of the intellect naturally made him repudiate the idea of inspiration. Thus in an article called "Professional, or . . ."[4] he makes fun of "the British worship of inspiration, which in literature is merely an avoidance of comparison with foreign literatures, a dodging of standards." In this, and in many other things, he showed himself a convinced anti-romantic.

There is hardly an opinion that he laboured more to inculcate in this period than the undesirability of personal Ideas and philosophies, not only

---

[1] MP, SE p. 287.   [2] Ibid. p. 286.   [3] RAN p. 183.   [4] *Egoist,* April 1918.

in poetry, but in criticism too.[1]   His review of Balfour's *Theism and Humanism*[2] is an interesting document, both because it was published at an early date, and so shows that we have here a preoccupation of long standing, and because the author tries to expound very general principles of aesthetics. What his arguments amount to is this: that the way in which we enjoy art and the reasons by which we justify to ourselves our enjoyment of art are to some extent dependent on our world outlook; but no type of philosophy can prevent our taking pleasure in art in some way. Eliot seems to regard the enjoyment of art as a pragmatic fact, and the philosophical views which may be superimposed on this enjoyment as almost irrelevant. As for the creative writer, Eliot tells us in many of his essays that what he needs is not ideas or a philosophy, but a point of view (which, I take it, is a familiarity with certain aspects of life, which helps the writer to see the world in perspective). Eliot does not hesitate to use superlatives in his praise of Henry James for avoiding ideas:

James's critical genius comes out most tellingly in his mastery over, his baffling escape from, Ideas; a mastery and an escape which are perhaps the last test of a superior intelligence. He had a mind so fine that no idea could violate it. — — — In England ideas run wild and pasture on the emotions; instead of thinking with our feelings (a very different thing) we corrupt our feelings with ideas; we produce the political, the emotional idea, evading sensation and thought. [Meredith and Chesterton are instanced.] James in his novels is like the best French critics in maintaining a point of view, a viewpoint untouched by the parasite idea. He is the most intelligent man of his generation.[3]

Similar praise is accorded elsewhere to Dante and Shakespeare, whilst Swinburne and Kipling are censured for having "concepts (Liberty, Empire) and oratory".[4] William Blake was too much his own philosopher, to the detriment of his art, whilst "the borrowed philosophy of Dante and Lucretius is perhaps not so interesting, but it injures their form less".[5] Goethe's *Faust* and Ibsen's *Peer Gynt* embody philosophies and "a creation of art should not do that: he [the artist] should replace the philosophy".[6]

Eliot at this point finds philosophies justifiable in poetry only if, as with Lucretius and Dante, they serve, not their own ends, but those of the poetry. Therefore it is safest for the poet to borrow his ideas, so as not to fall into the temptation of subordinating poetry to speculation. The Idea is dangerous, both when personal and when popularised. It is only compatible with art when it remains in its pure state; and "it can remain pure only by being stated simply in the form of general truth, or by being transmuted,

---

[1] For his views on criticism cf. "The Perfect Critic", SW.   [2] *International Journal of Ethics,* Jan. 1916.   [3] "In Mem. of H. James", *Egoist,* Jan. 1918. [4] "Kipling Redivivus", *Athenaeum,* May 1919.   [5] "Blake", SE p. 320.   [6] "Poss. of P. Dr.", SW p. 66.

as the attitude of Flaubert toward the small bourgeois is transformed in *Education Sentimentale*. It has there become so identified with the reality that you can no longer say what the idea is".[1]

To put it crudely, it is not the business of the poet to argue, persuade, teach or speculate. It is his business to *present* something — "permanent literature is always a presentation",[2] a statement which immediately puts us in mind of the Imagist movement. Accordingly, "the poet can deal with philosophical ideas, not as matter for argument, but as matter for inspection".[3]

It may be reasonably doubted whether Eliot would still say that permanent literature is always a presentation. The *Four Quartets* are rather an exploration, and I assume that the poet wishes them to be permanent. As for Dante and Lucretius, he has come to recognise them as unashamedly didactic.

In his early years, apparently, he considered human suffering to be the only genuine material of poetry,[4] in spite of his intellectualism. In any case, emotions and feelings were involved in the first phase of poetic composition (whatever he may have meant by the distinction between emotions and feelings in "Tradition and the Individual Talent"). The material of poetry, he said in his early manifesto, is partly or entirely the passions of the poet, though in the finished poem they may not and should not be recognised as being his.[5] But it was not enough to "look into the heart and write". The poet should also be a psychologist. He should be able to explore the human soul. "One must look into the cerebral cortex, the nervous system, and the digestive tracts",[6] penetrate to the sources of each tributary to the personality, passions, brains, nerves, instincts.

When we consider the actual process by which personal thought and emotion become impersonal "objective correlative" or "verbal equivalent", we find, as we have seen, that the author attributes a large place to the intellect and discredits inspiration. But at one stage in the creative process something mysterious seems to happen, which Eliot can only explain by a simile. The poet's mind is only a catalyst,[7] he says; or it is "a receptacle for seizing and storing up numberless feelings, phrases, images, which remain there until all the particles which can unite to form a new compound are present together". At which moment, we must suppose, there occurs a spontaneous fusion with the effect of "amalgamating disparate experience".[8] And "it is not the 'greatness', the intensity, of the emotions, the components, but the intensity of the artistic process, the pressure, so to speak, under which the fusion takes place, that counts".[9]

---

[1] Ibid. p. 68.   [2] Ibid. p. 64.   [3] "Dante", SW p. 162.   [4] Cf. "Dante", SE p. 262.   [5] TIT, SE p. 18.   [6] MP, SE p. 290.   [7] TIT SE p. 18.   [8] MP, SE p. 287.   [9] TIT, SE p. 19.

The introduction of this notion of "intensity of the artistic process" certainly looks like some form of aesthetic mysticism: the most important moment in the creation of poetry is removed from the sphere of reason and emotion, which psychology makes familiar to us, and attributed to what looks like a special artistic faculty which can only be known by its works. If we follow up this idea, we must conclude that poetry is not, as Babbitt would have it to be,[1] a matter of technique, at least not of conscious technique. "It is a concentration which does not happen consciously or of deliberation".[2]

Eliot, it must be admitted, comes near accepting the idea of supernatural inspiration.[3] But perhaps we should not pay too much attention to his use of the words "intensity" and "pressure" in this connection.

An important idea emerges, however: "feelings, phrases and images" are stored up together and finally fused. This can only mean that form and matter are born together in a single creative act, and that they are both integral and equally valuable components of the poetry that is created.

But we must now, before leaving Eliot's first period of criticism, turn our attention for a moment to what he calls his "Impersonal theory of poetry".[4]

The author begins his essay on "Tradition and the Individual Talent" by referring to the vague censure often implied when the term "traditional" is used. He finds an undue prejudice in favour of originality in literature. "Whereas if we approach a poet without this prejudice we shall often find that not only the best, but the most individual parts of his work may be those in which the dead poets, his ancestors, assert their immortality most vigorously". Tradition is thus something valuable. The poet must "be aware that the mind of Europe — the mind of his own country — a mind which he learns in time to be much more important than his own private mind — is a mind which changes, and that this change is a development which abandons nothing en route — —". The poet must continue to develop his consciousness of the past throughout his career; and what happens then "is a continual surrender of himself as he is at the moment to something which is more valuable. The progress of an artist is a continual self-sacrifice, a continual extinction of personality. — — It is in this deperson-alization that art may be said to approach the condition of science."

Eliot then goes on to study more closely the relation of a poem to its author (it is in this connection he uses the phrase "the Impersonal theory of poetry"). The creative mind of the poet, he says, "may partly or exclusively operate upon the experience of the man himself; but, the more perfect the artist, the more completely separate in him will be the man who suffers and the mind which creates". "It is not in his personal emotions, the emotions provoked by particular events in his life, that the poet is in any

---

[1] "The Critic & American Life".   [2] TIT, SE p. 21.   [3] Cp. UPC pp. 144—5;
EAM p. 142.   [4] TIT, SE p. 18.

way remarkable or interesting." And, on the other hand, "the business of the poet is not to find new emotions, but to use the ordinary ones and, in working them up into poetry, to express feelings which are not in actual emotions at all". Finally he says that "poetry is not a turning loose of emotion, but an escape from emotion; it is not the expression of personality, but an escape from personality. But, of course, only those who have personality and emotions know what it means to want to escape from these things".

The last statement sounds like that of a spiritual defeatist. I do not know whether Eliot ever felt any intensity of despair. But it would seem that his Impersonal theory at least in part springs from a deepseated abhorrence of his own personal freight at the time, and an intense distrust of the private and individual personality. Perhaps this distrust has something to do with doubt as to the spiritual nature of man. He certainly rejects belief in the separate human soul and in the personality as a definite entity. The point of view which he struggles to attack in "Tradition and the Individual Talent" is perhaps related, he says, "to the metaphysical theory of the substantial unity of the soul: for my meaning is, that the poet has, not a 'personality' to express, but a particular medium, which is only a medium and not a personality, in which impressions and experiences combine in peculiar and unexpected ways". If there is no individual soul it is obviously no irreparable loss to exclude from poetry what we are in the habit of calling personality. In fact, in such a case it is clear that tradition, even though it represents the second-hand,[1] is both more rich and more reliable than the private mind. And that an outside authority, such as is recognised in Classicism, is greatly to be desired.[2]

The Impersonal theory must have been a difficult one to uphold consistently, especially if, as I suspect, it lacked the support of a general philosophical theory. In several of the essays of the period there are statements which appear to contradict it. Thus Ben Jonson's works, we are told, cannot be appreciated without "knowledge of Jonson", which I take to mean "knowledge of the personality of Jonson".[3] And in a book review in *The Athenaeum,* the author declared that the arts require the Individual himself but refuse to accept him as "a member of a family or of a caste or of a party or of a coterie",[4] i.e. in any of the relationships which, one would suppose, are the nearest links of the individual with tradition.

Even a casual study of Eliot's poetry will make it clear that he is an individualist as well as a traditionalist, and it is hard to decide which he is chiefly. As far as his subject-matter is concerned, however, he seems to give both tendencies their due by erecting an objective, and to some extent traditionalist, structure on an individualistic basis. Thus he follows

---

[1] Cf. "Reflections on Contemp. Poetry", *Egoist,* Nov. 1917.   [2] Cf. SE p. 26.
[3] Cf. "Ben Jonson", SE pp. 157, 159.   [4] *Athenaeum,* May 1919.

his own critical precept, according to which a personal *donnée* should be transmuted into an impersonal work of art.

The case for individuality in literature is as good as the case for impersonality, if both be considered separately. But the ideal, of course, is a fusion of the particular and the common, the individual and the traditional. Indeed, only in such a fusion can literature subsist. The pleasure derived from reading consists to a large extent in a recognition of "similarity in dissimilarity", in variations within a traditional framework of references. And any deviation from the central compromise between individuality and tradition can only be a matter or degree. Thus Eliot's ideal of extinguishing the personality is impossible if it means more than a concealment of direct references to personal experience and emotions. A concealment of the personal is possible, but not a liquidation of it. Equally, individuality, if exploited to its limits, would result in mere babbling and incomprehensibility. Now presumably the personal psyche, if explored deeply and correctly, will reveal its similarity and essential oneness with all human nature, and reveal universality in individuality by the principle of *les extrêmes se touchent*. This, however, is not the way to universality that Eliot would have us travel. So that however one takes it, his Impersonal theory seems somewhat unsatisfactory.

In Eliot's more recent criticism, the personal passions of the poet are still regarded as being the transmuted but fundamental and only material of poetry. He speaks of Shakespeare as being "occupied with the struggle — which alone constitutes life for a poet — to transmute his personal and private agonies into something rich and strange, something universal and impersonal. The rage of Dante against Florence, or Pistoia, or what not, the deep surge of Shakespeare's general cynicism and disillusionment, are merely gigantic attempts to metamorphose private failures and disappointments".[1] And elsewhere he declares that "we all have to choose whatever subject-matter allows us the most powerful and secret release; and that is a personal affair". An original impulse which is entirely personal is transformed into a correlative which is entirely impersonal. But the idea of the private passions as the raw material of poetry no longer preponderates. The attention is focused more on the materials as *subjects* of poetry; and the eligible subjects are found to be many and diverse. From the start the sordid and the ugly were recognised. Now, as Eliot so strikingly shows us in his essay on Dante, he has come to see not only damnation, but purgation and beatitude as well, as fit subjects for a poet.[2] Further, one learns from the *Purgatorio,* he says, "that a straightforward philosophical statement can be great poetry".[3]

---

[1] "Shakesp. & Stoicism of Seneca", SE p. 137.   [2] SE pp. 252—3. 264.
[3] SE p. 252.

In one of his *Criterion* Commentaries Eliot declares that he "cannot think of art as either national or international — — but as racial and local".[1] But local colour in the subject-matter is no hindrance to universality of thought and feeling. Eliot wants poetry to express the "permanent and universal".[2] "The great poet, in writing himself, writes his time",[3] he says. But he objects to the prevalent tendency of treating "each work of art, especially those contemporary with ourselves, as a manifestation of the spirit of the age". "All great art", he continues, "is in a sense a document on its time; but great art is never merely a document, for mere documentation is not art. All great art has something permanent and universal about it, and reflects the permanent as well as the changing — —. And as no great art is explicable simply by the society of its time, so it is not fully explicable simply by the personality of its author: in the greatest poetry there is always a hint of something behind, something impersonal, something in relation to which the author has been no more than the passive (if not always pure) medium".[4] The sense of something absolute beneath the changing concrete phenomena has become very strong. And therefore "the essential advantage for a poet is not to have a beautiful world with which to deal: it is to be able to see beneath both beauty and ugliness; to see the boredom, and the horror, and the glory".[5] The poet may even be groping for the inexpressible, he may be "occupied with frontiers of consciousness beyond which words fail, though meanings still exist".[6] It is the truthfulness of his perception of reality that counts; for "we cannot be *primarily* interested in any writer's nerves — — or in any one's heredity except for the purpose of knowing to what extent that writer's individuality distorts or detracts from the objective truth which he perceives. If a writer sees truly — as far as he sees at all — then his heredity and nerves do not matter".[7]

Great poets, of course, transcend the limitations as to material that may be indicated for lesser craftsmen. They possess, or we expect them to possess, a "general awareness",[8] which enables them to move freely and securely, whatever subject-matter they choose or find. And if at the same time their awareness is coloured by Christian belief, then they will be "great Christian religious poets", in the sense in which Dante and Corneille and Racine were such poets "even in those of their plays which do not touch upon Christian themes".[9] For Eliot does not seem to place religious or specifically Christian themes higher than others. He wants "a literature which should be *un*consciously, rather than deliberately and defiantly, Christian". Such literature he will perhaps allow us to see exemplified in the work of François Mauriac and Graham Greene in fiction, and in his

---

[1] CRICOM, Oct. 1937.   [2] "Dialogue on Dram. P.", SE p. 46.   [3] "Shakesp. & Stoicism of Seneca", SE p. 137.   [4] CRICOM Oct. 1932.   [5] UPC p. 106. [6] MUS p. 15.   [7] "Baudel. in Our Time", EAM p. 67.   [8] EAM p. 97. [9] EAM p. 98.

own work in poetry. He does not think poetry should set forth a belief, but, as he puts it, "What poetry conveys is what it feels like to believe something".

The matter, or material, of a poem is that which forms the emotional or intellectual or sensual substance or content of the poem, possibly all these things combined. It may also be taken to include the purpose of the poem, if a purpose can be found, its object, and its idea. Obviously there must be a close connection between matter and form, and it is the author's views concerning this connection that we must now examine.

It may be a common impression that Eliot tries to "impose upon us a conception of poetry as some sort of pure and rare aesthetic essence".[1] This "essence", presumably, would have to be manifested in the formal elements of poetry. Now this impression is a very partial one, but it can be supported by numerous quotations from Eliot's prose. For instance: "Not our feelings, but the pattern which we may make of our feelings, is the centre of value";[2] "What is poetic about poetry is just the invention or discovery or elaboration of a new idiom in verse";[3] "Poetry begins, I dare say, with a savage beating a drum in a jungle, and it retains that essential of percussion and rhythm".[4] We have also Eliot's assurance that there are passages in his poetry which he "invented out of nothing because they sounded well",[5] and that his interest in poetry is "primarily a technical interest".[6] The supremacy of the formal element in poetic creation is here definitely indicated. Eliot's general idea seems to be this: that beauty of form provides a stimulus which, as far as emotional, sensual or intellectual content goes, is undifferentiated both to the writer and the reader. And each is allowed to differentiate the meaning to himself by his particular responses, much as is commonly done in the case of music. Eliot praises Shakespeare for appealing to different people on different planes. He himself planned a verse drama,[7] which should appeal to various categories in the audience in various ways.[8] But the fact that he did not succeed, at least that he never finished the play, may have been due precisely to his having planned it too deliberately beforehand: the idea or purpose became too prominent, and thus the effect of the play could not be left to the individual whom it was to affect; in other words, the formal appeal was not undifferentiated. Kipling, says Eliot, is a writer for whom poetry is an instrument. But, he goes on, "most of us are interested in the form for its own sake — not apart from the content, but because we aim at making something which shall first of all *be*, something which in consequence will have the capability of exciting, within a limited range, a considerable variety of responses from different readers. For Kipling the poem is something which is intended

---

[1] AC p. 119.   [2] Introd. to Valéry's *Le Serpent*, p. 12.   [3] LIS, Apr. 16, 1930.
[4] UPC p. 155.   [5] "Shakesp. & Stoicism of Seneca", SE p. 127.   [6] *Milton*, p. 6.
[7] *Sweeney Agonistes*.   [8] Cf. UPC p. 153.

to *act* — and for the most part his poems are intended to elicit the same response from all readers, and only the response which they can make in common. For other poets — at least, for some other poets — the poem may begin to shape itself in fragments of musical rhythm, and its structure will first appear in terms of something analogous to musical form; and such poets find it expedient to occupy their conscious mind with the craftsman's problems, leaving the deeper meaning to emerge, if there, from a lower level".[1]

With his eye on the outer influences affecting a poet, however, Eliot believes that the real, and not the formal, impulses are the original ones. Thus he declares that "any radical change in poetic form is likely to be the symptom of some very much deeper change in society and in the individual".[2] As for the relation of the formal elements to the private material employed by the poet, we learn that the purpose of complexity of form "must be, first, the precise expression of finer shades of feeling and thought".[3]

The last statement especially is hard to reconcile with the above quotations which indicate the primacy of form. But a more thorough examination reveals some consistency. Although the conscious attention of the poet may be fixed on the form and the meaning may be left to emerge, if there, from a lower level, this is not to say that the meaning is quite unimportant to the inception of the poem. It may even be the prime factor, though unconscious. Eliot thinks that a poem may be prepared unconsciously and then suddenly come to eruption. And, on the other hand, the fidelity of the expression to feeling and thought may be to feeling and thought *inherent* in the expression or created with it. This reconciliation of seemingly opposed statements leads us to the integral view of the relation between form and matter.[4]

At our first approach to this integral view, we are brought up against a barred gate: Eliot in one place explicitly distinguishes "between the thought and the clothing of it in elocution".[5] But we are forced to jump the gate, for we see a pathway beyond it. Eliot gives us a hand up himself, by means of a little equivocation: he speaks of the importance of "the distinction between form and substance, and again between material and attitude. — — In the perfect poet they fit — are the same thing; and in another sense they *always* are the same thing. So it is always true to say that form and content are the same thing, and always true to say that they are different things".[6] This helps us over the gate, so we need inspect it no closer, but proceed to cull such statements as these: from the poetic processes a masterpiece now and then results, "in which medium and material, form and content, are indistinguishable";[7] "The music of poetry is not some-

---

[1] *Choice of Kipling's Verse,* p. 18.   [2] UPC p. 75.   [3] *What is a Classic?* p. 16.   [4] Cp. p. 49.   [5] *Dryden* (1932) p. 64.   [6] Introd. to Pound's *Selected Poems,* p. ix.   [7] Ibid. p. xx.

thing which exists apart from the meaning. Otherwise, we could have poetry of great musical beauty which made no sense, and I have never come across such poetry";[1] "The music of verse is strongest in poetry which has a definite meaning expressed in the properest words";[2] "What matters, in short, is the whole poem".[3]

After all, a word is indissolubly a pattern of sound and a complex of meaning. And what enters into and makes the poetry, is a verbal combination of sound and meaning.

If it were possible to weigh Eliot's various statements against each other, I think perhaps a slight preponderance would be found in favour of the formal elements as the prime factors in poetry. But only in the integral view can he remain consistent, and, as we have seen, he is quite aware of the merits of this view.

Now it might be said that the integration of form and matter is in a sense a denial of both, for they both claim complete sovereignty for themselves. Their integration is a compromise, and a compromise which changes their very nature. For matter in the ordinary course of things is essentially loyal to what we call truth and reality, and now it cannot remain so. And form is defined by its loyalty to its parents space and time, and now that loyalty is questioned. To conclude that the marriage is a mesalliance or poetry a bastard would be heartless and intolerable to our love of beauty. But the only alternative seems to be to conclude that form and matter, when used in poetry, become different categories. This will need a more lengthy discussion in a later chapter.[4]

Perhaps as a result of the general subordination of purely aesthetic interests to metaphysical, political and cultural interests that has taken place in the author's criticism since about 1921, he has attempted more systematically than at first to relate his aesthetic opinions to his main beliefs and attitudes in other fields by speculating upon the very function of poetry.

In the chapter on "The Modern Mind" in *The Use of Poetry,* he quotes the views of various authorities to show how wide is the disagreement in modern criticism as to the function of poetry. Thus I. A. Richards, allying himself with Arnold, thinks "poetry is capable of saving us", i.e. that poetry has a cultural function to perform, a task of salvation (for which men previously looked to religion). M. Maritain, on the contrary, thinks "it is a deadly error to expect poetry to provide the super-substantial nourishment of man".[5] While the Abbé Brémond thinks of poetry as a mystical revelation, Dr. Richards asserts that it is nothing of the kind. Eliot himself continually hedges, but he cannot finally escape committing himself to fairly definite opinions.

---

[1] MUS p. 13.   [2] *Milton,* p. 19.   [3] MUS p. 17.   [4] Cf. pp. 209—210.
[5] UPC p. 124.

Concerning the origin of poetry, Eliot only tells us that it "begins, I dare say, with a savage beating a drum in a jungle"[1] — which really tells us nothing at all about the function of poetry, for the action of the savage may be prompted· by primitive instincts, or, on the contrary, by the awakening urges of civilisation. Elsewhere, however, in a number of contexts, we are told that poetry is essentially entertainment. In general, says Eliot, "a poet wishes to give pleasure, to entertain or divert people".[2] Thus Eliot adopts the conception of the use of poetry attributed by Jacques Rivière to the masters of the seventeenth century, such as Molière and Racine: "If in the seventeenth century Molière or Racine had been asked why he wrote, no doubt he would have been able to find but one answer; that he wrote 'for the entertainment of decent people' (*pour distraire les honnêtes gens*)".[3] And very definitely Eliot tells us in *The Music of Poetry* that "the end of understanding poetry is enjoyment, and — — this enjoyment is gusto disciplined by taste".[4]

The "contents" of the poem are almost irrelevant. "*If* poetry is a form of 'communication', yet that which is to be communicated is the poem itself, and only incidentally the experience and the thought which have gone into it".[5] And Eliot considers that at least in some kinds of poetry "the chief use of the 'meaning' of a poem may be — — to satisfy one habit of the reader, to keep his mind diverted and quiet, while the poem does its work upon him: much as the imaginary burglar is always provided with a bit of nice meat for the house-dog".[6]

He is particularly emphatic in asserting that art can be no *substitute* for religion or philosophy, or indeed for anything else that· is not art. "Literature can be no substitute for religion, not merely because we need religion, but because we need literature as well as religion".[7] He says the same thing repeatedly in *The Use of Poetry*. He stresses this point obviously because he finds that it is here abuses have been most common ("Our literature is a substitute for religion, and so is our religion"[8]). He puts the chief blame on Matthew Arnold for propagating this heresy by his attitude to poetry, and by his definition of it as "a criticism of life".[9] But in our secular age Arnold has had many followers.

Poetry should neither be a substitute for religion, nor should it be subordinate to it. The two domains are both sovereign and autonomous in their different spheres; and they should be kept apart. A *confusion des genres* results in treating the Mass primarily as art or the Bible primarily as literature, or turning poetry into magic. "You cannot take heaven by magic".[10] With religion may be grouped all beliefs and philosophies. "I believe", says Eliot, "that for a poet to be also a philosopher he would

---

[1] UPC p. 155.   [2] UPC p. 31.   [3] UPC p. 128.   [4] MUS p. 7.   [5] UPC p. 30.   [6] UPC p. 151.   [7] "Dialogue on Dram. P.", SE p. 48.   [8] Ibid. p. 44. [9] UPC pp. 111 ff.   [10] UPC p. 140.

have to be virtually two men".[1]   Even Coleridge, he declares, was only able to exercise the one activity at the expense of the other.

We must take poetry as we find it, he says, even if the poet perceives "possibilities of intensity through the elimination of meaning".[2]   But it must not be inferred that he holds with the doctrine of "art for art's sake".   By this he seems to understand the belief in "some illusory *pure* enjoyment".[3]   Pure enjoyment is impossible because poetry cannot divorce itself completely from meaning (and meaning, of course, is not necessarily a message).   Nor is it desirable, in Eliot's opinion, that it should attempt to do so, for "the music of verse is strongest in poetry which has a definite meaning expressed in the properest words".[4]

He goes so far as to find some necessary connection between religion and philosophy on the one hand and poetry on the other.   For one thing, we cannot "distinguish, as people sometimes do, between the occasions on which a particular poet is 'being a poet' and the occasions on which he is 'being a preacher' ".[5]   Dr. Richards thought *The Waste Land* effected "a complete severance between poetry and *all* beliefs".[6]   Eliot, with an unimportant reservation, thinks him wrong.   At the same time, however, he seems to suggest that a complete severance between poetry and all beliefs would have been a good thing for poetry if it had been possible: it would do "what all poetry in the past would have been the better for doing".   In other words, the connection between poetry and thought is a practical necessity, not an ideal necessity.   Therefore it should not artificially be made more pronounced and uncompromising than it actually is: "Any theory which relates poetry very closely to a religious or a social scheme of things aims, probably, to *explain* poetry by discovering its natural laws; but it is in danger of *binding* poetry by legislation to be observed — and poetry can recognise no such laws".[7]

The Romantic view of the poet as a seer or a prophet Eliot would reject.   But he does not entirely reject the idea of the ontological or noetic function of poetry.   Poetry *may*, occasionally, be related to mystical apprehension.   Eliot is very wary and non-committal on this point, but when he admits that "there is a relation (not necessarily noetic, perhaps merely psychological) between mysticism and some kinds of poetry, or some of the kinds of state in which poetry is produced",[8] he at least leaves a possibility open.   I asked him in an interview if he thought poetry had any ontological significance.   He replied that he did not think it had any such significance directly, but that poetry could help us to approach an understanding of an ultimate reality, and it could give the readers a sense that there was such a reality.

---

[1] UPC p. 98.   [2] UPC p. 151.   [3] UPC p. 98.   [4] *Milton*, p. 19.
[5] UPC p. 97.   [6] UPC p. 130.   [7] UPC p. 139.   [8] UPC p. 139.

He insists somewhat more specifically on the relation between "religion and literature" in the essay of that name. Most modern literature, especially fiction, has become quite secularised, he says. We completely separate our literary from our religious judgments. Yet, he declares rather illogically, "the separation is not, and never can be complete".[1] He means that though it may be complete on the conscious plane it remains incomplete on the unconscious plane — assuming of course that there *is* religion. For there is a common ground between religion and fiction, that of behaviour, or ethics. And ethical conventions, says one of the characters in *A Dialogue on Dramatic Poetry,* are necessary to art[2]: the dramatist (and poet) must have a frame of reference which enables him to communicate (or commune) with the public. But in the essay on "Religion and Literature", instead of dealing with the artistic usefulness of moral conventions, Eliot deals rather with the moral usefulness or harmfulness of literature: "Our religion imposes our ethics, our judgement and criticism of ourselves, and our behaviour toward our fellow men. The fiction that we read affects our behaviour towards our fellow men, affects our patterns of ourselves".[3] "And if we, as readers, keep our religious and moral convictions in one compartment, and take our reading merely for entertainment, or on a higher plane, for aesthetic pleasure, I would point out that the author, whatever his conscious intentions in writing, in practice recognizes no such distinctions. The author of a work of imagination is trying to affect us wholly, as human beings, whether he knows it or not; and we are affected by it, as human beings, whether we intend to be or not". Our reading necessarily "affects us as entire human beings; it affects our moral and religious existence".[4] By using the term "religious existence" the author shows that the effects he has described are independent of the faith or lack of faith of the readers of literature. From his point of view even unbelievers have a religious existence, a relation in their lives of a positive or negative character to the absolute truths of religion. It follows that, from Eliot's point of view, even a poet who on the conscious plane does away with all "meaning" must nevertheless exercise some subtle influence which touches on his own religious existence and that of others. For a "religious existence" which is able to remain unconscious can only be imagined as something that interpenetrates the entire personality, including the artistic sensibility.

Altogether, what the author wants "is a literature which should be *un*consciously, rather than deliberately and defiantly Christian".[5] This may be taken to mean, in accordance with his views on the objectivity of poetry, that he regards religion as a substratum of all life, which consequently must be recognised in poetry, if only by the poet's unconscious attitude. Eliot's position in this matter seems almost the opposite of Claudel's desire for

---

[1] EAM p. 99.   [2] Cf. op. cit., SE pp. 45, 54. The idea is also a leading one in *What is a Classic?*   [3] EAM p. 100.   [4] EAM pp. 101, 105.   [5] EAM p. 99.

a clearly religious literature, voiced in his somewhat effusive essay "Religion et Poésie".[1]

Eliot deliberately suggests a compromise between the view of poetry as entertainment and the view of it as a vehicle for instruction or "salvation": "Between the motive which Rivière attributed to Molière and Racine [*distraire les honnêtes gens*] and the motive of Matthew Arnold bearing on shoulders immense what he thought to be the orb of the poet's fate, there is a serious *via media*".[2]

It must not be supposed, then, that Eliot would disparage a poem simply because it contained a "message". On the contrary, he considers it a gain if poetry serves other purposes *over and above* that of being poetry: "Poetry is of course not to be defined by its uses. If it commemorates a public occasion, or celebrates a festival, or decorates a religious rite, or amuses a crowd, so much the better. It may effect revolutions in sensibility such as are periodically needed — —. It may make us from time to time a little more aware of the deeper, unnamed feelings which form the substratum of our beings to which we rarely penetrate; for our lives are mostly a constant evasion of ourselves, and an evasion of the visible and sensible world".[3]

At one time Eliot reacted against the "prevalent tendency in literary criticism — — to treat each work of art, especially those contemporary with ourselves, as a manifestation of the spirit of the age".[4] He has moved to a rather different position more recently, for he wrote in 1945 that "it is the business of the poet to express, and to criticise, the culture in which he lives and to which he belongs",[5] and this holds good even if his conscious purpose is another. (In passing, I must say I find it a little strange that Eliot should not have remarked in *The Use of Poetry* on the verse of his younger contemporaries who were, just about 1932, bursting into literature with a radical social and political purpose. It would seem that he disapproved of them in so far as their message was not merely incidental to their poetry.)

From one point of view — that of language in its relation to culture — he has no doubts as to the function of poetry. He even tends to regard the poet's task as being primarily an objective one connected with the cultural and social development of a community. This makes him declare that "the prime interest of a practitioner of verse like myself must be in the immediate future; — — — our first concern is always the perennial question, what is to be done next? what direction is unexplored?"[6] In other words the poet is a servant of the linguistic and cultural development of his nation. This has become quite a favourite idea with Eliot. It is "*the* social role of the poet", he says, to develop the language: "I think it is important for every language, if that language is to be worth preserving, to have its own

---

[1] *Positions et Propositions.*   [2] UPC p. 137.   [3] UPC p. 155.   [4] Cp. p. 52.
[5] SFP.   [6] MUS p. 6.

poetry — not simply for those who enjoy reading poetry, but for the sake of the people as a whole. — — it is through his service to people who do *not* read his poetry, that I assign to the poet his greatest *social* role". The reason is that the life of a people is intimately bound up with, and its intelligence and feelings in part dependent upon "the structure, the rhythms, the sounds, the idioms" of its language.[1] Poetry is, especially, the most *"precise* medium" for emotion,[2] and therefore it may be useful in teaching us, as citizens, to be critical of what we read and hear, and to distinguish an appeal to the emotions from an appeal to the intellect.[3] Altogether the poet's "first duty *qua* poet is to the language of his country. First, he has the duty to *preserve* that language — —. Second, he has the duty to *develop* that language, to bring it up to date, to investigate its unexplored possibilities. So far as he expresses, in his poetry, what other people feel, he is also affecting that feeling by making it more conscious: in giving people words for their feelings, he is teaching them something about themselves". But since the poet is at the same time different from other people, he can also "give his readers knowledge of feelings which they have never experienced".[4]

Eliot's emphasis on the social function of poetry has of late years overshadowed his interest in the personal aspects of the use of poetry. This is in consonance with his increased preoccupation with social questions in general. But it must not make us forget that his concern with the personal aspects was for long the more important, in fact almost exclusive. There is no opposition between the two aspects, of course. The idea of poetry as a means of relief from pain and anxiety for the poet, for instance, is quite compatible with the idea of poetry as a means of developing the language and consciousness of a people. But in practice, it will immediately be realised, there is a great difference between the poet with an individualistic attitude and the poet with a social attitude. It is possible that whatever poetry Eliot writes in the future will be more marked by his social sympathies than most of his poems have been up to the present, perhaps with the exception of "Little Gidding".

Faith and Aestheticism.

In spite of the developments that we have noticed, we find little change in Eliot's aesthetic ideas from first to last. His defence of the autonomy of poetry is maintained throughout. On the other hand, his philosophical ideas develop considerably in being merged in a new religious faith. We must therefore ask ourselves whether his aesthetic ideas are compatible with his

---

[1] SFP.   [2] SFP.   [3] *Poetry* pp. 12—15.   [4] SFP.

early philosophical outlook or with his later Christian creed, or perhaps with both.

As to his early philosophical outlook, there cannot be much difficulty, since it helped to fashion his aesthetic tenets. His disbelief in the personality as a separate and integral unit of consciousness made him reject it both as a definite point of departure and as an aim in poetry. His belief in transcendence in the Bradleyan sense made him adopt the notion of a poetical transcendence of private matter into something absolute and objective. And his acceptance of cohesion and completeness as criteria of perfection led him to his cult of tradition and also made him emphasise the formal elements of poetry. At the same time, Bradley's sceptical theories of knowledge no doubt had something to do with Eliot's refusal to take upon himself the prophet's task of pointing the way to truth and goodness.

When we come to his Christian creed, the relation between general philosophy and aesthetic becomes much more difficult to determine. On the whole, one receives the impression that the two continue to subsist side by side without much interaction or interference one with the other. But the question is: would it have been possible to weld them into a whole? Is Christianity compatible with an aesthetic such as Eliot's? Or at least, is the *modus vivendi* that Eliot has found justifiable? To answer these questions we shall first have to ascertain whether there is such a thing as an orthodox Christian philosophy of art, or an aesthetic theory that follows naturally from the main Christian doctrines as held by the churches and as they recommend themselves to the individual mind.

A cursory glance at the use of art made by the various churches is enough to convince us that they are not in agreement among themselves about the position of art in the universal scheme of things. Nor does there seem to be any very definite or authoritative opinion in any of the churches that matter on the general subject of art. And neither the Scriptural canons nor the writings of the Fathers can help us very far. This absence of aesthetic theory has to do with special directions and emphases of thought in the ancient world and the Middle Ages, which it would be outside the scope of this book to examine. Owing to these peculiarities of classical thought, we are forced to work by inference from more or less indirect statements bearing on the subject, and to turn to more recent philosophers for comprehensive views. We will first consult Jacques Maritain.

Saint Thomas defined beauty as *id quod visum placet,* which, in Jacques Maritain's analysis, becomes "une *connaissance intuitive,* et une *joie*".[1] If it is an "intuitive knowledge", it means that the intelligence is concerned, says Maritain; for only the intelligence can *know* in the full meaning of the word, though with human beings knowledge is not directly intuitive but must be transmitted through the medium of the senses. Beauty, then, is an

---

[1] AeS p. 35.

object of the intelligence, and an intellectual joy. And what it conveys to the intelligence, what the intelligence apprehends in knowing beauty, is a glimmering of the Divine:

— *splendor formae,* disait saint Thomas — —: car la "forme", c'est à dire le principe qui fait la perfection propre de tout ce qui est, qui constitue et achève les choses dans leur essence et dans leurs qualités, qui est enfin, si l'on peut ainsi parler, le secret ontologique qu'elles portent en elles, leur être spirituel, leur mystère opérant, est avant tout le principe propre d'intelligibilité, la *clarté* propre de toute chose. Aussi bien toute forme est-elle un vestige ou un rayon de l'Intelligence créatrice imprimé au coeur le l'être créé.[1]

God is the fountain of beauty, and beauty belongs to the transcendental and metaphysical order. Therefore, the fine arts, which are particularly ordered to beauty, have a special character among the other arts. They are like a horizon where matter comes into contact with spirit. They have a spiritual soul, and enable souls to communicate with each other, and to contemplate, with delight, the reality of the spirit. The fine arts, therefore, are an end in themselves and completely disinterested — a fruit, to be enjoyed as such.

"La poésie est ontologie",[2] says Maritain. Because they share the transcendental character of beauty, the fine arts are able to surprise a secret in nature, which is the secret of its hidden spirituality, and the "correspondances sans fin" of natural objects. Thus in every work of art, the artist "recompose *tel qu'en lui-même enfin la poésie le change,* un monde plus réel que le réel offert au sens".[3]

The creative idea is itself purely spiritual. Obviously, then, it is best realised in art which tends towards "purity", i.e. pure spirituality. Maritain praises Mallarmé for having endeavoured to do away with the merely contingent and to bring poetry into harmony with itself. The spirituality of art is best manifested in the purity of form, which is hidden in the material elements of art. It is practically the Symbolist doctrine in its most essential aspect that here finds scholastic support.

The fine arts, however, have also a material nature which it would be fatal do deny. They cannot be detached from the physical conditions of human existence. They should *tend* towards spirituality, but not rashly attempt to achieve it completely and all at once. Rather an equilibrium must be found between the opposite forces of their dual nature. This is what the modern world has not understood. Overweeningly proud of discovering Beauty, artists thought that they were not merely offering a fruit, but that they were giving humanity the Bread and Wine, everything that the spirit needed. Or, in more recent times, they denied the spirit altogether. But art cannot, like wisdom, attain to the perfect contemplation of

---

[1] AeS p. 38.   [2] *Frontières de la Poésie,* p. 13.   [3] Ibid. p. 21. Cf. also p. 62.

God; it is painfully bound to material existence. Nor, on the other hand, is it wholly determined by its material conditions. Only a right understanding of the double character of the fine arts can lead to their being rightly practised. And such an understanding is implicit in the simple striving to be a good workman.

It is not quite clear how Maritain can reconcile the autonomy of art with its dependent role in the total life of the spirit, since in the total life of the spirit the purpose of sanctification is paramount. Such a reconciliation, however, is possible if we do not understand autonomy in an absolute sense, but as denoting the relative independence of the fine arts of the other functions of the human spirit.

The fine arts can help us on the road to salvation by the secondary effects of the emotions that they arouse in us rather than as a fulfilment of their proper purpose. By those who understand, the objects of art can be read as signs of a transcendent reality, so that art can set us on the road to knowledge. And the purity of the artist, though it cannot save his soul, can reflect, and so prepare, moral purity. "Inutiles par eux-mêmes à la vie éternelle, l'art et la poésie sont plus nécessaires que le pain à la race humaine. Ils la disposent à la vie de l'esprit." [1]

The sole end of art itself is the work to be done and the beauty of the work. But in its human aspect, as residing in a person, art has a moral significance and is subordinate to the sanctification of man and to the human virtues. That is to say that "l'art n'a aucun droit contre Dieu". [2] If a conflict arises between the purposes of the artist creating his works of art and the needs of the man in his spiritual struggles towards the light, then the artist is in duty bound to give way. It is obvious that such conflicts will always arise in practical life, except perhaps in the case of the saint, whose every artistic impulse would be inspired by the love of God.

In the ordinary course of things, the intrinsic perfection of art is marred by sin. But if saintliness is not within the reach of all, at least grace is possible, and makes possible a Christian art, which is the art of humanity redeemed, and to which everything belongs, the profane as well as the sacred. The builders of cathedrals believed, and therefore their work "révélait la vérité de Dieu". Conversely, Maritain considers that "partout, lorsque l'art a connu, égyptien, grec ou chinois, un certain degré de grandeur et de pureté, il est déjà chrétien, chrétien en espérance, parce que tout resplendissement spirituel est une promesse et une figure des équilibres divins de l'Evangile". [3]

Implicit in Maritain's aesthetic is a fairly strong faith in the goodness of human nature and in the efficacy of human virtues, a faith which perhaps is natural to a Catholic. His views would have been unacceptable to a Protestant and Puritan philosopher like Søren Kierkegaard. But the

---

[1] *Réponse à Jean Cocteau*, p. 29.   [2] AeS p. 123.   [3] AeS pp. 110, 114.

disagreement between these two is not only a disagreement about human nature, but about the nature of art itself.

Common to all aesthetes, according to Kierkegaard, is their enjoyment of the appearance of the moment, their lack of personal integration and their failing sense of responsibility. The person who makes the enjoyment of art the main thing in his life is only one example of a far more widespread type, which comprises both the gross sensualist, the altruistic endower of charities and the sad sybarite stimulated by his very melancholy. The objects one enjoys cannot of themselves give anything of permanent value to the soul — a statement which applies to beautiful objects as well as to all other sources of pleasure. At bottom all aesthetic enjoyment is a disguising of despair. But it leads the thinking soul back into despair and hence to the problem of good and evil and a moral choice which may bring him to the "ethical stage".

In the ethical stage there are still aesthetic values, but here they are strictly subservient to ethical purposes. On the other hand, not till the ethical stage is reached can beauty be known for what it is. It is not as Saint Thomas said, *id quod visum placet*. It is the super-sensual rightness of persons and things moving individually towards perfection. Thus Kierkegaard's beauty is of a moral and abstract order. Nowhere does he more clearly express his ethical conception of beauty than in his preference — from the point of view of beauty — of the hard-working breadwinner to the idle lilies of the field.

Of art, or to be more specific let us say of imaginative literature, Kierkegaard has a poor opinion. There are poets who have reached the ethical and religious stages, but in general, he thinks, the "existence" of a poet lies in the obscurity of indecision, refusing the ethical choice. And "the poetic ideal is always a false ideal, for the true ideal is always real. When the spirit is prevented from soaring to the eternal realm of spirit, it dawdles on the way, gladdened by the images which are reflected in the clouds, and weeping over their transience. Therefore a poet's existence is by its nature an unhappy existence —".[1] Kierkegaard goes still further. He declares that "from a Christian point of view — — a poet's existence is one of sin, the sin of imagining instead of being, of approaching goodness and truth through the imagination instead of realising them, that is to say, of existentially striving to realise them".[2]

His recognition of imaginative literature, including poetry, rests on the important condition that it should serve the high purposes of religion. But in the religious stage the aesthetic point of view is fraught with the gravest dangers. For the path of the Christian here on earth is the narrow way and his lot that of suffering, and art has no business to camouflage this fact. Nor can celestial bliss be pictured by art, for then it becomes less a goal

---

[1] *Enten-Eller*, p. 227.   [2] *Sygdommen til Døden*, p. 213.

than an object of present and false satisfaction. Only an art, therefore, which is one with its purpose and perfectly transparent is allowable in religion. Art is a very humble servant of the Lord.

Maritain and Kierkegaard represent two extremes in Christian thought. They do not differ greatly in their concepts of beauty, which to both is chiefly the splendour, perceptible to the intellect, of that which is right and good, and derives ultimately from God himself. But Maritain gives it a wider significance, including also the satisfaction of the senses. And the two philosophers are entirely at variance as to the function and value of art. Are they talking about different things, is there something wrong with their premisses, or can their views be finally reconciled?

It seems unquestionable that aesthetic good may be united with moral evil. If we think of the poetry we have read, we are sure to find passages which seem to show that evil can be enjoyed aesthetically. Thus even Dante, exulting in the sight of his enemies being tormented, achieves a beauty which to us seems almost horrible. And Baudelaire's descriptions of the disgusting are not without beauty. But are not our impressions in such cases so mixed that the sense of beauty only partly accounts for them? And is not the beauty itself undefiled, though it may appear in repulsive company? What is properly aesthetic in the case of Dante is not his desire to see his enemies punished, but the power of his imagination and the just proportions of his composition; it is the harmony which invests his subject-matter. And what is beautiful in the case of Baudelaire is not his rotting carcases, but the very magnitude of their repulsiveness, his audacity in describing them, the aptness of the imagery for their disgusting purpose and the words and rhythms in themselves:

> Les jambes en l'air, comme une femme lubrique,
> Brûlante et suant les poisons,
> Ouvrait d'une façon nonchalante et cynique
> Son ventre plein d'exhalaisons. (Une Charogne.)

Beauty is found on close scrutiny to reside in relational and quantitative factors perceptible to the intelligence rather than in sentimental and qualitative factors peceptible to the feelings and the senses. I do not deny that the latter factors play an important part, nor would I suggest that form and content can or should be separated; but I think only the reader's relative sensitiveness to subject-matter and form respectively can determine whether a poem like "Une Charogne" is to be, for him, preponderantly beautiful or preponderantly ugly.

Form in poetry is the pattern of lines, sounds, images, ideas, and the pattern of lines, colours, etc. in the images called up; it is harmony, correspondence, symmetry, balance, in dynamic self-assertion. Maritain suggests that these things can reach, or enable us to reach, the realms of the spirit. Is this possible? Can mere pattern make "words or music reach the stillness", as Eliot puts it in "Burnt Norton"? Perhaps. Geometry has a finality and perfection which may put us in mind of the absolute. But perhaps we must be mentally aware of formal perfection before we can recognise and enjoy it (for instance, in geometrical figures), and perhaps the idea of a higher glory must have entered into our minds before we can see it reflected in a formal pattern. Our experience seems to tell us that what is already in our minds is seized by. the aesthetic emotions and lifted up to be bathed in the light of beauty. Dr. Hans Ording says that "art employs undifferentiated aesthetic ideas, so as to create an emotion which can move freely in relation to various contents. — — It is incorrect to say that art expresses the inexpressible: really it only prepares the ground for the individual to be moved in his inmost self".[1] This, I think, is true, but it is only part of the truth. Art is not just a whirlwind which stirs up dead leaves. It arranges and brings into harmony the contents of our mind, and so enables us to build them into new understanding and new intuitions. And if the mind, at the moment of being moved by aesthetic emotions, is turned towards spiritual things, it receives the necessary impetus to reach higher into the realms of the spirit. Art *qua* art is not devotion. But art to a devout mind may be devotion. And art in a church, where the mind is turned to religious things, may be devotion — if it is not distraction.

Because art gives us the impetus, but not necessarily the contents, and perhaps not the direction, it is powerless alone to save us. This is what most Christian thinkers have realised, though the Catholic thinkers suggest that art can effect a sort of intermediate or special and partial salvation.

On the whole, art is more or less edifying in a general spiritual sense according to the greater or less predominance of formal elements of beauty and their more or less clear recognition.[2] But pure art cannot help us very far. If we could imagine contents which were morally or spiritually neutral, we could perhaps imagine also a kind of "uplift" caused by the pure beauty of form. Such contents, however, are a practical impossibility even in music, because the contents are not only given by the art but are also present in the minds of the listeners, just as in conversation the contents, or meanings, of the individual works spoken to us are present in our minds beforehand, together with a host of other things, and what we hear only presents them to us in a new order. Art, then, is clearly edifying in a spiritual sense only if it involves edifying contents, that is to say, either if it finds edifying contents (which may be the same thing as a mood of devotion) in the mind of the enjoyer, or if it puts such contents into that mind. In either case it is enough that there should be a general awareness of certain things, a general upward direction of interests, even scattered fragments of ideas or emotions — for art will integrate them. Not only is a didactic poem not art in its didactic aspect, but it is not necessary to the effect of edification that

---

[1] *Estetikk og kristendom* p. 211.   [2] Cp. Hulme: *Speculations,* p. 8.

there should be a clear belief or purpose in the mind of the enjoyer or in the poem. For instance, if the contents of a poem are such as to engage the mind on a religious plane — not instruct or influence or challenge or puzzle, but merely engage — the beauty of the poem will create a sense of value on that plane, and hence edify.

It seems that the truth, in the question of the value of art from a Christian point of view, lies somewhere between the typical Catholic and the typical Puritan positions. A similar mean will give the best answer to the question of the autonomy of art in relation to religion.

The scholastics believed that the will could be free only if it acted under grace, and analogously the writers of antiquity believed that beauty was liberated in the bonds of necessity. Thus there is not "free" or "pure" poetry on the one hand and didactic or "impure" poetry on the other, because freedom and autonomy are not outer distinctions, but a state of mind. The poet's state of mind and the reader's state of mind determine the actual autonomy or freedom of poetry. If the poet is in a state of grace, or, to put it more psychologically, if the personality is dominated by faith, then the poet is free, from the point of view of Christianity, to write about whatever it occurs to him to write about. So both Maritain and Kierkegaard are right: art is autonomous but art is also subjected to religion.

In Christianity both the Church and the individual are of paramount importance, and it is impossible to set one above the other. It is right to say, with the Puritans, that the soul of the artist matters supremely. But art itself is not personal. You can convert and save the artist, but you can neither convert nor save art any more than you can convert or save a right-angled triangle. Consequently art is and must be autonomous from the impersonal point of view, which is that of theory, but not from the personal point of view, which is that of practice.

To return now to T. S. Eliot. He began by declaring, in effect, that religion was of no importance to the artist. In a book review of 1916, he admitted that one's enjoyment of art must obviously be coloured by one's philosophy, but asserted for his own part that he saw no reason "why a man's enjoyment of art should be atrophied by a naturalistic philosophy or stimulated by a theistic one". "The feeling and the belief", he explained, "are different things in different categories of value. We enjoy the feeling, and we cannot rest content unless we can justify it by exhibiting its relation to the other parts of our life. Having made this attempt, we then enjoy the theory we have made".[1] A few years later he asserted that "a poet who is also a metaphysician, and unites the two activities, is conceivable as an unicorn or a wyvern is conceivable: he is possible like some of Meinong's *Annahmen;* but such a poet would be a monster —".[2]

---

[1] *International Journal of Ethics,* Jan. 1916, pp. 285—7.   [2] Introd. to *Le Serpent,* p. 13.

Eliot never really gave up this view of art and religion as belonging to two distinct spheres. But of course he came to treat religion in a less cavalier fashion, to see that it mattered to art more than he thought at first, and, now and again, almost to change his ground by subordinating art to dogma and belief. Thus in *The Use of Poetry* he gave it as his opinion (his "eccentricity", he said), that aesthetic studies should be "guided by sound theology",[1] and in his essay on "Religion and Literature" he exhorted all Christians to maintain consciously, in literature, "certain standards and criteria of criticism over and above those applied by the rest of the world".[2] Since he would not make these standards and criteria binding on everybody, however, we may assume that he does not think them proper and essential to art, but only to religion in its dealings with art. He approaches a more general ruling when he says that "anyone who is committed to religious dogma must also be committed to a theory of art which insists on the permanent as well as the changing",[3] but there is really nothing in such a bare insistence on permanence which art might not have formulated for itself. In the ninth Chorus of *The Rock*, the poet speaks of the various branches of art, and asks:

> LORD, shall we not bring these gifts to Your service?
> Shall we not bring to Your service all our powers
> For life, for dignity, grace and order,
> And intellectual pleasures of the senses?
> The LORD who created must wish us to create
> And employ our creation again in His service
> Which is already His service in creating.

The creative activity in itself is here regarded both as a gift of God and as service of God; besides which it may, and should, be employed again more specifically in his service. And this is not only a stray banal idea in a poem; for in *After Strange Gods* Eliot apparently subjects art to the rule of religion by deliberately and judicially applying the criterion of Christian orthodoxy to a number of writers as the supreme test of the value of their works. Even as early as 1922 he stated in an article on "The Lesson of Baudelaire" that "all first-rate poetry is occupied with morality" and that what most matters to a poet is the problem of good and evil.[4]

But we are told with far greater insistence that art is independent and supreme in its own sphere. In "The Function of Criticism" the author "assumed as axiomatic that a creation, a work of art, is autotelic".[5] And in one of his Commentaries he observes that "from the point of view of art, — — Christianity was merely a change, a provision of a new world with new material; from the point of view of communism as of Christianity, art

---

[1] UPC p. 150.   [2] EAM p. 110.   [3] CRICOM, July 1932, p. 678.   [4] *Tyro*, 1, 1922.   [5] SE p. 30.

and literature are strictly irrelevant".[1] A Christian, he says in the same article, is free to allow for inconsistencies in the affairs of this world, such as the appearance of good art even where there is a bad philosophy. Again and again Eliot points to the difference between art and belief. Having read Maritain's *Situation de la Poésie,* and incidentally warned poets against the study of aesthetics, he goes on:

I would make a distinction which Maritain has omitted to make: that between the possible interests of the poet at the times when he is not engaged in writing poetry, and the direction of his attention when writing. — — Certainly, in the effort of composition — — the poet can only properly be occupied with how to say it; and must be sufficiently interested in the thing made, for its own sake, to be content if his readers think the poem means something different from what he thinks it means to him. The problem of which he can afford to be most conscious is the problem of what he can do with his language.[2]

A clearer answer could not be given to those who think that Eliot tries and intends to teach Christianity in his poems. He believes in the real and full sovereigny of art in relation to religion, not just Maritain's qualified autonomy or the special autonomy which we arrived at in our discussion of Christian aesthetics. The above quotation shows that Eliot regards not only impersonal art, but the person of the artist as well, in so far as he is engaged in his work, as exempt from the supremacy of religion. Naturally he does not think that a Christian artist would forget his Christianity as soon as he began to create, but it need no longer, indeed it *should* no longer, be a primary concern with him.

Now this is a view which can be accepted only if by Christianity is meant such things as the articles of the creed, Christian knowledge, Christian morality, etc. If something more is meant, if Christianity is a quality of goodness that should penetrate into all the divisions, aspects and actions of the personality, even to the use of artistic technique, then it is obviously unacceptable. I think Eliot wavers here between different attitudes. Because he is half inclined to free the personality of the artist in his moments of creation from religious allegiance, he tends occasionally to regard sin and evil as an aesthetic good, as instruments in the orchestration of emotions. His "Sin is Behovely" in "Little Gidding" is spoken as much by the aesthetician in him as by the mystic. And because Christian philosophy is reduced to a mere subject of art, he finds other philosophies, such as that of Lucretius, or the Forest Philosophers of India, equally acceptable in poetry, at least theoretically.[3]

Behind his mask of impersonality and orthodoxy, behind his attitude of interpreting the outlook of a generation, Eliot is really quite personal, and the fact that he presents us with the semblances of general ideas does not

---

[1] CRI, Jan. 1933, p. 246.   [2] NEW, 27 April, 1939.   [3] Cf. Introd. to G. W. Knight: *The Wheel of Fire,* p. xiv.

alter the fact that it is his private ideas and emotions he exploits as an artist. The person of the artist is supreme. By stressing the self-completeness of poetry as he does, Eliot renders himself open to the charge which he himself has brought against Matthew Arnold and I. A. Richards, of substituting poetry for religion. Had he been less critical, and less humble before divine mysteries, he might have imitated Joyce's Stephen Dedalus in actually making art his religion and himself its priest.

It is possible that Eliot's views have again been modified of recent years. At any rate it is only fair to add that in some of his statements he does find a place for poetry in a general scheme of things, which is governed by religion. He thinks of art as "one of the essential constituents" of the soil in which religion flourishes.[1] And it is noteworthy that in one of his latest essays, "Cultural Forces in the Human Order", he finds that both aesthetic sensibility and spiritual perception can be so deepened and merged with each other that "in the end, the judgment of a work of art by either religious or aesthetic standards will come to the same thing".[2] This is an idea that we should like to see developed, but unfortunately there is, up to now, only this passing suggestion.

As we saw (p. 57), the author does not commit himself to sweeping assertions about the noetic significance or non-significance of poetry. He thinks that poetry can help one to realise that there is a transcendent reality, and that it can embody already existing beliefs. But he rejects the idea of literature "as a means for eliciting truth or acquiring knowledge" or as "the expression of philosophical or religious intuition". He prefers to see it as "a means of refined and intellectual pleasure".[3] Perhaps his different attitudes to the noetic significance and the salvation value of poetry can be integrated in his desire for "a literature which should be *un*consciously, rather than deliberately and defiantly Christian". At any rate he realises the need for a compromise (cf. p. 59). But he gives us no determinate opinion on the relation between poetry and Christianity.

When I asked him whether he believed in the possibility of divine inspiration in poetry, he did not reject this idea, but neither did he positively assent to it. Only quite exceptionally is it found in his criticism, even as a suggestion.[4]

In his statements on Christianity and aesthetics, he speaks rather as a poet than as a critic. He also speaks as a Christian, but as one for whom there is no need to emphasise his own Christianity. This partly accounts for his frequent failure to show the connection between art and religion; the practical connection between the two nobody can fail to recognise, and it does not need expatiating upon. Besides, there are only too many

---

[1] "Notes towards a Def. of Culture", NEW, 11 Feb. 1943.   [2] Reckitt (ed.): *Prospect for Christendom*, p. 64. Cp. NDC p. 30.   [3] "Exp. in Crit.", *Trad. & Experiment*, p. 200.   [4] Cf. EAM p. 142.

people who welcome Eliot's art as a contribution to Christian propaganda, or decry it for the same reason. It is natural that the poet should react against such people and that his reaction should colour his statements. But when we have allowed for these things, there still seems to be a residue of aestheticism unaffected by the conversion to Christian orthodoxy, and a certain discrepancy (which may, however, be now disappearing) between the beliefs of the man and the attitude of the poet.

Eliot is relatively communicative on the question of the place of philosophy and belief in poetry. This question, however, is so important that we will devote a separate chapter to it. On other points, such as the nature of beauty, the author is silent or almost so. He is in agreement with the Christian aesthetic which we have adumbrated, in favouring the formal elements of poetry, but though he might accept the idea of the edifying and revelatory power of formal beauty, there is not much in his criticism to indicate his adherence to this idea. His chief divergence from a definitely Christian aesthetic lies in his tenacious clinging (contradicted at times, it is true) to the separateness of poetry from other domains of life and from philosophy and metaphysics. However, his theory is really too fragmentary and uncertain in this matter to make a fair comparison possible. It will be more rewarding to study his practice.

III.

Poetic Belief.

Being an attempt to ascertain the ways in which ideas and philosophy may be involved in poetry.

Sir Philip Sidney simply demonstrated that poetry did not ask to be believed literally, and left it at that. Coleridge required that there should be "a suspension of disbelief". And I. A. Richards introduces the idea of "emotional belief". There is here an interesting growth in psychological subtlety, which may, by a kind of inter-play, have gone hand in hand with the development of poetry itself.

How far are we required to believe the things we read about in poetry, and how definitely must the poet believe what he writes? Is there any essential connection between belief and enjoyment? The questions may not have been of great moment in former times, but in our age, with its scientific attitude and its corrosive scepticism, they are of vital significance to the continued existence of poetry. Whether or not there is such a thing as "emotional belief" as distinct from "intellectual belief", it is clear that the Muses must find a justification for their flights of fancy or else be doomed from henceforth to walk upon the ground.

We may start by limiting our field of investigation to the kinds of poetry where the question of belief may be doubtful. That means excluding on the one hand the religious, philosophical or didactic poetry whose purpose is primarily to instruct and teach, and on the other hand historical, narrative and descriptive poems where complete realism and veracity are clearly aimed at. In all these cases the sincere poet believes what he says and the reader is asked to accept and assent in recognised ways. We may also exclude poems which are so obviously extravagant that belief in any usual sense is certainly not expected. That leaves us, as our main objective, with poems which incorporate seemingly reasonable or rational statements of various kinds, but which may be thought to aim chiefly at artistic effect. In the immediate focus of our interest we will find such philosophical poetry as does not directly aim at instruction, and our main problem is to know when and how belief is involved in such poetry.

We may have to distinguish later on between many kinds of belief. But from the first it will be both convenient and necessary to distinguish between the belief of the poet and the assent of the reader, i. e. between the poet's attitude to what he writes about, and the reader's attitude to what he thinks he finds in the poems.

Eliot's Exclusion of Belief from Poetry.

T. S. Eliot frequently discusses the question of belief in poetry, and tells us that neither the poet nor the reader is obliged to believe in the ordinary way in the ideas which have been assimilated into the poetry, or on which the poetry more or less tacitly rests. There is an obvious connection here with his Impersonal theory.

I would suggest that the history of his own spiritual development might throw some light on his views. In his younger days, his days of agnosticism, he read Dante and found that Dante's ideas, his medieval theology and philosophy, would stand in the way of enjoyment if they had to be believed in. He could not believe in these things, but nevertheless he recognised the greatness of the poetry, helped in this, perhaps by Santayana and Pound. So he decided that real belief was unnecessary. And further he decided that Dante need not have believed in these things himself. The theory of poetic belief which was thus indicated may not have originated with Eliot. But he probably found it congenial; useful, too, as a sort of fortification around his own poetry, enabling him to conceal himself in his works and to ward off mere prying.

Altogether, there seems to have been a constant sceptical and analytical tendency in Eliot's early speculations about belief and meaning. The tendency is discernible in several domains. Thus in the paper on "The Interpretation of Primitive Ritual" which he wrote for Josiah Royce, he tried "to show that in many cases no interpretation of a rite could explain its origin".[1]

---

[1] Introd. to *Savonarola*, p. viii.

In his essay on "The Development of Leibniz's Monadism" he made a point of proving that Leibniz's metaphysics and his scientific achievements represented "two different values".[1] And — most significant of all in this connection — in 1919 he wrote that "it is not true that the development of a writer is a function of his development as a man".[2] In other words, what the writer believes may spring from the same sources as what the man believes, but the beliefs of the one are not just derived from those of the other. Consequently, a work of art is a fact which exists apart from the beliefs of the artist as a private citizen.

Later, when Eliot was drawn into a discussion with I. A. Richards on the question of poetic belief, he somewhat modified his early views, but they were not fundamentally revised.

It is natural that his thoughts regarding this problem should have been brought to a focus about the time of his entering the Anglican communion. In "A Note on Poetry and Belief" published in *The Enemy* for January 1927, the author is concerned with the nature of belief, which he finds to have "been in constant mutation" throughout history. This he finds indicated both by the history of poetry and by the history of Christian dogma, as he had earlier found it proved by the study of primitive ritual. Belief was in many ways a different thing to Dante, Crashaw, and Christina Rossetti, and it is yet another thing to Eliot, for whom even "doubt and uncertainty are merely a variety of belief". Christianity, he thinks, "will probably continue to modify itself". The author's point of view is psychological rather than dogmatic (actually he fails to distinguish between belief as personal conviction and belief as impersonal dogma), and from this point of view it is natural to regard matters of belief as being in a state of flux determined by individuality and historical climate. This way of looking at belief makes it a kind of constantly repeated interpretation of dogma in relation to the spirit of the age. And for such a task of interpretation the poet, we may conclude, is peculiarly fitted, for it demands a great deal of intuition and sympathetic imagination. Thus, by what he implies perhaps, rather than by what he actually says, Eliot relates the psychological nature of belief much more closely than is usual to the nature of poetic imagination.

This, of course, only means that belief is made to look less fixed and static than we are used to regard it; it does not reduce the poetic imagination into a technique for metaphysical speculation. Such speculation, according to Eliot, is no business of the poet's: "a poet who is also a metaphysician — — would be a monster". Valéry, at any rate, was no monster, for Eliot found no philosophy in his poetry. Nor need the poet actually believe in the ideas he uses. Dante's poetry certainly contains philosophy; but Eliot maintains that Dante's beliefs as a man are not identical with his beliefs

---

[1] *Monist* Oct. 1916, p. 542.   [2] "Reflections on Contemp. Poetry", *Egoist*, July 1919.

as a poet: "his private belief becomes a different thing in becoming poetry".[1] Shakespeare is another poet whose philosophy must not be accepted too literally. In "Shakespeare and the Stoicism of Seneca" the author gives it as his "own frivolous opinion" "that Shakespeare may have held in private life very different views from what we extract from his extremely varied published works; that there is no clue in his writings to the way in which he would have voted in the last or would vote in the next election; and that we are completely in the dark as to his attitude about prayer-book revision". "I admit", adds Eliot, "that my own experience, as a minor poet, may have jaundiced my outlook; that I am used to having cosmic significances, which I never suspected, extracted from my work — —; and to having my personal biography reconstructed from passages which I got out of books, or which I invented out of nothing because they sounded well — —".[2] In the same essay, the cases of Donne and Chapman are found to be similar to those of Dante and Shakespeare. In Donne the author, after investigation, found only "a vast jumble of incoherent erudition on which he drew for purely poetic effects". And Professor Schoell had shown Chapman "lifting long passages from the works of writers like Ficino and incorporating them in his poems completely out of their context".[3]

In fine, Eliot doubts "whether belief proper enters into the activity of a great poet, *qua* poet. That is, Dante, *qua* poet, did not believe or disbelieve the Thomist cosmology or theory of the soul: he merely made use of it, or a fusion took place between his initial emotional impulses and a theory, for the purpose of making poetry".[4] Indeed, as we have seen, Eliot thinks it a blemish if a personal belief is too apparent in poetry. "With Goethe, for instance, I often feel too acutely 'this is what Goethe the man believed', instead of merely entering into a world which Goethe has created".[5]

Not that the poet may not have some axe to grind, or a very definite purpose in writing. Eliot admits that these things are compatible with even the greatest poetry,[6] only they have to comply with the conditions set by the work of art, and not intrude as foreign elements. It is not the proper function of poetry to teach, or present a philosophy. Nevertheless there is a necessary connection between poetry and belief.[7] In Eliot's words: "we are forced to believe that there is a particular relation between the two, and that the poet 'means what he says'. If we learned, for instance, that *De Rerum Natura* was a Latin exercise which Dante had composed for relaxation after completing the *Divine Comedy,* and published under the name of one Lucretius, I am sure that our capacity for enjoying either poem would be mutilated. Mr. Richards's statement (*Science and Poetry,* p. 76 footnote) that a certain writer has effected 'a complete severance between

---

[1] SE p. 258.   [2] SE p. 127.   [3] SE p. 139.   [4] SE p. 138.   [5] SE p. 258.
[6] Cf. Book review CRI, July 1931; and SFP.   [7] Cp. p. 57.

his poetry and *all* beliefs' is to me incomprehensible".[1] The last sentence refers to Dr. Richards's opinion of Eliot's *Waste Land*. And the whole passage shows that Eliot is no fanatical devotee of aestheticism: the view that he expresses here is such as might be expected of a believer in Catholicism and an upholder of tradition and Classicism; whereas his inclination to cut poetry adrift from rational belief reveals the Romanticist in him.

The "particular relation" between poetry and belief appears, on analysis, to fall under several heads. There is first the poetic use of philosophical ideas as a kind of game. This is how Donne used his chequered learning, according to Eliot.[2] The game consists in making a kind of pattern of ideas, and for this purpose it is evident that borrowed ideas — and emotions — may serve the poet's turn as well as his own.[3] Since everything is proffered in play, the question of sincerity does not arise.

Secondly, there is the emotional rendering of the poet's philosophy, which, as in the case of Lucretius or Dante, appears as a *fusion* between the philosophy of the poet and "his natural feelings".[4] Eliot thinks that poems in which such a fusion has taken place "were not designed to persuade the readers to an intellectual assent, but to convey an emotional equivalent for the ideas. What Lucretius and Dante teach you, in fact, is *what it feels like* to hold certain beliefs; what Virgil teaches you [in his *Georgics*] is to feel yourself inside the agrarian life".[5] (Elsewhere, however, Eliot has recognised Dante's didactic purpose.[6])

The third possible and legitimate relation between poetry and belief is that of the poetic illustration of a philosophy which is already existent and moreover generally accepted, so as to need no rational presentation or justification. In this case it is not so much the poet's belief as the belief or ethos of the age he lives in that is exploited poetically. "When a poet has expressed successfully a philosophy we find that it is a philosophy which is already in existence, not one of his own invention".[7] Eliot mentions Dante's ideas on the Freedom of the Will and the order of the seven deadly sins as something that Dante may have simply borrowed from Aquinas without vouching for their credibility in the ordinary sense; and the theory of the soul in Dante as deriving from Aristotle's *De Anima*.[8] He admits that "the 'truest' philosophy is the best material for the greatest poet",[9] but "truth" is not all-important, for he considers Dante and Lucretius fully justified in "using other men's philosophies cheerfully without bothering too much about verifying them for themselves".[10]

In fact, "a philosophical theory which has entered into poetry is established, for its truth or falsity in one sense ceases to matter, and its

---

[1] "Dante", Note, SE p. 269. Cf. also NPB.   [2] Cp. "Donne in Our Time", *Garland for J. Donne*, pp. 8, 12.   [3] Cf. TIT, SE p. 21.   [4] "Idea of Lit. Review", CRI, Jan. 1926, p. 37.   [5] SFP. Cf. also *Poetry*, p. 13.   [6] Cf. UPC p. 96.   [7] SFP.   [8] "Dante", SE p. 259.   [9] PP p. 37.   [10] Introd. to *Le Serpent*.

truth in another sense is proved".[1] Eliot might have adopted the statement "Beauty is truth, truth beauty". (But he would have had to pervert Keats's meaning, for neither Keats nor his contemporaries really distinguished between different kinds of truth.) The sense in which he thinks that poetry can prove the truth of a philosophy is primarily aesthetic. A Christian, he says, will not think of Dante as proving Christianity, or a materialist of Lucretius as proving materialism or atomism. "What he will find in Dante or Lucretius is the *esthetic* sanction: that is the partial justification of these views of life by the art to which they give rise. — — what poetry proves about any philosophy is merely its possibility for being lived — for life includes both philosophy and art." It is a very limited sanction that poetry gives to the ideas it successfully embodies, if we understand the author to say that philosophy in art merely proves that philosophy can be used in art. But he also means that art, by its imaginative testing and illustration of a philosophy enables us to realise more fully the practical implications of that philosophy. Poetry, he says, "is not the assertion that something is true, but the making that truth more fully real to us".[2] To the reader this means that something may be made to seem real without being accepted as true.

A poem, as Eliot acknowledges, is a different thing to the reader from what it is to the poet. This is inevitably so, but of course one may strive to make the difference between the poet's and the reader's experiences as small as possible. Theoretically it is tenable that the reader would get the greatest enjoyment out of poetry if he were able to recapture the emotions and thoughts of the author, and the state of tension in which he created the poem. Eliot, however, does not think the writing of poetry in itself enjoyable, and apparently would hardly think it desirable for the reader to recapture the poet's emotions. He is perfectly content to let the reader enjoy poetry in his own way, provided his appreciation is not too one-sided.

The reader's appreciation of poetry may be determined in the first place by the attention he gives proportionately to art and meaning, enjoyment and understanding. Eliot finds that "the legitimate responses of the reader vary very widely" between two extremes. At one end of the scale are those who, like Mr. Belgion, "like poetry merely for what it has to say", at the other end those who, with Dr. Richards, "like the poetry because the poet has manipulated his material into perfect art". "Between these extremes occurs a continuous range of appreciations, each of which has its own limited validity".[3] In a more recent essay, Eliot continues to recognise a wide variety of responses, but warns us emphatically against the extremes at either end. It is wrong to think "that it is simply the value of the *ideas* expressed in a poem which gives the value to the poetry, or that it is the *truth* of [the poet's] view of life — by which we ordinarily mean its congruity with our own view — that matters". And it is also wrong to think

---

[1] MP, SE p. 288.   [2] PP pp. 36—7.   [3] PP p. 33 .

"that the ideas, the beliefs of the poet do not matter at all; that they are rather like some alloy, necessary for the poet in order to manipulate his true. material, which is refined out of the poetry in the course of time". The author comes to the conclusion that a *good* poet presents a certain ambiguity. "At moments", he says, "I feel that his language is merely the perfect instrument for what he has to say; at other moments I feel that he is simply making use of, even exploiting, his beliefs for the sake of the verbal beauty in which he can express them. He appears to be both inside and outside his beliefs. and interests. Where this doubt about the attitude of the poet cannot arise, one is tempted to suspect the poetry".[1]

Eliot is generally sceptical of all "interpretation", though he regards it as unavoidable, because we are urged to it by a restless instinct.[2] This being so, it is as well to recognise that a poet is as much in the dark as anybody else about many things that go to the making of a poem, and that "what a poem means is as much what it means to others as what it means to the author".[3] The reader, therefore, has a certain scope for finding his own beliefs in what he reads and colouring it with his own view of life. But in many cases he comes up against ideas or beliefs which cannot be meddled with, and which he must either accept, or pretend to accept, or reject. And this brings us into the centre of the problem of the reader's poetic assent.

"There is a difference", asserts the author in his essay on Dante, "between philosophical *belief* and poetic *assent*".[4] And in the Note to Section II of this essay, he explains his position as follows:

If there is "literature", *if* there is "poetry", then it must be possible to have full literary or poetic appreciation without sharing the beliefs of the poet. That is as far as my thesis goes in the present essay. — — —
If you deny the theory that full poetic appreciation is possible without belief in what the poet believed, you deny the existence of "poetry" as well as "criticism"; and if you push this denial to its conclusion, you will be forced to admit that there is very little poetry that you can appreciate, and that your appreciation of it will be a function of your philosophy or theology or something else. If, on the other hand, I push *my* theory to the extreme, I find myself in as great a difficulty. I am quite aware of the ambiguity of the word "understand". In one sense, it means to understand without believing, for unless you can understand a view of life (let us say), without believing in it, the word "understand" loses all its meaning, and the act of choice between one view and another is reduced to caprice. But if you yourself are convinced of a certain view of life, then you irresistibly and inevitably believe that if anyone else comes to "understand" it fully, his understanding *must* terminate in belief. It is possible, and sometimes necessary, to argue that full understanding must identify itself with full belief. A good deal. it thus turns out, hangs on the meaning, if any, of this short word *full*.

---

[1] SFP.   [2] Cf. Introd. to G. W. Knight: *The Wheel of Fire*, p. xiv.   [3] UPC
p. 130.   [4] SE p. 257.

In short, both the view I have taken in this essay, and the view which contradicts it, are, if pushed to the end, what I call heresies (not, of course, in the theological, but in a more general sense).

After considering a number of literary examples, in which he finds that his understanding and acceptance of the propositions they enunciate, or his lack of understanding and acceptance, affect his sense of beauty, Eliot continues:

So I can only conclude that I cannot, in practice, wholly separate my poetic appreciation from my personal beliefs. Also that the distinction between a statement and a pseudo-statement is not always, in particular instances, possible to establish. — —
— — Actually, one probably has more pleasure in the poetry when one shares the beliefs of the poet. On the other hand there is a distinct pleasure in enjoying poetry as poetry when one does *not* share the beliefs, analogous to the pleasure of "mastering" other men's philosophical systems. It would appear that "literary appreciation" is an abstraction, and pure poetry a phantom; and that both in creation and enjoyment much always enters which is, from the point of view of "Art", irrelevant.[1]

We see that in Eliot's opinion it is not only pleasant, but necessary too, in a way, to entertain beliefs that one does not actually hold. He finds the use of poetry in this respect similar to that of philosophy. We study different philosophies "largely for the exercise in assumption or entertaining ideas", and "only by the exercise of understanding without believing, so far as that is possible, can we come in full consciousness to some point where we believe *and* understand. Similarly with the experience of poetry. We aim ideally to come to rest in some poetry which shall realize poetically what we ourselves believe; but we have no contact with poetry unless we can pass in and out freely, among the various worlds of poetic creation".[2]
Eliot here makes an important point. He does not think, however, that *any* philosophy should be acceptable to the reader, as he tells us in *The Use of Poetry:*

We may be permitted to infer, in so far as the distaste of a person like myself for Shelley's poetry is not attributable to irrelevant prejudices or to a simple blind spot, but is due to a peculiarity in the poetry and not in the reader, that it is not the presentation of beliefs which I do not hold, or — to put the case as extremely as possible — of beliefs that excite my abhorrence, that makes the difficulty. Still less is it that Shelley is deliberately making use of his poetic gifts to propagate a doctrine; for Dante and Lucretius did the same thing. I suggest that the position is somewhat as follows. When the doctrine, theory, belief, or "view of life" presented in a poem is one which the mind of the reader can accept as coherent, mature, and founded on the facts of experience, it interposes

---

[1] SE pp. 269—271.   [2] PP p. 37.

no obstacle to the reader's enjoyment, whether it be one that he accept or deny, approve or deprecate. When it is one which the reader rejects as childish or feeble, it may, for a reader of well-developed mind, set up an almost complete check.[1]

Eliot is not doctrinaire or one-sided in this matter. He does not think "culture" requires us to make "a deliberate effort to put out of mind all our convictions and passionate beliefs about life when we sit down to read poetry".[2] As usual, he brings a number of qualifications to bear on his main position. But it remains true that he does definitely advocate a suspension of disbelief and the adoption of a poetic assent as a condition of poetic enjoyment. Of Dante he says that "you cannot afford to *ignore* Dante's philosophical and theological beliefs, or to skip the passages which express them most clearly; but on the other hand you are not called upon to believe them yourself. It is wrong to think that there are parts of the *Divine Comedy* which are of interest only to Catholics or to medievalists. — — In reading Dante you must enter the world of thirteenth-century Catholicism — —. You are not called upon to believe what Dante believed, for your belief will not give you a groat's worth more of understanding and appreciation; but you are called upon more and more to understand it. If you can read poetry as poetry, you will 'believe' in Dante's theology exactly as you believe in the physical reality of his journey; that is, you suspend both belief and disbelief. I will not deny that it may be in practice easier for a Catholic to grasp the meaning, in many places, but that is not because the Catholic believes, but because he has been instructed".[3] Eliot repeats in *The Use of Poetry* that "it is not essential to share Dante's beliefs in order to share his poetry" (and he calls Dante "about as thorough-going a didacticist as one could find").[4] This is a cardinal point in his critical writings, and has a general application: "Some of the early Buddhist scriptures affect me as parts of the Old Testament do; I can still enjoy Fitzgerald's *Omar,* though I do not hold that rather smart and shallow view of life".[5] Eliot regards it as a personal prejudice of his that he takes the greatest pleasure in "poetry with a clear philosophical pattern". But though he prefers a "Christian and Catholic" philosophy, he is quite prepared to enjoy "that of Epicurus or of the Forest Philosophers of India" as well.[6]

The theory of poetic assent is applicable not only to the thought contained in poetry, but also to the feelings Thus Eliot declares that he enjoys Shakespeare's poetry to the full extent of his capacity for enjoying poetry. "But", he adds, "I have not the slightest approach to certainty that I share Shakespeare's feelings".[7]

---

[1] UPC p. 96.   [2] UPC p. 97.   [3] SE p. 257.   [4] UPC p. 95.   [5] UPC p. 91.   [6] Introd. to *The Wheel of Fire* p. xiv.   [7] UPC p. 115

General Discussion.

Eliot's views on poetry and belief are rather fumblingly discussed by M. Louis Grudin in a book called *Mr. Eliot Among the Nightingales,* and rather captiously by Mr. Yvor Winters in his essay on "The Illusion of Reaction". But a number of critics more interesting to the student have entered the general debate from various angles of approach. Among those who are more or less in agreement with Eliot is I. A. Richards.

Dr. Richards, Mr. Eliot and, incidentally, A. E. Housman and Mr. Middleton Murry,[1] are agreed in thinking that strict belief need not be accorded to the ideas or philosophy employed by a poet. But Richards goes a step further than Eliot in repudiating the rational meaning of poetry, which makes Eliot accuse him of wanting poets to create in a vacuum.[2] What Richards actually contends is briefly this: "It is never what a poem *says* which matters, but what it *is.* The poet is not writing as a scientist". Poetry is produced by and in turn acts on an intricate system of interests in the mind, and its worth is a matter of the degree to which it moves the mind "towards a wider equilibrium". Now the human mind cannot find equilibrium and order unless it believes in something. We may believe in true statements, which to Richards are scientific statements, or in false statements, which he calls "pseudo-statements". "On the whole true statements are of more service to us than false ones. None the less we do not and, at present, cannot order our emotions and attitudes by true statements alone. — — This is one of the greatest dangers to which civilization is exposed. Countless pseudo-statements — about God, about the universe, about human nature, the relations of mind to mind, about the soul, its rank and destiny — pseudo-statements which are pivotal points in the organization of the mind, vital to its well-being, have suddenly become — — impossible to believe as for centuries they have been believed." Only scientific knowledge can now command belief in anything like the old sense, but this knowledge is not sufficient for a fine organisation of the mind. It cannot be trusted "to give support to our lives — a support we now recognise as largely emotional". The only remedy, therefore, "is to cut our pseudo-statements free from that kind of belief which is appropriate to verified statements". We must distinguish between different modes of belief if we are to survive morally.[3] Accordingly, Richards distinguishes between "intellectual belief" and "emotional belief". "In primitive man — — any idea which opens a ready outlet to emotion or points to a line of action in conformity with custom is quickly believed. — — This acceptance, this use of the idea — by our interest, desires, feelings, attitudes, tendencies to action and what not — is emotional belief. So far as

---

[1] Cf. Housman: *Name & N. of Poetry* and Murry: *Countries of the Mind, II.*
[2] Cf. PP p. 30; and NPB.   [3] *Science & Poetry* pp. 31—90.

the idea is useful to them it is believed, and the sense of attachment, of adhesion, of conviction, which we feel, and to which we give the name of belief, is the result of this implication of the idea in our activities". "An emotional belief is not justified through any logical relations between its idea and other ideas. Its only justification is its success in meeting our needs." Emotional belief, of course, can be accorded — and actually is accorded, if we will only recognise it — to pseudo-statements, thus enabling us to benefit by such statements without coming into conflict with our knowledge of scientific truth. But emotional belief must be "kept from interfering with the intellectual system. And poetry is an extraordinarily successful device for preventing these interferences from arising", because it charms us into something more than Coleridge's "willing suspension of disbelief": "the question of belief or disbelief, in the intellectual sense, never arises when we are reading well".[1] Poetry, therefore, is "capable of saving us". And "the tradition of poetry is the guardian of the supra-scientific myths",[2] which are necessary to our mental well-being.

Whereas Richards distinguishes between intellectual belief and emotional belief, Eliot does not reject intellectual belief in poetry, but distinguishes instead between what we may call genuine belief and assumed, or temporary belief. He repudiates Richards's idea of separating sensibility and intellect and finds his division of belief into two kinds both unnatural and unhistorical. Belief is not just a matter of two distinct categories, but of infinite gradations from doubt to assent. And irrespective of the rise of modern science, it "has been in constant mutation — — from the beginning of civilisation", and will continue to change in the future. Dr. Richards's distinctions cannot help anyone to believe, since "it takes application, and a kind of genius, to believe anything". For belief, I understand Eliot to mean, is something that concerns all circumstances of life at a given time, including both science and poetry.[3]

The distinction between intellectual and emotional belief certainly seems rather factitious. On the other hand, as long as Eliot maintains the distinction between real and assumed belief, his ideas of the gradation and mutation of belief are not sufficiently radical solutions of our problem: the problem of poetic belief in relation to an individual poet or reader. I would suggest that the idea of different categories of belief be given up. The actual movement of belief is always an affair of the emotions, as even Richards recognises when he defines belief as "the sense of attachment, of adhesion, of conviction, which we feel". What he calls "intellectual belief" is really an emotional belief caused by the perception of cohesion, completeness and harmony between ideas. This perception is related to the perception of beauty in art; only, in one case the intellect is primarily instrumental

---

[1] *Pract. Criticism* pp. 275—7.   [2] *Science & Poetry*, p. 90.   [3] Cf. NPB and PP.

in arranging the matter for our understanding, whilst in the other case the senses are also at work. "Intellectual" or "scientific belief" has, in the last analysis, nothing more certain about it than any other kind of belief, certainty, too, being an affair of the emotions. It is true that the matter of scientific belief belongs to a closed system of thought distinct from, let us say, the matter of religious belief. But the whole system of thought may, for all we know, be as mythical in the case of science as in the case of religion, or, conversely, as absolutely valid in the case of religion as in the case of science.

It will be apparent that the chief objections we must lodge against earlier discussions of the nature of belief concern false distinctions. The distinction between belief and knowledge served its purpose until modern psychology revealed it as a fiction, since when it has become suspect. But it cannot be replaced by a new fiction, such as the distinction between intellectual and emotional belief. One is rather surprised to find Dr. Richards make this distinction, since, in his *Principles of Literary Criticism,* he insists so strongly on the similarity between aesthetic experiences and experiences of any other kind, and on the essential oneness of all psychic or, as he prefers to call it, neural activity. But Richards is probably led off his course by his worship of science, as so many others are led astray by misapplying their loyalties. We cannot allow Richards to set scientific knowledge apart for special definition any more than we allow ourselves to set religious knowledge apart as psychologically taboo.

Belief must be conceived of more or less on the same lines as F. H. Bradley conceives of thought. Thought to Bradley is "different from thought discursive and rational". It does not predicate, it gets beyond mere relations and reaches something other than truth. It is "absorbed into a fuller experience" which also comprises feeling and will.[1] In the same way we must regard belief as different from rational assent; it comprises thought, feeling and will in a higher emotional experience which reaches something other than truth. Eliot's striving to "get *beyond poetry*"[2] may be seen as a striving to appeal to this kind of belief.

As a matter of fact, Eliot sometimes approaches a conception of belief similar to the one I am trying to define. Thus in *The Music of Poetry* he regards the reader's emotion as the criterion of the significance of a poem: "If we are moved by a poem, it has meant something, perhaps something important, to us; if we are not moved, then it is, as poetry, meaningless".[3] He almost says here (though he avoids saying it explicitly) that meaning in the semantic sense is dependent on emotion. It would have been more intelligible, and probably have covered his intention as well, if he had said that belief is dependent on emotion. In his "Note on Poetry and Belief" he holds, as we have seen (pp. 73, 81), that belief as a psychological pheno-

---

[1] A&R p. 171.   [2] Cf. ATSE p. 90.   [3] MUS p. 15.

menon varies with times and individuals, and he implies that it is a matter of sympathetic understanding, not of mere rational demonstrability. He even includes more within the concept of belief than I am prepared to do, by classing doubt and uncertainty as a variety of belief, just as the phenomenologists class the non-existent as a variety of Reality. Psychologically doubt and uncertainty may be very near to belief, but psychically, if we may make this distinction, the characteristic mark of belief is nevertheless its quality of *positive* attraction or assent. In other words, an individual may need to take only a step to pass from doubt to belief, but he does pass from one thing to something different. And it is this fact that counts from the point of view of aesthetics.

Mr. John Crowe Ransom has done much to answer the question we are here dealing with. He suggests that "the differentia of poetry as discourse is an ontological one. It treats an order of existence, a grade of objectivity, which cannot be treated in scientific discourse". The signs used by art, he says, "are 'icons' or images", and poetry, by means of these icons aims at imitating actual life. Therefore, whilst "in scientific discourse we deal with a single value-system at a time", in art "the work itself goes beyond its paraphrase into the realm of the natural objects or situations themselves, which are many-valued".[1] By resolving the problem in such terms, Ransom retains the unity of belief (or, as he would prefer it, "speculation" and "hypothesis") as an activity of the mind, whilst distinguishing between its different ways, and the varying comprehensiveness, of its relating itself to fact.

Mr. Ransom sees poetic truth and scientific truth as different orders of the same thing. His ideas have thus some similarity with other views in which poetic truth is held to be another or a higher form of intellectual truth. An extreme view is stated by Matthew Arnold, who cherishes the poetic idea and looks to poetry to interpret life for us.[2] A commoner and more plausible view is that of the Abbé Brémond, who thinks poetry can give a direct, intuitive knowledge of the highest mysteries.[3] That such a notion, in an attenuated form, is quite seriously entertained by many people, is shown by an interesting report on *Doctrine in the Church of England* made by the Commission on Christian Doctrine appointed by the Archbishops of Canterbury and York in 1922. The Commission, which published its report in 1938, regarded the language of devotion as "more nearly akin to poetry than to science", and both the language of devotion and that of poetry as presenting truth in a symbolical way.[4]

Richards regards such solutions as subterfuges and the product of poor thinking.[5] He is not satisfied with merely distinguishing between different aspects or ranks of truth which all presuppose the same kind of unqualified

---

[1] RAN pp. 281—293.   [2] Cf. *Essays in Criticism, Works,* IV, pp. 1—2.
[3] Compare Bergson's theories.   [4] Op. cit., p. 35.   [5] Cf. *Science & Poetry,* p. 69.

belief. And we may admit that he is right to some extent: there is a difference between the way in which we believe in a poetic statement, and the ways in which we believe in other kinds of statements — religious, scientific, journalistic, legal, etc. But it is not the difference between intellectual and emotional assent. However, before going into that, we must consider a powerful piece of criticism that has been levelled against both Eliot's and Richards's positions.

Mr. Montgomery Belgion (and perhaps we may see an ally of his in Mr. Yvor Winters) contends that "there is no meaning, in the sense of import or significance, in a poem, apart from its 'logical meaning' ". The imaginative writer may not believe in what he writes, but at any rate "his conception of what is going to be most effective in his work will vary according to the philosophy of life he happens to hold. In other words, when the imaginative writer appears to be aiming, and may suppose he is aiming, at no more than the production of an effect in his reader, he is actually seeking to philosophize or moralize." As for the reader, if the imaginative writer is to produce in him the effect he aims at producing, "the reader must accept the philosophy of life which the imaginative work illustrates, he must accept it as a true philosophy". The reader's belief becomes no different just because he has been moved emotionally into adopting it. But he may be moved so subtly that he does not realise that he has been influenced, and that he thinks he has always considered those things to be true which actually the writer has convinced him of.[1] We enjoy literature, according to Belgion, only in the measure we think it true to life. But the things we believe to be true to life are often a mere deception. So the poet is an "irresponsible propagandist", who often persuades us illicitly.[2]

Some of Mr. Belgion's main opinions are shared by Mr. Edmund Wilson.[3] The arguments of these men are weighty, but yet they seem one-sided. This is probably because both are attacking what they regard as grave misconceptions. Belgion is alarmed by "a statement contained in the theory of art most favoured in England today, the statement that a philosophy, once it is incorporated in a work of art, ceases to be a philosophy, and is no longer *qua* philosophy either true or false, but is only true or false aesthetically".[4] Belgion is justified in attacking this view, but he goes too far in the opposite direction, and denies common experience, which tells us that we are in most cases able to tell fairy-tale from history.

It ought to be possible to find a solution which avoids the faults of the extreme views. And here we may return to Dr. Richards, who, in his book *Mencius on the Mind,* tells us that we must acquire the habit of mind "of regarding all thinking — even the most seemingly autonomous — as pur-

---

[1] *Our Present Philos. of Life,* pp. 31—47.   [2] Cf. *The Human Parrot* p. 85.
[3] Cf. AC p. 119.   [4] *Our Present Philos. of Life,* p. 30. Cp. Eliot: MP, SE p. 288.

posive; and of expecting the form of the thinking to be not independent of the purpose".[1] Now this leads to a different train of thought from that induced by the distinction between intellectual and emotional belief. It leads us to think of all statements as appealing equally to the same kind of belief (which, we have determined, is emotional) but by a great number of different ways, or, to use another concept of Richards's, in a great number of different tones. "Tone", with Richards, is one of the ways in which the meaning of a poem is conveyed, and it includes the many different devices and clues by which the author reveals his attitude to his subject and to his readers. Clearly tone can be shaded off into almost infinite modifications, which our mind can register correctly, but which language can only approximately describe. And the same applies to what Richards calls purpose, or intention, which is the general plan and aim of the poet when writing a poem, and the organising principle of the other kinds of meaning: sense, feeling and tone.

To the spectrum of "tone" answers a spectrum of belief. To acquire the habit of mind of regarding all thinking as purposive means to modify our belief indefinitely in accordance with the sort of thinking we come up against. Or rather, since belief is essentially the same thing in all cases, it means modifying the mental machinery by which belief is operated, so as to make belief more or less permanent, more or less temporary, more or less intermittent, and to regulate its strength through all degrees from complete disbelief to intense belief. The mental machinery by which this is done is primarily judgment, which may be either an abstract ability to recognise perfection (the intelligence) or a more concrete ability to find satisfaction (the senses). Of course, in a poem, the poet has already judged for us to a certain extent, as he shows by his tone, and he wishes us to accept his judgment. This we generally do; and it is one of the pleasures of reading poetry to escape the trouble of judging. But a good reader will know directly, or any reader will know from habit, that the poet's judgments have not been tested, and very likely would not stand testing from the point of view of scientific veracity. Therefore he accepts them with a certain restraint. And this may be why poetic belief *seems* different from other belief.

Our common scientific attitude is really no more than a tacit social convention by which we agree to discriminate between "truths" to which we can accord a very strong belief, because derived from so many sources — evidence of the senses, hearsay, custom and constant corroboration — and other kinds of truth or falsehood. Belief in, let us say, religious truths can also be very strong, but for different reasons, and therefore appears in a different modality. Poetic belief has yet other modalities, and so on. When Blake was asked whether, when the sun arose, he did not see a round disc of fire somewhat like a Guinea, he replied, "O no, no, I see an innumerable

---

[1] Op. cit. p. 91.

company of the Heavenly host crying, 'Holy! Holy! Holy is the Lord God Almighty!" There may be a stronger, but not necessarily a better reason for one answer than for the other. And, in the final analysis, as F. H. Bradley forcibly demonstrates in the first part of his *Appearance and Reality*, scientific truth is no more reliable than any other sort. It is based on an illusory, or as we might say, imaginative, apprehension of Reality, and we recognise it as emotional in its movement of assent. All this leads us to conclude that scientific belief is only one mode of belief among so many others.

Belief in relation to its object is essentially one thing and indivisible. But as was the case with the sense of beauty, to which it is obviously akin, it can appear in the company of many strange and mixed emotions. Thus, in relation to the person who believes, it is modally qualified. Perhaps Eliot has some such idea as this at the back of his mind when he uses the expression *"belief attitude"*.[1]

In theory there is an infinite modality of beliefs. In practice we find systems, or clusters, of modal beliefs, which clusters may or may not hang together among themselves. Thus we hold one cluster of beliefs when in "intellectual" or "scientific mood", another when in fairy-tale mood, etc. In this sense, then, we may speak of "intellectual belief"; but not as opposed to "emotional belief". The latter expression is indeed something of a pleonasm, since all beliefs, i. e. all value-attachments, are ultimately emotional.

The tone of a poem is an indication of the system of beliefs in which we may incorporate the statements of the poem. If it fails to put us right, our judgment has to be called upon. That will always be a disturbing element so long as it functions, but having functioned, and having put us in the right mood, it will enable us to appreciate a poem all the better. Much poetry, especially modern poetry, only reveals its beauty after we have studied it.

Eliot is quite right, from an historical point of view, to speak of mutations of belief. The common moods of thought and belief change with the times. In former ages, before rational and scientific thought became a well-defined convention, the ideal of exact and truthful thinking was subtly different from what it is to us, and must have been applied very differently to many everyday statements which involved strong emotions or perhaps stock responses. It is only because our thinking to-day is governed so rigidly by reason that we are tempted to look upon rational belief as something fundamentally distinct from poetic belief or religious belief. It is all part of a general movement of thought. It is typical, perhaps, that people nowadays, more than formerly seems to have been the case, tend to ask of poetry: *what* does it say? *what* does it mean? and forget, because they

----

[1] "Dante", SE p. 259.

feel these rational questions to be so urgent, to attune themselves to the right mood of appreciation.

It is true, as I. A. Richards and Middleton Murry assert, that it is impossible to believe in the old things in the same way as our forefathers. But this is not only because we have gained greater insight into reality. It is also because we have adopted a new illusion: the primacy of scientific belief. Richards recognises that scientific belief is not enough for human kind. Man shall not live by bread alone. But he regards scientific truth and scientific belief as being in a class entirely apart, and scientific statement as the only "true" statement in a sense which I cannot see that he has defined. Admittedly it meant progress, a deeper insight into the reality of things, when we learnt to differentiate various modes of belief, but we must go further and recognise not just two clearcut modes of belief, but an undivided scale of moods of belief. Otherwise we shall only increase our confusion. The job must be done thoroughly or not at all. If I am not mistaken, there are strong currents in modern psychology which would support this argument, though it would probably be on a materialistic basis.

As far as what he calls "emotional belief" is concerned, Richards would say that our needs and impulses determine what should be believed in. But, we must ask, what justifies our needs and impulses in the first place? Are they to be merely accepted in the lump, the good with the bad, or can we assume that they are all good? To a psychologist who defines good as that which satisfies our impulses, there is no answer, no way out of the vicious circle. To a Christian the answer is so obvious that one must beware of applying it in too sweeping a fashion: our needs and impulses must also to some extent be determined by our dominant belief, or creed, that is to say, some must be encouraged and others discouraged. This involves dangers: it may lead to morbid repressions and inhibitions. But perhaps the best way to avoid these dangers is to recognise the modality of belief, which will enable imaginative, or poetic belief to operate successfully in draining and sublimating the undesirable urges within us.

I must insert an explanation here concerning the claim of religious truths to absolute validity. My insistence on the modality of belief does not run counter to this claim. On the contrary; when Christ said, "I am the way, the truth, and the life", he said that all truth was in him, that consequently all belief should be directed to him, and that belief was equivalent to emotional attachment. Through all the modes of belief the highest is aimed at. And if one mode, the religious mode, is more appropriate to religious knowledge than the others, it is neither completely distinct from the others, nor does it deny them. I have tried to define the modes of belief from a human, psychological point of view. This does not mean that what we believe or try to comprehend is inherent in our faculties of belief and comprehension. There is a transcendent reality which remains unaffected by our efforts to define the ways in which we may attain to belief in that reality.

With our considerations of the nature of belief in mind, we may now turn to the contents of poetry to determine their appeal to belief and their truth-value.

Mr. Murry regards the contents of a poem, in so far as they represent a philosophy, as meaningless. He declares that "the fact that we can and do continually refuse the philosophy and accept the poetry points to the likelihood that the philosophy merely serves the same office in philosophical poetry as the plot or myth in other kinds",[1] in other words that it merely serves structural purposes. Eliot does not go so far as this, but his ideas tend in the same direction.

But surely, what our attention is chiefly directed to in a poem — if we think at all, and we cannot suspend disbelief to the point of putting our thoughts entirely to sleep — is the plot and the general background, not the details, even in such works as *The Waste Land,* where the details seem to reign supreme. In the same way, in the glimpses one catches from a train, one finds a unity, which is the general impression of the country one is travelling through; in the reports and articles of a newspaper one finds a unity which is the general history of the day; and a film or story is concentrated by our attention, and for our attention, in the main outlines of the plot and the general atmosphere. The philosophy of a poem, even if it functionally only serves the structure, is therefore no matter of indifference to the consciousness of the reader. It is there for him to believe or refuse to believe, and the tone and purpose of the poem must lead him to do this in the right mood. We must also remember that thought has a tendency to move in images. The language of poetry therefore represents no deviation from normal thought processes, as we sometimes imagine. Rather it corresponds to an ingrown habit of thought. This may be one reason why we often pass over statements in poetry without "noticing" them as statements. We have not been lulled to sleep, we have not suspended belief and disbelief, but we have been persuaded more easily than in ordinary discourse. For the language of images that poetry employs is very convincing. An image can explain many things better than a statement or an argument can, so that it is frequently more precise than these in its correspondence to the ideal meaning.

The convincing quality of poetic language makes it all the more incumbent upon us to believe poetic statements in the right mood. Only thus can we cooperate with the poet to complete the poem. A drama is not complete till the actors perform it on the stage. In a much lesser degree the reader is asked to fill in the blanks of a poem. He has to contribute by his associations something, which is elicited not just by the poetry, but by the words as they are. And the words are not created by the poet, they are everybody's property. Poetic belief in what the poet has to say will make

---

[1] *Countries of the Mind,* II, p. 47.

the reader pull out the appropriate stops for his associations, whereas disbelief will make him pull the wrong stops and produce mere discord.

For practical appreciation and criticism of poetry we must find the tone and purpose in each particular case and adjust our attitude accordingly. Richards says as much in his *Principles*. And Eliot advocates a similar idea when he says that we must be able to "pass in and out freely among the various worlds of poetic creation".

Consequently, when we apply ourselves to reading a poem, the whole personality must be engaged to begin with. We must open our minds as wide as possible, like a big target, to receive the unknown communication. Only thus can the impact of the poem be registered where it directly strikes us. And after one or two readings the proper mood is given, through which belief is filtered. If we sit down with the distinction between intellectual and emotional belief in mind, we may miss the impact altogether. We must start by opening our minds, and the consequent crystallisation of an attitude within us is largely unconscious. In this sense it is right to say with Eliot and Richards that when we read poetry in the right way the question of belief simply does not arise. Belief is enjoyment.

The whole personality of the poet need not be engaged in the same way in the work of creation. It will be clear from the above considerations that whatever he can feel attached to is an object of belief with him, and accordingly something that he may write poetry about. And when we define belief in this wide sense, we must demand of the poet that he should be undeviatingly sincere, i. e. true to his beliefs, in what he writes. This is a demand both beneficial and necessary to the standard of his art. You cannot write good poetry by pretending to like things that you dislike — at least you must transpose yourself for a moment into a mood of liking them. But since such transposition is constantly possible thanks to the imagination, what it all amounts to is that the poet must be faithful to the whims of the moment. I emphasise that this is all that can be positively demanded of him. The deeper his personality and his thought, and the more dependent his moods on his basic view of life, the deeper, too, will be his sincerity and the more constant his loyalty to what is permanent in him. Also the bigger, in length and scope, the poem that he composes, the more must it be governed by his permanent beliefs. But a short lyric may be governed by nothing more permanent than a caprice and yet be beautiful poetry.

There is one thing in Eliot's general ideas that helps to justify his claim that the poet should be held independent in respect of belief in his poetic ideas — namely the notion that poetry may be created by an unconscious process. If this notion holds good, the final result of the creative process is something which is almost as new to the poet as to the reader,[1] so that

---

[1] Cp. UPC p. 126.

the former may be excused for feeling that any ideas contained in the poetry are not his own in the same way as ideas to which he has given his conscious assent. But this again raises an interesting problem: cannot the emanations from the subconscious be regarded as equally appropriated or believed in as are consciously accepted ideas and attitudes? Aren't they even more thoroughly assimilated and a more genuine expression of the artists's mind than the superficial thoughts? And if the poet cannot be held responsible for everything that surges from his subconscious, mustn't he at least recognise it as forming, in a way, part of his belief? I think it may be said that if the theory of unconscious creation holds good, it is all the better for much of the poetry that is written; for poetry in which unconscious inspiration plays a large part is likely to be sincere.

I have not been using the word sincerity in Richards's sense of a general harmony of the personality. I doubt whether this kind of sincerity can be more than a striving, a goal to be aimed at. In order that such harmony should be complete, the subconscious would have to be something which merely duplicated conscious beliefs, perhaps in terms of symbols rather than of ideas. But for such a correspondence to subsist between the spheres of the conscious and the subconscious, a person would have to be spiritually integrated and undivided to an extent which only saints, maniacs and possibly geniuses can be imagined as compassing. Ideally one might demand of a poet that he should be such a person, and undoubtedly he would write the best poetry if he were (A. E. Housman points out that the four men whom he recognises as true poets in the eighteenth century — Collins, Smart, Cowper, Blake — were all mad [1]). But under more average circumstances, a poet usually has the choice between discarding his inhibitions and revealing the "inner truth" about himself and his outlook, or else working under intellectual control and embroidering his surface reactions. He can perhaps do both at the same time; but he cannot fuse the two; and the inevitable tension that will arise is, so far from being detrimental to his work, highly beneficial to it.

Of course, there will always be certain domains, varying with various persons, in which the whole personality is integrated. It might be demanded that the poet should limit himself to such domains. If he did we might expect poetry of a serene and confident type if directed inwards, of an indignant, wrathful or elegiac, but none the less unified kind, if directed outwards towards disharmony in the environment. One would not expect such an integrated attitude to be common in the domain of religion. At least the belief in original sin makes one regard human nature as too divided to reach this perfect wholeness in a main sphere of belief. Hence the tormentedness of much religious poetry and of much poetry of a religious nature (witness Baudelaire), and, on the other hand, the banality and lack of deep

---

[1] *Name & N. of Poetry*, p. 38.

genuineness of another great mass of devotional poetry. Perhaps it would not be wrong to say that good, and genuine, and happy religious poetry at least presupposes a background of unhappiness. For instance, the joyful thankfulness for salvation springs from the realisation of what one has been saved from. T. S. Eliot speaks of Dante using beatitude as a theme. He could hardly have done so in *Paradiso* without having described despair and suffering in *Inferno*.

The conclusions we have arrived at concerning poetic belief take their natural place in the Christian aesthetic which we sketched in the preceding chapter. If belief is regarded as emotional attachment it should be particularly responsive to beauty, and it thus becomes easier to understand how the contemplation of beauty can lead us to believe in its divine source. The impact of formal beauty is undifferentiated and elicits an emotional response (belief) which is also undifferentiated, though both the impact and the response are usually accompanied by secondary impressions and emotions, so that they appear modally particularised. In order that impulses and beliefs shall be permanently edifying, the mind must be prepared beforehand, and able to exercise judgment. And this is where Christian tradition and Christian doctrine come in. To a Christian the whole system of his religion forms a single, comprehensive unit to which he gives, or should give, belief. This dominant belief may then be allowed to guide his particular responses. Thus belief is supreme, art has its sovereignty, and yet religion, too, is supreme.

The Question of Belief and Eliot's Poetry.

Eliot, as we saw, was doubtful about Dante's belief in what he wrote. But he brings in no evidence to show why Dante should be sceptical in private life as to the beliefs he assumed in the *Divine Comedy*. I prefer to think that Dante wrote from sincere belief. Thus his comedy became a poem rather than a drama (a poem is usually based upon a more integral view of life than a drama, in which division and uncertainty have free play). Dante's beliefs were not all filtered through a religious mood. A good many of them, I am prepared to admit, were "merely poetic". But a poem of the scope of the *Divine Comedy*, we argued, could hardly have been written unless it was governed fairly consistently by a philosophy which the poet held permanently.

In the same way, I am prepared to find in Eliot's longer poems the impress of permanently held ideas or a settled attitude to life, especially when the same or similar ideas or moods recur in various poems (and, of course, in the prose writings); while I am also prepared to find a good many incidental views held with less settled conviction and employed for their poetic worth. As for the shorter poems, it is fairly easy to see whether they agree in outlook with the longer ones. Eliot, as we have seen, sets at a discount the belief of the poet in what he writes. But, for reasons which I hope have been made clear, we must not let his opinion in this matter deter us from seeking his beliefs in his poems. They may not make up an organised philosophy, and they may have been very much changed in the process of composition. But they are there. The poet's views and attitudes must colour what he writes, and they cannot be so much changed that one can mistake their general direction. Thus far, at least, Mr. Belgion is right, though I disagree with him on most other points.

As a matter of fact, Eliot, like so many other poets, thinks and believes in his poetry in a far more primitive manner than that of adult and civilised reasoning. His imagery often shows a *nostalgie de l'enfance,* which in turn may be interpreted as a longing for childish knowledge and childish assurance. He tries to escape the perplexities of "is and seems", and to cling only to what *is,* i.e. to what is to him an object of belief. His poetic insight and outlook resemble the insight and outlook of children in recognising in practice the direct emotional nature of belief.

He shows in his poetry, he says, what it feels like to believe in anything — but precisely that is the belief, or at least the degree and mood of the belief. We believe in so far as we feel positively. And when Eliot defines behaviour as belief, as he does in "The Three Senses of 'Culture' ",[1] he must be understood to include the actual behaviour of our emotions. He must also be understood to include the behaviour of a poet *qua* poet; for the way in which a poet writes, if he is sincere, may be regarded as a reflection of his beliefs.

Eliot may hold certain beliefs principally for their value to his poetry. They may even form a system or cluster of beliefs more or less distinct from what he "ordinarily" adheres to. But they are none the less beliefs, and the fact that they are determined by a poetic mood does not prevent them from entering into other domains of his life than poetry. Nor does it prevent them from affecting his readers in other domains besides that of poetic enjoyment.

For the enjoyment of Eliot's poetry — or that of any other poet — it is not necessary for the reader to trace minutely what the poet in various ways has believed in, or what statements and attitudes the poetry presents in a more or less recondite fashion. Nor is it necessary for the reader, in the ordinary course of things, to believe scientifically, religiously or in any other specific way the statements and attitudes that the poetry of itself reveals to him, except in such a degree and with such permanence as the particular poem requires in order to be enjoyed. I find it hard to accept, as Eliot suggests, that the reader can enjoy poetry without at least for a time sharing the feelings, experiencing the emotions of the poet. One cannot entirely enjoy Shakespeare without being moved by something more than

---

[1] NDC p. 32.

verbal beauty. The passions of poet and reader have to enter into sympathetic reaction. But this does not mean that the reader can or should recapture the whole of the poet's experience, nor does it make it any less necessary to the reader to add his own interpretation to what the poetry gives him.

Ordinarily, I repeat, the reader need not speculate about the poet's ideas or try to find a philosophy in his poetry. But when poetry has become as influential as Eliot's, both in inspiring other poets and perhaps in affecting our general view of life, it is time to enquire what ideas and moods it incorporates, and where it will lead us if those ideas and moods, consciously or unconsciously, and coming as they do in the convincing language of poetic imagery, are allowed to affect us permanently. And for the sake of poetry itself, it is necessary from time to time to examine successful poetry to see what ideas and attitudes can receive the sanction of art.

IV.

Vision and Mood.

Being the first of three chapters in which we endeavour to ascertain the attitudes views, ideas and beliefs which chiefly make up the "meaning" of Eliot's poetry.

It is obviously useless labour to try to detect and reconstruct all the experiences, feelings and thoughts that were originally in a poet's mind when he wrote his poems. This is especially the case so long as we are debarred — as we must be with a living poet — from prying into his private life. Private experiences obviously go to the making of poetry, and Eliot has told us often enough that they have entered into his. The conception of a kind of impersonal core in the poet's soul whence his inspiration proceeds, though it may be a useful check to critics of the extreme biographical school, is a dangerous oversimplification, and perhaps a product of wishful thinking. Poetry is autobiographical. "But", as Eliot says, "this autobiography is written by a foreign man in a foreign tongue, which can never be translated".[1]

Even this statement we would like to qualify. If it were strictly true, we should be confined in the interpretation of poetry merely to the impressions of various readers. We should have to believe that comparison and analysis, Eliot's favourite instruments of criticism, could yield us no understanding of the poet's own intentions which could not be had equally well by a sensitive reading of a poem. But we refuse to be put off in this way. We give up gladly enough, since it must be so, a detailed knowledge

---

[1] *Nation & Athenaeum*, 12 Feb. 1927.

of the poet's private experiences. We do not pretend that we can always tell what is fact in his poetry and what is fiction, what is *Dichtung* and what is *Wahrheit*. We do not demand that he should permanently believe all the statements that he makes in his poetry. Nor do we suppose that his poetry reveals to us his views on particular persons and topics. But we do think his poetry as a whole shows us his general feelings and his general opinions, his view of life and his main philosophical positions. And so far from having to resign ourselves to these generalities, we are glad to be confined to them. They are precisely what interests us here: for it is the general attitudes and the general principles whose imaginative presentation produces the greatest repercussions, in individual minds and cultural life.

We cannot take refuge, then, in the fact — also recognised by Eliot — that a poem, as far as its meaning goes, is as much the reader's property as the writer's; for in this case we wish, to some extent, to understand the writer's own premises, and not just the circumstances which make us our- selves understand the poems in such or such a way. If we read thought- fully, however, I think our interpretation will only come to rest in identifying itself ultimately with what we discover to be the poet's meaning. I emphasise the fact that this only applies to one aspect of the poetry, that which, broadly speaking, can be labelled meaning. And I repeat what I said at the beginning of this book, that I am not here concerned primarily with helping towards the appreciation of the poetry as poetry. In the total appreciation, the reader's background of private experiences must play such a large part that any identification of the significance of the poem to him with its significance to the poet is impossible.

The investigation of Eliot's outlook as it appears in his poetry is for several reasons more difficult than are similar investigations in the cases of other poets. Eliot commends Byron's *Don Juan* for revealing the poet's self,[1] but he himself prefers to conceal his presence in his works. He is the "I who am here dissembled" of *Ash-Wednesday*. A powerful self- criticism and a certain fear of exhibiting himself which struggle with his urge to write are the real causes of much that is difficult and esoteric in his poetry. And his theory of the transmutation of personal into impersonal matter has certainly tended to encourage his "deliberate disguises".[2] As a result, his ideas are often concealed and camouflaged in such a way as to be difficult to recognise and dangerous to guess at.

In the process of transmutation, thought may be recreated into feeling,[3] or feeling into thought. Minor subjects may release major emotions,[4] or major emotions may appear, when objectified, as something of minor im- portance. Often one is tempted to ask whether the poet can have felt any passion at all, so thoroughly has he suppressed or transformed it. One way

---

[1] Cf. "Byron", *From Anne to Victoria* (ed. B. Dobrée).   [2] HM II.   [3] Cf. SE pp. 286, 290.   [4] Cf. Introd. to M. Moore: *Sel. Poems.*

of doing this is by using a lyric theme in a more or less dramatic way, as has been done, for instance, in "The Love Song" and "Portrait of a Lady".[1]

A poetic theme may appear simple enough, but usually has complex sources. "A love affair", says Eliot, "might cause a successful or bad investment; it cannot, without a great many other and alien experiences of which the ordinary man is incapable, cause good poetry".[2] All these experiences, or the impressions they have left, have to be combined. A fusion takes place between disparate elements, and the results of the fusion may be very difficult indeed to analyse. Perhaps the least puzzling fusion is that which takes place between a poet's philosophy and his natural feelings.[3]

The original experiences which Eliot draws upon may be either the chance impressions of life, or carefully sought-for and selected events. In the former case one would expect that only the poet himself could find significance in them, and that his attempts to transmute them into something objective and "rich and strange" must be foiled. Some of the people mentioned in "Gerontion", the old white horse in "Journey of the Magi" and a number of other motifs, seem to represent private memories whose hidden meaning is fully apparent to the poet alone. The effort of objectification, therefore, must begin with the choice of subject-matter, if the reader is to find a meaning. I do not mean that the poet must perform a conscious labour of construction or must *invent* his "objective correlatives". He is at liberty to *discover* them even in his chance experiences provided he recognises something inherent in those experiences (not something merely due to his accompanying moods and associations) which answers to the idea or the emotion he wishes to present. A "correlative" or symbol of this kind can express a subjective experience in terms of an objective observation and a subjective truth in terms of a general truth. The idea or emotion is made concrete in another context than that of the poet's original experience. Thus, as Eliot has told me, the phrase "La figlia che piange" was the name given to an old relief preserved in a museum of Northern Italy. Eliot, travelling in Italy, was advised by a friend to go and see this piece of sculpture, but failed to find it. However, the name stuck in his mind, and he used it as a suggestive title to one of his poems. The fact that he only heard the phrase by accident does not make it any less expressive in the poem, for we feel that he was struck by it precisely because it represented something personal to him. A chance thing like the Figlia phrase may be *found*, instead of being expressed from within, but it still expresses some inner experience, because it is found to correspond to that experience.

The process of transmutation, we see, is no arbitrary affair, or when it is, it results in nearly unintelligible imagery. The process is traceable here and there, as in "La Figlia" or, still more clearly, in *The Waste*

---

[1] Cp. H. R. Williamson: *Poetry of T. S. E.*, p. 66.   [2] *Nation & Athenaeum*, 12 Feb. 1927.   [3] Cf. PP p. 37.

Land, where imagery which elsewhere appears to be closely connected with personal emotions becomes part of a general idea. In so far as the process results in intelligible imagery, it is successful and fully justified, that is to say in so far as the private experiences of the poet are transmuted while some idea or attitude still attaches to the images. And this we will usually find to be the case in Eliot's poetry.

The objectification of meaning will sometimes appear to occur in three stages. There is first the original experience, then the general attitude of the poet abstracted from that and similar experiences (i.e. depersonalised but still possessed by the poet) and finally a common attitude or idea, which may be the expression of the spirit of the age. The first stage is not, on the whole, our concern, but the two next stages are. Where they both occur, they give the poems two strata of meaning. On the surface appears the completely generalised meaning, but on a deeper level the meaning which is generalised while still belonging to the poet. In *The Waste Land*, as we shall see, the general idea or attitude which appears on the surface is that of the disillusion of a generation of human beings. Deeper down we find the poet's feelings and ideas, abstracted from his particular experiences. We must be aware all the time of both strata of meaning, but it is the deeper one that chiefly calls for scrutiny.

We shall consider in a later chapter the relation of construction and other elements of technique to meaning and purpose. Let it suffice to say here that although Eliot often presents us with a "music of ideas", as Dr. Richards has it, this does not remove the meaning or invalidate the significance of the ideas. As we discovered in our discussion of poetic belief, even the handling of ideas as in a game requires some degree of belief in them. We may therefore, for the present, minimise the distinction between form and content, between ideas and attitudes dominated by technique, and ideas and attitudes which seem to rise above technique. In this way we shall be able to treat as one whole the poetry which was written for its own sake and the poetry written for special occasions, the "prosy" and straightforward passages and the more typically lyrical passages. For our present purpose, which is the investigation not of particular statements or fantasies but of general views and attitudes, this lack of discrimination does not entail great dangers.

The Poet's Vision.

"All art originates in an act of intuition, or vision. But such *intuition* or vision must be identified with *knowledge*, being fully present only when consciously objectified. This act of vision or intuition is, physically, a state of concentration or tension in the mind".[1] These words of Herbert Read's express, to my mind, an important truth about the poet's activity.

---

[1] Read: *Form in Mod. Poetry*, p. 39.

At or very near the beginning of poetic creation there is the poet's
vision of phenomena in the outer world and in his own mind and body. This
comprises both his manner of perceiving these things, the way in which
they impinge upon his senses and mental organs of receptivity, and the way
in which he subsequently arranges the phenomena in his mind. It also
comprises the emotive colouring in which he comes to "see" them, i. e.
his moods. We will begin by examining Eliot's vision primarily as perception,
leaving, for the moment, its modal quality to be treated separately. Of course
both vision and mood have some connection with the poet's general view of
life and philosophical leanings.

⟨ According to Eliot's Bradleyan idealism, perception, or feeling, transcends itself to become thought, and in the incessant union of feeling and
thought "we have the ideality of the finite, and that is the life of the mind".[1]
In aesthetic language Eliot speaks of the transmutation of feeling into thought
or vice-versa. In other words, he would naturally regard philosophy as a
transcendent phase of perception.⟩ "Our philosophy should spring from our
point of view", says Eeldrop.[2] To us it may be more natural to see his
vision as guided by his philosophy than the other way about. In any case
we cannot ignore the relation between vision and philosophy, so that though
the latter will be more closely examined in the next chapter, it has a natural
bearing on the subject of the present chapter as well.

Eliot's vision of phenomena is a very characteristic feature of his early
poetry, where vision begins definitely with sense-impressions, but seems
to expand at once into mental images. The best word for it is probably
"awareness", which we meet quite a number of times in the poems: "I am
aware of the damp souls of housemaids" ("Morning at the Window"),
"I was aware of becoming involved in her laughter" ("Hysteria"), "the
awareness / Of things ill done" ("Little Gidding"), etc. We also find the
word used significantly in his prose.[3] With Eliot awareness is a mode of
perception, related to intuition, and distinct from full consciousness and
from plain knowledge. Awareness involves a strong impression, usually
of the senses, which translates itself immediately into what one might almost
call an obsession, a state of consciousness which absorbs all the activities
of the mind in the moment's concentration on an object. Especially in his
early poetry there is a strong element of impressionism, which is served well
by this kind of awareness. One feels that Eliot sees objects as they appear
to the mind, an impression which is emphasised by the fact that many of
his poems, or parts of them, are given as mental soliloquies. In this respect
it might be profitable to compare the technique of "The Love Song" with
the "stream of consciousness" technique of Joyce's Ulysses.

"The natural wakeful life of our Ego is a perceiving." This line from
Husserl, quoted by the poet in "Triumphal March", may serve to indicate

---

[1] Church: "Eliot on B's Metaphysic", HA, Dec. 1938, p. 26.   [2] Little Review,
May 1917.   [3] E. g. SE pp. 16, 242—3.

the importance that Eliot attached to the sense-perceptions. He was supported in this by all the philosophers who, as opposed to the Platonists and others, have stressed the reliability of our direct impressions of the outer world. Thus Lucretius believed that the senses cannot be deceived, whereas the *inferences* that we draw from sensation are often wrong. But above all Aristotle would tend to turn the interest of his readers to the sense-perceptions. To Aristotle also the perception of the objects of sense is free from error, while thinking may be erroneous. He finds nothing in existence that is not inherent in sensible spatial magnitudes, and asserts that the objects of thought are in the sensible forms. By a "sense" he means "what has the power of receiving into itself the sensible forms of things without the matter"; in other words, the actuality of things actually exists in sensation, so that we receive in sensation not only a pale reflection of reality, but reality itself. And conversely, mind, in so far as it is knowledge, only becomes actual in sensation, for knowledge is identical with its object.[1] A poet trained in such views as these, as was Eliot, might confidently announce, as Eliot did, that poetry may legitimately be concerned with actuality and criticism with principles. For actuality, being real, might be expected to reveal of itself the order and reasonableness of the universe. If it failed to do so, of course, *tant pis*. The loss would be that of the philosopher, not necessarily that of the poet.

Now Eliot was not content merely with Aristotle's relatively primitive conception of reality. In his treatise on Bradley's metaphysic, he recognises that knowledge and its object are one in immediate experience, but not that immediate experience is simply the unqualified sense-perceptions. For what we experience immediately is not just objects, but relations, and the wholeness of a sentient experience is not just a sum of various sensations. Much that we generally call ideal has immediate reality.[2] And so perception and knowledge mean a complicated awareness of both particularity and relationships, of sensations, emotions and thoughts. It would be rash to say that the poet has illustrated these ideas according to his philosophy, but I think we may find them reflected in his poetry, especially in the constant attempt to find a common organisation in disparate experiences, or to find a revelation of the essential in the particular and fortuitous. Thus the two observers of life in "Eeldrop and Appleplex" (which, because of its imaginative character, can only be classed with Eliot's poetry) watch from their window for the exceptional here and now when life actually sallies into their silent street, and when people detach themselves from their classifications and reveal themselves as real individuals, with histories of their own: "It is these moments which we prize, and which alone are revealing. For any vital truth is incapable of being applied to another case: the essential is unique."[3]

---

[1] Cf. esp. *De Anima,* III, 3, 5, 8; II, 12.   [2] Cf. Church: "Eliot on B's Metaphysic", HA, Dec. 1938.   [3] *Little Review,* May 1917.

It was not the general truth the poet was after, but the vital truth. And this is why he studied individual persons and phenomena, the exceptional in the setting of the ordinary: a Prufrock, a Sweeney "among the nightingales" — as if the spotlight on them would bring out their vital secrets. Unfortunately, he was not quite convinced that the unique *was* real, or that the individual was valuable. Even Aristotle seemed not to have made up his mind whether the individual or the specific was real.[1] And in Eliot's poetry the spotlight singled out the individual, and the x-rays "threw the nerves in patterns on a screen", but obstinately refused to reveal more than hollow men. So his perception to a great extent remained merely perception of the individual and unrelated and fragmentary fact; which enabled him to become an admirable Imagist, and admirably to follow Hulme's precept, "to prove that beauty may be in small, dry things",[2] as well as Poe's recommendation to write short, static poems;[3] but which kept his vision between relatively narrow confines, and for many years frustrated his philosophical inspiration.

In his early poetry he writes of "smell of steaks in passage-ways", "broken blinds and chimney-pots" and so on, and no effort to force these things to join together can deprive us of the impression that we have to do with odds and ends in a vast jumble of particularities, in spite of the fact that they do make up a "picture". The picture of reality may be coherent, but the reality is itself incoherent. And frequently the picture too, or the scene, is given only in flashes and glimpses. "The Love Song", though narrative in a way, proceeds fitfully, with numerous digressions from the "story" if not from the nebula of vision. In "Rhapsody on a Windy Night" the glimpses of a concrete night scene are almost submerged in the roaming thoughts and memories of the protagonist. Here, if anywhere, immediate perception may be said to be ideal as well as real, but it is no less fragmentary for that reason. The senses are all at work, bringing in impressions of sight and hearing, of taste, smell and touch, and though the poet may be aware of several of them at once, there is no other principle than his awareness that unites them, and they can be readily analysed into their component parts. We may find the same tendency to grasp the particular rather than the general in Eliot's prose.

Eliot thinks that "perhaps one reason why Donne has appealed so powerfully to the recent time is that there is in his poetry hardly any attempt at organization; rather a puzzled and humorous shuffling of the pieces; and we are inclined to read our own more conscious awareness of the apparent irrelevance and unrelatedness of things into the mind of Donne".[4] The sense of the irrelevance and unrelatedness of things is not undisputed in Eliot's early poetry, but it is certainly very powerful up to, and including, "Coriolan".

---

[1] Cf. "Devel. of L's Monadism", *Monist*, Oct. 1916. [2] Hulme: *Speculations*, p. 131. [3] Cf. *Chapbook*, April 1921. [4] "Donne in Our Time", *Garland for J. Donne*, p. 8.

One feels that the vision of unrelatedness must have something to do with a general view of life which has refused to submit to Absolute Idealism or any other integrating philosophy. If it was inspired or confirmed by any philosophy at all, it would most probably be by that of "the weeping philosopher" Heraclitus, whose belief in flux and change evidently found a strong echo in Eliot's mind.

"These fragments I have shored against my ruins", says the "I" of *The Waste Land*. And it strikes us that the poet himself must have frequently felt something like this. In some of his moments of intense awareness he saw life as the broken fragments of what might have been originally a harmonious whole, but which it was impossible now to piece together. And only fragments of various philosophies fought in his mind, as, at the end of *The Waste Land,* do the Catholic philosophy of Dante, the eroticism of *Pervigilium Veneris,* the hopelessness of Gerard de Nerval's "El Desdichado", the mysticism of the *Vedanta.* Eliot's view of life at this stage seems to have been almost atomistic, and this impression becomes all the stronger if we compare the poems of his pre-Christian phase with those of his Christian period. In the latter we see the effect of an organising and unifying principle which is almost absent from the former, as Eliot found it absent from Donne's poetry.

It would not be idle to speculate whether the Epicurean atomism of Lucretius might not have had something to do with Eliot's perception of an un-unified universe. He constantly reverts to *De Rerum Natura* in his criticism, and what the mind is much occupied with is, as we have seen, almost a matter of belief. In the philosophy of Epicurus and Lucretius, the particles of matter which compose the universe are only united by accident, and disintegrate again readily to form new bodies. Even the soul is merely made up of solid atoms and void, in which transient images and notions are formed by repeated impressions. This is not very different from Eliot's view of the soul in his third "Prelude", where he speaks of "The thousand sordid images / Of which your soul was constituted". And it agrees with his apparent conception of the soul and his rendering of mental processes in nearly all the non-Christian poems.

A further support for an atomistic view of life may have presented itself in Hulme's "theory of discontinuity".[1] But more important, no doubt, was the teaching of Santayana, who in turn owed a great deal to William James. In James, Santayana admired a peculiar "sense of the immediate", of "the unadulterated, unexplained, instant fact of experience". And here I will cite a passage from Santayana which is like an unconscious commentary on the poems of Eliot's younger days:

Actual experience, for William James, however varied or rich its assault might be, was always and altogether of the nature of a sensation: it possessed a vital, leaping, globular unity which made the only fact, the flying fact, of

---

[1] Cf. "Pensées", EAM p. 158.

our being. Whatever continuities of quality might be traced in it, its existence was always momentary and self-warranted. A man's life or soul borrowed its reality and imputed wholeness from the intrinsic actuality of its successive parts; existence was a perpetual re-birth, a travelling light to which the past was lost and the future uncertain. The element of indetermination which James felt so strongly in this flood of existence was precisely the pulse of fresh unpredictable sensation, summoning attention hither and thither to unexpected facts. Apprehension in him being impressionistic — that was the age of impressionism in painting too — and marvellously free from intellectual assumptions or presumptions, he felt intensely the fact of contingency, or the contingency of fact. This seemed to me not only a peculiarity of temperament in him, but a profound insight into existence, in its inmost irrational essence. Existence, I learned to see, is intrinsically dispersed, seated in its distributed moments, and arbitrary not only as a whole, but in the character and place of each of its parts.[1]

This philosophy, or part of a philosophy, would naturally be a very good starting-point for a revolutionary young poet who was intent on breaking up the complacencies and conventions and all too coherent views of life of his predecessors. A useful platform, as well, for a poet experimenting with his technique and desirous of using his subject-matter freely: a view of life which decomposed it into immediate facts of experience would enable him to bring objects and ideas together at the dictate of his formal needs and not according to the relatedness of the objects and ideas among themselves.

A certain solipsism would naturally accompany an atomistic philosophy. If the soul consists of combinations of material particles, it can have no real communication with other souls, and if its particles are combined in accidental groups, souls cannot be essentially but only superficially alike in organisation. Thus the mind which experiences is to itself the only actual universe. And this perhaps helps to explain why, from "The Love Song" to *Ash-Wednesday*, Eliot's poems are staged in the mind of the poet.[2] The people and objects that we meet are really subjective: "Tenants of the house, / Thoughts of a dry brain in a dry season".[3] Most of Eliot's poems are in the first person and spoken as monologues, apart from the dialogue of the plays. In the last poems, however, the *Four Quartets,* the impression of communication has replaced the earlier impression of solitary rumination.

The trouble was that though an atomistic philosophy might benefit a poet for a time, it could not in the long run satisfy the constructive poet, and hardly the man, unless he were content to make of scepticism a belief.

The French Symbolists believed in the inter-relatedness of things. And it is quite apparent in Eliot's poetry that, in spite of his atomistic view of life, he searched for connectedness as well, for that fusion of disparate elements which would really make them one. His perception of immediate facts co-existed with a reaction against their fragmentariness, which made

---

[1] "Brief Hist. of My Opinions", *Philos. of Santayana*, pp. 14—5.   [2] Another partial explanation, of course, is the poet's interest in psychology.   [3] "Gerontion".

him join impressions as it were by force, perhaps in an effort to find a hidden significance in them. "The evening is spread out against the sky / Like a patient etherised upon a table", a "smile falls heavily among the bric-à-brac", housemaids have "damp souls". The images are often extremely successful. And they do give a limited meaning — but only a meaning which describes one fragment in terms of another.

Another device by which an effect of identity is often obtained is that of juxtaposition. There is a good example of this in "The Fire Sermon", where the typist's gramophone, by the mediation of Ariel's music in *The Tempest,* turns into the fishmen's pleasant mandoline. In "Rhapsody", the moon, without a transition, becomes a bedraggled prostitute.

Sometimes there seems to be an attempt at interpretation by inter-penetration, when the poet renders external objects as subjective impressions and subjective impressions as objective. Thus in "Morning at the Window" there is a "smile that hovers in the air". It is the smile of a passer-by, but really it is only the poet's lingering impression of that smile that seems to hover in the air, as he moves his glance upwards. The boundaries between subjective and objective have been broken down, and there is an illusion of some secret revealed, but no more. Another image in the same poem comes nearer to finding a real significance. The street is seen as a sea where people are drowned. This is interpretation of life. But on the whole the effort to find a hidden meaning in or behind the freakish phenomena of life results in little more than a pretence that the meaning is there. When, for instance, in the third "Prelude"; the experiences of a city dawn are gathered in the lines "You had such a vision of the street / As the street hardly understands" it remains no more than an assertion to the reader, though the word "vision" may stand for a remembered moment of exaltation or illumination to the poet himself.

Now the facts of existence, as observed by the phenomenologists, *have* no ulterior significance. And unique, vital truth as it appears to an individualist or an empiricist is gratuitous and essentially useless: Eliot says so himself in "Eeldrop and Appleplex". On the other hand, the phenomenologist Meinong particularly emphasises the fact that we do perceive things in their relations, and not only as isolated objects — "dass mit zwei Vorstellungen auch deren Relationen zueinander gegeben sind" [1] — and we have seen Eliot argue this fact in his dissertation on Bradley. Where no other meaning is found, such relations can be taken to indicate at least a principle of order. There are the beginnings of integration in them. So Eliot extracted as much poetry as he could from "pure observation" (a phrase from "Eeldrop") but he also went further and tried to exploit poetically the relationships that he found or forged, between objects and experiences.

---

[1] Meinong: *Abhandlungen zur E. und G.* I, p. 46. Cf. also II, p. 388. Bradley has a similar view, but speaks of wholeness instead of relations, "relations" to Bradley being mere appearance; they disintegrate experience.

There was always Bradley to urge him still further. "From the very first beginnings of intelligence it is the type that operates and not the image", says Bradley. "The lower we descend in the growth of our own functions, or in the scale of animate nature, the more typical, the less individual, the less distinct, the more vaguely universal and widely symbolic is the deposit of experience".[1] Eliot, possibly in a moment of revolt against Bradley, declared in "Eeldrop" that the general and universal was superficial and without interest. But he obviously found it difficult to get everything that he wanted out of the particular, if only an intuitive assurance that its existence was justified. And there were loud voices, Plato's perhaps most persuasive amongst them, telling him that reality was not in the particular, as most modern philosophers asserted, but, on the contrary, in the universal. His own longing for metaphysical certainty, we may assume, made it impossible for him to ignore these voices. And so we see that in one way he does manage to integrate his sensations even in his early poetry. Amid the confusion of fragments and particularities, he generally selects for us those experiences which point to something typical, something that we can all recognise. In presenting the particular as the type of a great number of phenomena of the same kind he not only achieves the aims of the satirist, but he begins to create symbols. And in so doing he imposes the beginnings of order upon his universe.

A general vision of urban life is rendered by means of concrete scenes recognised as typical. The conventional drawing-room of polite society, with its interminable tea-drinking — "you have the scene arrange itself" — is glimpsed in "The Love Song", "Portrait of a Lady" and "Mr. Apollinax". The women straying about "talking of Michelangelo", make a fitting background to Prufrock, with his desperately conventional appearance: "My morning coat, my collar mounting firmly to the chin, / My necktie rich and modest, but asserted by a simple pin —":

> For I have known them all already, known them all:
> Have known the evenings, mornings, afternoons,
> I have measured out my life with coffee spoons;
> I know the voices dying with a dying fall
> Beneath the music from a farther room.
> So how should I presume?
> And I have known the eyes already, known them all —
> The eyes that fix you in a formulated phrase

And so, amid "the cups, the marmelade, the tea", Mr. Prufrock's individuality founders miserably, just as the housemaids, in "Morning at the Window", are reduced to "sprouting despondently at area gates". Even when a death occurs, the undertaker "was aware that this sort of thing had occurred before" ("Aunt Helen").

Somewhat lower down on the social scale, indoor life is typified by "smell of steaks in passageways", by "dingy shades / In a thousand furnished

---

[1] *Princ. of Logic*, p. 37.

rooms", and by the rattling of breakfast plates in basement kitchens. The smells and noises penetrate to the street, which we are intermittently reminded of in "The Love Song" and "Portrait of a Lady", and which is the scene of several other poems.

The poet's vision of the street is not only of its intrinsic sordidness, but of its sameness, its appalling unimaginativeness. The streets "follow like a tedious argument". There are "the sunsets and the dooryards and the sprinkled streets", where a street piano "reiterates some worn-out common song". The "Preludes", "Morning at the Window" and "Rhapsody" must be read in their entirety to fill out the picture of the typical street in its various aspects, "at four and five and six o'clock", morning, afternoon, evening and night. For the better-off citizens out-door existence is perhaps slightly less grimy, but hardly less trivial:

> Let us take the air, in a tobacco trance,
> Admire the monuments,
> Discuss the late events,
> Correct our watches by the public clocks.
> Then sit for half an hour and drink our bocks.[1]

These glimpses of modern urban life chiefly typify a phase of civilisation. They also vaguely outline a view of life itself, whilst retaining their character of direct impressions.

When a poet's vision results in the fusion of the individual and the universal in memorable images, his creatures sometimes assume mythical proportions. This is what Prufrock has achieved in our age. And even Sweeney is something of a mythical figure. The comparisons with other heroes of legend and history — Theseus, Agamemnon, Christ — and the suggestions of supernatural powers are not wanting. La Figlia, too, is a mythical figure, and remains so throughout Eliot's production. But whereas the myth in the cases of Prufrock and Sweeney is that of humanity deified, or mock-deified, in the case of La Figlia it is rather of divinity humanised. In both cases, however, the myth arises from a wish to control and explain the universe. If the wish is unfulfilled, it results merely in criticism of actual life. But even that implies that there is some meaning to justify criticism; there is at least some imagined perfection. "The myth", says Eliot, "is imagination, and it is also criticism, and the two are one".[2]

The poet's interest in Symbolism was no doubt mainly formal at first. But Symbolism drew him on to try to express the inexpressible. And gradually the basis of his poetry changed: a Christian philosophy supervened. His vision changed at the same time. Instead of a jumble of irrelevancies life began to look like a complete system in which even sin was "behovely" and nothing was irrelevant. The poet found a pattern when the man found

---

[1] "Portrait of a Lady."   [2] "The Romantic Englishman", *Tyro,* 1, 1922.

a faith. One of the main effects of Christianity in Eliots' poetry is the provision of a unifying principle to his vision. In comparison with this such things as the presentation of doctrine in his poems are altogether insignificant.

His vision is now, apart from the imagery in which it is clothed, far less concrete than it used to be. It endeavours to grapple with pure ideas, and in this endeavour it changes itself into symbols and mental images. This means that it is both more indirect, more synthetic and more reminiscent than formerly. At the same time as the philosophical pendulum may be said to have swung from Aristotle to Plato, the poet's manner has swung, on the whole, from impressionism to expressionism; and there would seem to be some natural connection between these changes.

We still, no doubt, find the obscurity of vision which used to characterise his poetry in spite of the clarity of sensual impressions, but now it is caused by a different kind or degree of metaphysical ignorance. It seems to have a luminosity about it.

The Poet's Moods.

[The poet's moods are determined by his vision and in turn act upon his vision.] A mood of despondency may be nourished by the perception of inconsequence in life, and again such a perception will readily present itself to a person who is in a mood of dejection.

In Eliot's poetry up to *Sweeney Agonistes* we rarely find beautiful subjects. And only exceptionally is the atmosphere tragic or solemn, at least on the surface. [The subjects of the poems are trivial, trite, ugly, ludicrous. And the mood, accordingly, is predominantly one of irony or disgust, more rarely one of serious concern.]

In the *Prufrock* collection the irony is often levelled against the "I" of the poems. [But the poet also directs it against his age and the sort of life which surrounds him. In some of the poems, and in most of the 1920 collection, irony turns into a feeling of nausea and disgust both with the age and with life in general. The bitter satire of *The Hollow Men* makes this poem one of the gloomiest that Eliot has ever written] while the satire of *Sweeney Agonistes* is facetious, yet with an undertone of solemnity. [Despair and bewilderment, even fear, are apparent in many poems, and in some there is a pronounced note of melancholy, of sadness, disillusionment and nostalgia, for instance in "Gerontion"]

[The origins of these dark moods were probably very complex. In part they may have been constitutional and possibly strengthened by experiences of a private character.] Mr. Edmund Wilson, who is inclined to blame Eliot's Puritan background, hints at the "regret at situations unexplored" and the "dark rankling of passions inhibited"[1] common to so many New

---

[1] AC p. 102.

England writers. [Then partly Eliot's pessimism was deliberately assumed in protest against the facile "cheerfulness, optimism, and hopefulness"[1] which he so much disliked in the nineteenth century.] In contrast to the vapidity of English Romantics and Victorians, he found many of the French writers strangely bracing. Baudelaire's prostitutes and corpses, the spleen of Verlaine and Laforgue, Flaubert's corrosive view of the small bourgeoisie appealed strongly to him, and undoubtedly much of his dismal outlook is directly caused by literary influences.[2] But plainly Eliot's despondency had very tangible causes in the outer world as well.

[One of the deepest needs of human nature is for society and communion, and Eliot, reticent as was his disposition, must have felt it keenly. But in life as it was actually lived — and not only after the first World War — human intercourse was as inconsequent and unrelated as everything else. Complete communication between mind and mind and complete union between heart and heart were impossible. And so the soul's incurable loneliness became one of the main themes of his poetry.]

[We may imagine that we have friends, and that friendship is real, as the lady in the "Portrait" does. "Without these friendships — life, what cauchemar"; the further development of the poem is a sufficient commentary on this remark, for the friendship that she has believed in proves illusory. Friendship is "faithless as a smile and shake of the hand",[3] a phrase which has added a great load of bitterness to Laforgue's "sans foi comme un bonjour". [And at any rate friendship is destroyed by age and death and bloodshed, as so many friendships were brutally destroyed during the Great War.] "I that was near your heart was removed therefrom", says Gerontion, — "I have lost my sight, smell, hearing, taste and touch: / How should I use them for your closer contact?" In "The Love Song" lonely men in shirtsleeves lean symbolically out of the windows of their isolation, smoking meditatively.] In The Waste Land, men herd in crowds, but a crowd is no company: "each man fixed his eyes before his feet".] And in The Family Reunion, Harry is haunted by a "sense of separation, / Of isolation unredeemable, irrevocable".[4]

[There is no communication, though all are equally miserable:

> In this last of meeting places
> We grope together
> And avoid speech
> Gathered on this beach of the tumid river.[5]]

It is impossible for human beings to share their deepest feelings with each other. "Formulated phrases", yes, and talk about Michelangelo, but Prufrock wonders

---

[1] SE p. 262.   [2] Cp. his treatment of Tourneur, SE p. 190.   [3] "Figlia".
[4] FR p. 99.   [5] HM IV.

> — how should I begin
> To spit out all the butt-ends of my days and ways?
> And how should I presume?

The need and longing to communicate, to establish contact, is still there, but it is frustrated, and therefore can only cause suffering, and the wish to escape still further from the company of men:

> I should have been a pair of ragged claws
> Scuttling across the floors of silent seas.

It is only natural that the relation between man and woman, in which the closest union between human beings is generally thought to be possible, should be used by Eliot to illustrate the theme of loneliness. At one end he depicts the prostitution of sex: Sweeney and his paramours in a number of poems, the "pneumatic bliss" of Grishkin, the typist and other figures of *The Waste Land*. In the latter poem, rape, artificial abortion, homosexuality, impotence and frigidity are indicated. At the other end there are the inane dialogue, the lack of understanding and sympathy of such poems as "Portrait of a Lady" and "Conversation Galante". Between them we have such sterile love as that of "Lune de Miel".

Even true love is doomed to futility. The episodes of "La Figlia", of the "hyacinth girl", of "Dans le Restaurant" (where the situation is directly connected with the boyhood love of Dante for Beatrice [1]) are really variants of one episode, which has also lent features to most of the true love relationships in the other poems and the plays. Even the purest affection cannot lead to the consummation of a complete union between two human beings.

But the poet's isolation is still more complete than it immediately appears in many of his poems. For he learned from Laforgue the trick of a *"dédoublement* of the personality",[2] which enabled him to commune with himself. Thus the "you and I" of "The Love Song" are not two persons but one. Gerontion addresses, not another person, but a god who is a figment of his own brain. In the story "Eeldrop and Appleplex" the two characters are different sides of the author's personality, or perhaps his self and his not-self. It is obvious that Eliot, both in prose and poetry, favours a dialogue form. It is a convenient form for objectifying emotions and personal experiences. In fact all the seemingly "objectively" conceived characters even in such works as *The Family Reunion* are self-portraits to a greater extent than is probably the case in most dramas.

The *"dédoublement* of the personality" may be enjoyable. Mr. Roy Basler even thinks that "The Love Song" is a love song to the poet's self and that the main emotion of the poem is pleasurable — an enjoyment of the undisturbed possession of self.[3] If the same conception be applied to Eliot's

---

[1] Cp. "Dante", SE p. 273.   [2] CRICOM, April 1933. Cp. "Eeldrop", *Little Review*, Sept. 1917, p. 19.   [3] *Basler:* "Psychol. Pattern in 'The Love Song —'", Knickerbocker: *20th Cent. Eng.*

other poems, we get a quite different picture of them from the customary one. However, though there is no doubt about the presence of an *element* of self-enjoyment, this by no means exhausts, or even dominates, the emotions of the poems. There is no narcissism. For to the introspective mind "every moment is a new and shocking / Valuation of all we have been".[1] The division of the personality can only cover up, it cannot cure, the soul's incurable loneliness. The mind perceives, but it feels cut off from what it perceives, and one must go far to find a remedy.

"The natural wakeful life of our Ego is a perceiving." This line from "Triumphal March" is pathetically ironic in its context. For what is the use of perceiving if what we perceive is invariably superficial, the perception of a crowd waiting with its stools and sausages, aware of "5,800,000 rifles and carbines, 102,000 machine guns" and so on, but quite unaware of what is "hidden under the dove's wing"?

A certain comfort and invulnerability may be found, perhaps, in a misanthropic pose, and Eliot's misanthrophy may be largely a pose of this kind. But misanthropy can only be a substitute for happiness. It cannot itself generate pleasure.

Not only are human beings isolated from their fellows, but nature also appears unfeeling and unsympathetic. The evening sky in "The Love Song" is described as "a patient etherised upon a table". And in "Rhapsody on a Windy Night", "la lune ne garde aucune rancune", for

> "The moon has lost her memory.
> A washed-out smallpox cracks her face,
> Her hand twists a paper rose,
> That smells of dust and eau de Cologne,
> She is alone
> With all the old nocturnal smells
> That cross and cross across her brain."
> The reminiscence comes
> Of sunless dry geraniums
> And dust in crevices,
> Smells of chestnuts in the streets,
> And female smells in shuttered rooms,

"She is alone" — the same key-note again. But it would perhaps be dangerous to stress this point too much in its application to nature, because natural objects are used in these poems mostly to provide supporting imagery, and rarely for their own sakes. What we can safely say is that the poet finds no comfort in nature. There is no "impulse from a vernal wood", and no "society, where none intrudes".

While reading Eliot's poetry, we probably give provisional assent to his description of human intercourse. On second thoughts, however, many of

---

[1] EC II.

his readers will be inclined to demur. Communication and communion do not appear so impossible to them as they do to the poet. Eliot, they might say, has merely projected his personal emotions into the social scene, he has transmuted his private experiences so as to make them seem objective. Be that as it may, the poet has formed a view of human life which appears as a view and not merely as a mood in his poems. But the bitterness with which it is invested perhaps indicates that the original and obscurely persistent emotion of the poet was love of individuals and of mankind — a love that was sadly disappointed in his contacts with the world.

It seems certain, at any rate, that Eliot's love of tradition and culture was at the root of his despairing view of modern civilisation, just as his avowed affection for London was at the bottom of his gloomy picture of the city in *The Waste Land* and elsewhere.

Tradition and culture as Eliot ideally imagined them, as he may have dreamt of them from across the Atlantic, were beauty, and order, and purposeful living: the "inexplicable splendour of Ionian white and gold"[1], "the Rialto", "the eagles and the trumpets", the "fishmen" in the heart of the City.[1] Not the beauty of the countryside, the order of the natural universe, the purposeful life of simple rustics. These things meant little to Eliot except as parts of his childhood memories. He wished to find his ideals manifested in human society and in man-made civilisation. But what did he actually see? The Paris of Baudelaire and of *Bubu de Montparnasse*, in a spring-time glow, yet with its soiled pleasures, its vices, its diseases. A drab London of swarming, aimless existences and joyless activities.

Modern civilisation is a civilisation of dingy streets and sooty houses, all alike, enlivened only by a street piano, "mechanical and tired" (Laforgue's piano, reduced to this!); of genteel teas, of "faint stale smells of beer", of "restless nights in one-night cheap hotels". The images of this paltry "civilisation" are legion. Life here is trivial, monotonous and pointless. "In a thousand furnished rooms" people do exactly the same mechanical things. We walk about in a fog of unknowing, damp of soul, and our smiles vanish aimlessly above the roof-tops.

In the 1920 *Poems* Eliot stresses the ugliness and corruption of our age compared with previous ages. The key-note in these poems is the decay that has taken place. The degenerate race of to-day, the race of modern cities, is represented by such individuals as the Jew Bleistein and the phthisic Princess Volupine, Sweeney and his hysterical lady and *le garçon délabré*. Behind them stand the shadows of Shylock, Nausicaa and Polypheme, *Phlébas, le Phénicien*, Hercules, Ariadne, Agamemnon, Napoleon and a number of others — an altogether more impressive assembly. The heroes of Homer were worth writing poetry about. Eliot feels that he can only ridicule *homo sapiens* of 1920, and in fact the poems of this collection are

---

[1] WL III.

more grotesque than anything he wrote either before or since. He does not
merely compare his own age with the past of history, however. He knows
well enough what corruption was seen in Carthage and in the England of
Elizabeth. Therefore it is an ideal past rather than a real past and ideal
heroes rather than real heroes which give him matter for comparison.]

Into this pitiful world came the turmoil of the Great War to increase
its likeness to a vast Inferno.] It was not for nothing that the *Prufrock* poems
were inscribed to a victim of the War. There are not many references
to actual fighting in Eliot's poems. "Gerontion" has some, and *The Waste
Land* some.)It does not look as if the War itself was regarded as the greatest
evil. In fact, in "Gerontion", the fighting at "the hot gates" and "in the
warm rain" is felt as a salutary activity contrasted with the decay by which
the "old man" is surrounded. But the decay is associated with the fighting,
as were the estaminets of the enemy-occupied towns of Antwerp and Brussels.
The civilisation which remained after the War was hollowed-out from within.
It was inevitable that the note of disillusion should be strong in this civilisation, especially among town-dwellers. Only speculating industrialists and
contractors, smart tradesmen, militarists and amusement-caterers could really
like it. On the other hand, the post-War period was, as Eliot has pointed
out,[1] just as much a period of illusions as of disillusion. Its effete, effeminate,
romanticising society was castigated in Benda's *Belphégor,* which Eliot
much admired.

Eliot does not see post-war people in quite the same way as for
instance Fitzgerald, Hemingway, Huxley and Waugh. There is more grey
uniformity about Eliot's types than about the characters of these novelists,
or they are phantom-like in their disembodied neuroses as is the portrait-
gallery of "Gerontion". But often, too, we meet the fast, hardboiled, dis-
illusioned members of the lost generation in his poems — Sweeney in the
Buenos Aires bar and with the London prostitutes, the Lithuanian girl in
The Waste Land, etc. However glamorous they may appear to themselves,
there is a dreariness and sordidness about them of which the poet is perfectly
aware. And not only their private lives are tainted by it, but the whole
of the civilisation to which they belong. Our age is one of superstition and
necromancy, haunted by a feverish death-wish: ἀποθανεῖν θέλω.[2] No wonder,
then, that poets are called to an "endless battle to regain civilisation.[3]

There is no need for us who have lived through the last three or four
decades to expatiate any further on the many excellent reasons for a sensitive
person to feel discouraged in this period. In outer facts and concrete events
there were reasons enough. In Eliot's poetry, however, there are not only
moods of discouragement, but there is also such a consistent attitude of
despondency that we are forced to look for more than contingent reasons.

[1] "Last Words", CRI, Jan. 1939, p. 271.   [2] "I wish to die"; from the epigraph to WL.   [3] NEW, 27 April 1939.

We have already suggested his temperamental make-up and his literary bias. As we shall now see, there is also a close connection between his philosophical ideas and the moods that he expresses. And just as his vision not only determined his thought but was also determined by it, so his moods, too, must have been partly determined by his ideas. The various ways in which moods and ideas can be combined may best be called attitudes.

In 1933 Eliot wrote in a Commentary: "It is the use of irony to give the appearance of a philosophy of life, as something final and not instrumental, that leaves us now indifferent".[1] I see here an acknowledgment on the part of the author of the fact that his ironical mood was earlier felt to be part of a philosophical outlook. To Eliot the poet philosophy was, and to a great extent still is, a matter of emotion and not just of thought. That is one of the reasons why Indian philosophy exercised such a potent spell on him.

At first it seems that it was the negative aspects of Indian mysticism that appealed to Eliot, as we shall see in a moment. But still more important, perhaps, was the fact that his whole philosophical bent was negative and inverted, as if he despaired of metaphysics and clung to his very despair. If the interests evidenced in his writings are to be trusted, he more or less gave up metaphysics for art about 1917. In 1916 he wrote that no philosophy could make anything either more or less valuable to us than we actually find it to be.[2] He had obviously searched the realms of philosophy without finding a secure footing anywhere, and so he decided that a poet must give himself entirely up to art and cut himself off from everything else. But his liberation was not successful, and he admits as much in "Whispers of Immortality", which is obviously something more than a literary pastiche. Doubt and uncertainty were at the origin of Eliot's aestheticism. But "doubt and uncertainty", he tells us, with especial reference to these attitudes in *The Waste Land,* "are merely a variety of belief".[3]

He has Christian belief in mind in this context, and it may be that his despair of metaphysics was more particularly a despair of Christianity (though he also seems to have suffered a revulsion from Bradley's idealism). One of his "Preludes" contains a clear indication of this:

> I am moved by fancies that are curled
> Around these images, and cling:
> The notion of some infinitely gentle
> Infinitely suffering thing.
>
> Wipe your hand across your mouth, and laugh;
> The worlds revolve like ancient women
> Gathering fuel in vacant lots.

The "infinitely gentle, infinitely suffering thing" suggests both Jesus and the Virgin Mary. It is the objective correlative of an emotion, which

---

[1] CRI, April 1933, p. 469.   [2] *International Journal of Ethics,* 1916, p. 287.
[3] NPB.

is again transmuted from an idea, that of Christianity. But the whole complex of emotion, idea and symbol is rejected in the three final lines.

No doubt Eliot's Protestant and Unitarian scepticism made it hard for him to accept Christianity. His philosophical training would also make it difficult to give adherence to any definite belief. Perhaps such scepticism as that of Heraclitus meant something to him, and perhaps he was struck by the anti-religious fervour of Lucretius. There are several echoes of Lucretius's "nil posse creari de nilo" in his poetry.[1] And his early poems reflect, as we have seen, an atomistic view of the soul.

Yet there can be no question, even without his own statement about doubt being a variety of belief, but that he was much occupied with the Christian view of life. His *alter ego,* the bank clerk Eeldrop in "Eeldrop and Appleplex" takes an interest in theology, like himself. It may have been primarily an intellectual interest with Eliot. But Christianity is not mainly a philosophical system, and no degree of assent to it or repudiation of it can be exclusively intellectual. For the matter of that, Eliot thinks that "the intellectual soul" must necessarily experience moments of despair and disillusion in its development. His recognition of Pascal's despair as more terrible than Swift's is very self-revelatory: it is more terrible, he says, "because our heart tells us that it corresponds exactly to the facts and cannot be dismissed as mental disease".[2]

[The despair caused in the early phase by the loss or lack of a philosophy, particularly a Christian philosophy, is manifested in intricate ways in the poems. Much of it is projected into the portrayal of the various characters encountered there. Thus what is felt to be wrong with Sweeney, Bleistein, Mr. Eugenides, the "small house agent's clerk" and their numerous company, is not so much their immorality, or sexual perversion, as the fact that they have no sense of immorality or perversion, lacking knowledge of Good and Evil. This is an idea dear to Eliot, and it has also been exploited by other writers, for instance by Graham Greene in *Brighton Rock.* Eliot finds in Baudelaire a perception of the fact "that what distinguishes the relation of man and woman from the copulation of beasts is the knowledge of Good and Evil (of *moral* Good and Evil which are not natural Good and Bad or Puritan Right and Wrong). Having an imperfect, vague romantic conception of Good, he was at least able to understand that the sexual act as evil is more dignified, less boring, than as the natural, 'life-giving', cheery automatism of the modern world. For Baudelaire, sexual operation is at least something not analogous to Kruschen Salts".[3] Eliot's characters lack Baudelaire's awareness, and it would hardly be far-fetched to assume that they are partly an objectification of his irreligious as seen by his more enlightened self. The direct sense of guilt is absent from the Sweeney myth.

---

[1] E. g. "I can connect / Nothing with nothing" — WL III.   [2] "Pensées", EAM p. 152.   [3] "Baudelaire", SE p. 390.

It is far more prominent in the Figlia myth, from which the "Puritan" idea
of "Right and Wrong" is absent, but in which the aestheticist seems to be
at odds with the Christian moralist and mystic.

In "Gerontion" disbelief in the Christian faith is a central theme.
History, says Gerontion,

> — gives when our attention is distracted
> And what she gives, gives with such supple confusions
> That the giving famishes the craving. Gives too late
> What's not believed in, or if still believed,
> In memory only, reconsidered passion. Gives too soon
> Into weak hands, what's thought can be dispensed with
> Till the refusal propagates a fear. —

Knowledge and understanding of religion is often given too late — when
belief has passed, and it becomes lifeless theological learning. Wolf Manko-
witz, commenting on this poem, states that "the whole of Gerontion's complex
inquisition really would seem to constitute an apology for his failure to
passionally believe, or having intellectually conceded the required belief, his
constitutional inability to accept its corollary in faith".[1]

"After such knowledge, what forgiveness?" There would seem to be
none. Instead, there is punishment, there are "Rocks, moss, stonecrop, iron,
merds". Here, for the first time, we clearly find the idea of the corruption
of civilisation being due to the decay of religion, an idea which is more fully
developed in *The Waste Land.* Again we have to do with personal emotions,
of disbelief and consequent fear, objectified as an idea. And in *The Hollow
Men,* the "eye" that is feared, whatever else it may represent, is the eye
of God. Because it is avoided, everything is barren and hollow:

> Here the stone images
> Are raised, here they receive
> The supplication of a dead man's hand
> Under the twinkle of a fading star.

In poem after poem we find, behind the impersonal ideas, a note of the
personal suffering that Eliot thought must be the true subject of poetry.
How genuine is this suffering and how real are its causes?

It seems obvious that suffering and horror can be intensely imagined
without being painfully felt. It is less certain that they can be turned into
convincing poetry if they are only masquerading for the purposes of poetry.
Yet the contented and presumably placid life of Eliot the bank clerk seems
hard to reconcile with a lasting mood of despair. The explanation is probably
that a surface and, so to speak, civilian contentment was accompanied by a
more deep-seated unrest which was normally dormant, but which was roused

---

[1] F3 p. 134.

in periods of creation. In such periods despair might feel like a burden of which the poet wished to relieve himself.[1])

Eliot was also an intellectual uncommonly capable of sensing the emotional value-implications of philosophical and theological theories (a fact which goes far to explain his double role as philosopher and poet). Long before he believed in Christian orthodoxy he deplored "the decline of orthodox theology and its admirable theory of the soul", because owing to this decline, "the unique importance of events has vanished".[2] The decay of Christianity was a personal as well as a cultural problem.

It is tempting to mention the name of Oswald Spengler in connection with Eliot's early poetry. Eliot's criticism, however, is noticeably silent about Spengler, and it is doubtful whether he had read *Der Untergang des Abendlandes* before its author won international renown by its re-publication in 1923. This does not prevent the similarities between Eliot's views and those of Spengler from being frequently quite striking. Thus the cultural decline of the West was in Spengler's view associated with the exhaustion of what is the vital energy of all culture: religion. And one of the phenomena of decay was the rootless, barren life of the modern metropolis. The civilisation that Eliot describes might well be the same as civilisation according to Spengler's terminology: a culture that has passed its peak and is doomed to extinction.

⌠Eliot's metaphysical despair was linked with his sense of loneliness. And while he still cut himself off from the communion that may be found in religion, he must have felt that he had partly himself to blame for his isolation:

> We think of the key, each in his prison
> Thinking of the key, each confirms a prison⌡

These lines from *The Waste Land* are related, in a note, to Bradley's philosophy. Eliot quotes from *Appearance and Reality:*

My external sensations are no less private to myself than are my thoughts or my feelings. In either case my experience falls within my own circle, a circle closed on the outside; and, with all its elements alike, every sphere is opaque to the others which surround it . . . In brief, regarded as an existence which appears in a soul, the whole world for each is peculiar and private to that soul.

Such solipsism only becomes actual to a philosopher, in other words, it only appears if one thinks of it — "Thinking of the key, each confirms a prison". But the idea of such utter isolation cannot help stirring the emotions, and Eliot shows us very clearly what it feels like to believe in it. The "I" of "Portrait of a Lady" listens to the lady's effusions:

---

[1] Cp. UPC pp. 144—5.   [2] "Eeldrop & A."

> "I am always sure that you understand
> My feelings, always sure that you feel,
> Sure that across the gulf you reach your hand."

But she is sadly mistaken. Whatever others may say, think, or do, and whatever may happen to other people,

> I keep my countenance,
> I remain self-possessed

And the word "self-possessed" is given an extra weight of meaning: "I remain shut-off and impregnable" is what it conveys.

The lady of "A Game of Chess" hysterically demands

> "What are you thinking of? What thinking? What?
> "I never know what you are thinking. Think."

Only Agatha, and those who have learnt what she has learnt, know by what means one may "try to penetrate the other private worlds / Of make-believe and fear".[1]

It took the poet some time to learn this. Wanting a positive belief, he seems to have been haunted not only by misanthropy, but by a feeling of determinism, and even fatalism:

> Every street lamp that I pass
> Beats like a fatalistic drum,[2]

Our actions are mere reflexes, like those of animals:

> So the hand of the child, automatic,
> Slipped out and pocketed a toy that was running along the quay.[3]

The determinist view is terrifying, but it is also comforting because it relieves one of responsibility. "History to blame", is Stephen's comfort in Joyce's *Ulysses*. And in a way it is Gerontion's comfort too — as well as his nightmare. History deceives us and "guides us by vanities". And

> Neither fear nor courage saves us. Unnatural vices
> Are fathered by our heroism. Virtues
> Are forced upon us by our impudent crimes.

There seems to be a fatal development which we cannot resist. The symbol of the wheel is often used — notably in *The Family Reunion* — to express a sense of determinism. Harry and Agatha feel it very strongly until they are released by the illumination of faith:

---

[1] FR p. 92.   [2] "Rhapsody".   [3] Ibid.

To and fro, dragging my feet
Among inner shadows in the smoky wilderness,
Trying to avoid the clasping branches
And the giant lizard. To and fro.
Until the chain breaks.
                            The chain breaks,
The wheel stops, and the noise of machinery,
And the desert is cleared, under the judicial sun
Of the final eye — [1]

The poet's despondency, from a disappointment with human intercourse
and modern civilisation, broadens into an all-embracing pessimism, which
certainly owes something to Indian, especially Buddhist, philosophy. His
interest in Buddha was of long standing. As a boy he came across a poem
for which he has preserved a warm affection: "The Light of Asia" by Edwin
Arnold, a long epic on the life of Gautama Buddha. "I must have had a
latent sympathy for the subject matter, for I read it through with gusto,
and more than once".[2]

The symbol of the wheel was often used in Hindu and Buddhist
scriptures to denote the hopeless round of unredeemed life and death. The
whirlpool of Eliot's "Death by Water" and the "water-mill beating the
darkness" of "Journey of the Magi", to mention only two examples, are
among the Protean forms of the same wheel. The Buddha's "Fire Sermon"
he has directly drawn upon in *The Waste Land*. All things, says the Buddha,
are on fire, visible things are on fire, the ear and the tongue and what they
perceive, the body and the mind, everything is on fire "with the fire of
passion, say I, with the fire of hatred, with the fire of infatuation; with
birth, old age, death, sorrow, lamentation, misery, grief, and despair are
they on fire".[3] And in another famous passage the Buddha declares:

This, monks, is the noble truth of suffering: birth is suffering; decay is
suffering; death is suffering; presence of objects we hate is suffering;
separation from objects we love is suffering; not to obtain what we desire
is suffering.
In brief, the five aggregates which spring from grasping, they are painful.
This, monks, is the noble truth concerning the origin of suffering; verily
it originates in that craving which causes the renewal of becomings, is
accompanied by sensual delight, and seeks satisfaction now here, now there;
that is to say, craving for pleasures, craving for becoming, craving for not
becoming.[4]

We are reminded of Eliot's constant insistence, both in his prose and
his poetry, on pain and suffering. Awareness is painful, creation is painful, sincerity is painful, doubt is painful, belief is painful. In "Journey of
the Magi", we hear of the hardships of the journey, the pain of conviction,
the discomfort of belief. Life is death, as in *The Hollow Men*, and both

---

[1] FR p. 108.   [2] "What is Minor Poetry?", *Welsh Review*, Dec. 1944.
[3] From the *Maha-Vagga*, Warren: *Buddhism in Translations*, p. 352.   [4] Quoted
from Ballou's *World Bible*.

terrible to those who have not passed over the river to "death's other Kingdom".

The human mind is perpetually driven between two desires, between two dreams each of which may be either a vision or a nightmare: the vision and nightmare of the material world, and the vision and nightmare of the immaterial. Each may be in turn, or for different minds, a refuge to which to fly, or a horror from which to escape. We desire and fear both sleep and waking; the day brings relief from the night, and the night brings relief from the day; we go to sleep as to death, and we wake as to damnation.[1]

Eliot knows that insensibility, obtuseness, stupidity would bring relief, as they bring relief to a Sweeney "letting his arms hang down to laugh" — before he has become the philosopher of *Sweeney Agonistes* — or to the chattering uncles and aunts of *The Family Reunion*. He knows that Grishkin's "friendly bust / Gives promise of pneumatic bliss". But he has heard "whispers of immortality", he is above the mob, he disdains the vulgar pleasures which cost us all our human dignity. Nirvana attracts him, the quiescence of "dried tubers" under the snow in winter. Simeon says: "I am tired with my own life and the lives of those after me", and asks only for the peace of obliteration. The protagonist of *Ash-Wednesday* also at first wishes to be freed from the eternal cycle and to find peace in oblivion:

> Because I do not hope to turn again
> Because I do not hope
> Because I do not hope to turn
> Desiring this man's gift and that man's scope
> I no longer strive to strive towards such things

However, the poetic belief in Nirvana is challenged by other beliefs, particularly by Christian ideas of a hereafter. The peace of winter cannot last: "In the juvescence of the year / Came Christ the tiger".[2] The contemplation of Nirvana is disturbed, and peace of mind must be found elsewhere.

In any case, the poet recognises oblivion, too, as a mode of flight, and as unworthy of a philosopher. It resembles too closely the death-in-life of the "hollow men" or of the crowds flowing over London Bridge. Better then to follow the example of the Stoics and recognise life for what it is without being discouraged. Better still, perhaps, to embrace suffering as being itself a virtue, in the spirit of the Christian mystics, until we learn to see that "la sua voluntate e nostra pace".

The outcome of it all, to begin with, was that the poet gave himself up, with a certain heroism, to a pessimism which, in the opinion of at least one critic, is the most absolute and despairing since Swift.[3] And this in spite of F. H. Bradley, who thought that pain was not real, that it was transcended

---

[1] *Revelation* I, p. 31.   [2] "Gerontion".   [3] Häusermann: *Oeuvre p. de T. S. E.*, p. 2.

by something higher, and that there is a preponderance of pleasure in the universe.[1]

A philosophical pessimism of this kind presupposes, not necessarily religious belief, but certainly a religious attitude and point of view. T. E. Hulme realised this when, in his *Speculations,* he pictured human life as a plane with roads radiating from a centre, the roads wrongly imagined by the romanticists to lead indefinitely to perfection, but recognised as being blind alleys by those who have a religious attitude. "Such a realisation", he says, "has formed the basis of all the great religions, and is most conveniently remembered by the symbol of the *wheel."* But "this symbol of the futility of existence is absolutely lost to the modern world".[2]

It is "the Catholic philosophy of disillusion" which Hulme here has in mind, and the corresponding, but much stronger philosophy of disillusion in Brahmaism and Buddhism. The despondency engendered in Eliot by the difficulties of embracing Christianity was supplemented by this "Catholic philosophy of disillusion" which he found exemplified in Dante's *Vita Nuova,* and which may be summed up in the precepts: "not to expect more from *life* than it can give or more from *human* beings than they can give; to look to *death* for what life cannot give".[3] This philosophy is not necessarily bitter. It softens the bitterness of disappointed expectations in life. But it demands a high degree of resignation. In his early poems Eliot shows little of this resignation, though his constant preoccupation with the theme of death draws him towards it. Even in such poems as *Ash-Wednesday* he finds resignation difficult. But in time the Catholic philosophy of disillusion, with its tranquil recognition of the world for what it is, engulfs his more rebellious and bitter disillusion. This has happened in the *Four Quartets,* where the author has also taken a further step and expressed a mood or experience of beatitude only occasionally glimpsed before.

The Catholic philosophy of disillusion is connected, of course, with the doctrine of sin. [The Eastern religions are more aware of evil as suffering than as unrighteousness, as personal than as social, and this view seems to predominate in Eliot's poetry.] But in his later poems, at least, the note of gloom is often struck by the idea of sin. It appears already as "the shadow" in *The Hollow Men* (though this also stands for an aspect of Bradleyan philosophy). In *Ash-Wednesday* the realisation of sin is fully conscious and informs the prayers of the poem: "Pray for us sinners now and at the hour of our death." "Marina" mentions such definite sins as hatred, vanity, gluttony, and lust. And in Chorus V of *The Rock* there is a very keen feeling of sinfulness: "the heart is deceitful — — and desperately wicked."

On the whole, it seems as if sin is inextricably bound up with existence in time. It is *original sin,* the heritage of mankind. "Animula", however, indicates another point of view: that childhood is a period of innocence.

---

[1] Cf. A & R p. 199.   [2] Op. cit. pp. 33—4.   [3] "Dante", SE p. 275.

when the soul which has issued from the hand of God retains its purity and simplicity — whereas experience of this life and adult age bring corruption. The poem may be interpreted, it is true, as a general statement of what temporal existence does to man, who was originally shaped in the image of God. But it would be hard to deny that it shows some belief in the basic goodness of human kind.

Eliot's view in this case is influenced by Aristotle.[1] In his younger days he may also have inclined to the Romantic notion that man is essentially good but is corrupted by his environment. But as far back as his poetry takes us he was obviously drawn much more strongly to the opposite view, that man is fundamentally imperfect but can be improved by civilisation.

The conviction of sin is not always conscious. The Magi and Simeon, for instance, are not aware of their own evil. Simeon, on the contrary, has a strong sense of his own righteousness:

> I have walked many years in this city,
> Kept faith and fast, provided for the poor,
> Have given and taken honour and ease.
> There went never any rejected from my door.

But the Magi feel that "this Birth was / Hard and bitter agony for us, like Death, our death", obviously because they realise subconsciously how worthless they are in comparison with the perfection they have seen. Simeon, we must suppose, has some such realisation too, though he does not explain it in terms of agony and death, but in terms of tiredness. It is the old man's fear, also seen in "Gerontion", which is thus camouflaged.

In the early poems, the subject of sin is rarely introduced directly. Nor is the contemplation of death (which is fairly constant) frequently connected with the idea of doom. But in "Gerontion" and occasionally in *The Waste Land* we do find such a connection between death and the judgment for sins. "The tiger [i.e. Christ] springs in the new year", says Gerontion: "Us he devours." And Madame Sosostris admonishes her clients to "Fear death by water", with a similar meaning. There is not only fear attendant on sin, however. The possibility of damnation is also "so immense a relief in a world of electoral reform, plebiscites, sex reform and dress reform, that damnation itself is an immediate form of salvation — of salvation from the ennui of modern life, because it at last gives some significance to living".[2] Eliot's concern with death and doom in his poetry is partly due to his desire to find a meaning in life.

There is also the death-wish pure and simple, but whether as felt by the poet himself, or as observed by him in post-war society, it is hard to decide at first sight We touched above on the subject of Nirvana. The longing for Nirvana is obviously a personal one. And one may ask whether

---

[1] Cf. "Dante", SE pp. 259—261.   [2] "Baudelaire", SE p. 389.

the death-wish recognised by psychoanalysis is not also, necessarily, individual. A whole society may perhaps be thrilled and enthralled by the prospect of destruction. There seems to have been some of this fascination in European countries in 1939. But I would suggest that it was not a super-individual phenomenon, but rather something that resulted from the sum of individual emotions. The philosophy or ethos of a society can be really super-individual, more or less ignored by the majority and only held consciously by an élite. With the emotional urges of individuals in a society it is a different matter. They can spread, and do spread, by the contagion of suggestion, but they remain personal.

Eliot may have exploited theories of mass psychology, but we can safely assume that the death-wish in his poetry, especially in *The Waste Land* and *The Hollow Men,* has been personally experienced. It is not, however, identical with the fascination of destruction. As befits a post-war period, and in accordance with the poet's temperament, it is rather a feeling of fatigue, like the tiredness of Simeon, or like the infinite weariness of the Sibyl who figures in the epigraph of *The Waste Land.* There is a certain similarity with the disdainful refusal of life of many of the French Symbolists and decadents, for instance de l'Isle-Adam, whose *Axel* seems to have lent a number of images to *The Waste Land,* and Huysmans.[1] It is likely enough that these writers in their way, and Webster, Tourneur and other Elizabethans in theirs, helped to induce a mood of morbidity in Eliot. But the mood is none the less personal. This is borne out by Eliot's views on Cyril Tourneur in his essay on that playwright. *The Revenger's Tragedy,* he says, "is a document on humanity chiefly because it is a document on one human being, Tourneur; its motive is truly the death motive, for it is the loathing and horror of life itself. To have realized this motive so well is a triumph; for the hatred of life is an important phase — even, if you like, a mystical experience — in life itself".[2] The triumph would seem to consist in Tourneur's ability to experience mystical feelings. And it appears to be implied that Eliot has personally experienced the same feelings, else he could hardly have understood them.

A number of critics, among them Dr. Richards, have pointed to Eliot's preoccupation with sex. One cannot help noticing this preoccupation, and it is hard to avoid the impression that sex is regarded as in itself evil and sinful. This impression, however, is easily exaggerated if we imagine the sinfulness of sex to be inherent in Christian doctrine or philosophy. Apart from the doctrine of original sin, which perhaps has a special application to sex, there is no such teaching in Christianity. Catholic dogma, despite the doctrine of the Immaculate Conception, does not regard sexual intercourse as in itself tainted or sinful. Anglo-Catholic theology as expounded

---

[1] Wilson's treatment of these writers in AC is very interesting in this connection.
[2] SE p. 190.

in *Doctrine in the Church of England,* emphatically does not. [And I do not think Eliot very often had sinfulness in mind when he wrote about or alluded to the abuse of sex. If a philosophy is required to explain this preoccupation, it will sooner be found in the Oriental ideas of desire as suffering and as distraction from the path of holiness. [We must also remember that the sexual imagery of Eliot's poems stands for a number of other things besides physical copulation, especially for his view of spiritual communion.]

Mr. Edmund Wilson voices a common Freudian view when he says that "the drying up of the springs of sexual emotion" may cause a "straining after a religious emotion which may be made to take its place".[1] There is no doubt much truth in this claim, but there is no need to apply it to Eliot's poetry. It is at most irrelevant, and possibly quite false. It might with equal justice be maintained that the drying up of the springs of religious emotion causes a straining after sexual emotion which may be made to take its place. Very little is gained by either explanation. [And at any rate an interest in metaphysics, and religious emotions, positive or negative, are as original in this poetry as sexual emotions.] The positive faith that informs Eliot's later poetry might be explained in terms of sex without the supernatural reality towards which it is directed being made any less real (or more real, for that matter). We may admit, and Eliot admits, a connection as in an ascending scale between sexual love and divine love,[2] but this does not make either a substitute for the other. We shall therefore, in the following chapter, regard Eliot's metaphysics as an independent sphere of interest and emotion. But before closing this chapter it may be useful to attempt a general interpretation of the main work of the poet's early phase, in the light of what we have here discussed.

The Waste Land.

[Eliot himself has pronounced on two interpretations of *The Waste Land* both of which he declares to be incomprehensible to him. The first is that of I. A. Richards, who said that Eliot "had effected a complete severance between his poetry and all beliefs"; and the second is the common interpretation of the poem as the expression of the "disillusionment of a generation".]

In Richards's opinion, Eliot felt a sense of desolation because it had now become impossible to hold the beliefs of bygone days, and his readers derived the same sense of desolation from his poetry. Richards later explained that when he spoke of "a complete severance between his poetry and all beliefs" he was "referring not to the poet's own history, but to the technical detachment of the poetry". [And what Eliot had achieved, he said, was to find "a new order through the contemplation and exhibition of disorder".[3]]The

---

[1] AC p. 105.   [2] Cf. "Baudelaire", SE pp. 391—2. The idea is not only the Freudian idea of sublimation, but may also have some connection with the theory of transcendence as taught by F. H. Bradley.   [3] *Science & Poetry,* p. 70.

latter statement sounds unconvincing. As for the idea that the meaning of
the poem should be severed from all belief, we have Eliot's own statement
that "a 'sense of desolation', etc. (if it is there) is not a separation from
belief; it is nothing so pleasant. In fact, doubt, uncertainty, futility, etc.,
would seem to me to prove anything except that agreeable partition; for
doubt and uncertainty are merely a variety of belief".[1] We need discuss
this no further. The question has already been dealt with in the present
chapter and in that on "Poetic Belief"; and the general considerations there
are fully applicable to *The Waste Land*.

The notion of *The Waste Land* as the expression of the disillusionment
of a generation, Eliot simply calls nonsensical. What he objects to is the
term "generation".[2] A poet expresses his own ideas and emotions, not those
of a generation, if it may be said to have any. A great poet may be writing
his time, but he does so in writing himself, and anyhow the outlook of a
"time", or an age, is not identical with the outlook of a "generation", which
suggests a mob.

Since the view was first popularised by "the more approving critics",
it has become almost axiomatically accepted that *The Waste Land* expresses
the disillusionment of a generation, more particularly of the "lost generation"
of the first post-war era. Those who repeat this view usually disregard the
fact that most of the essential moods and other features of the poem were
present already in the poems that Eliot wrote before the Great War. Their
point of view tends to make the poem seem rather superficial, as it does seem
to Dr. Routh, who has written an otherwise excellent appreciation. "The
poem", he says, "despite its erudition, is essentially superficial. Eliot not
only overlooks the undercurrent of inventiveness and humanity, which is
struggling against the curse of Adam, but he trifles with the symptoms of
our alleged demoralization — —; blemishes which always have and always
will disgrace society even at its best —".[3] This objection might have been
justified if Eliot had been concerned with merely presenting "social aimlessness", as Dr. Routh puts it. But it is precisely this explanation of the poem
that is superficial. Eliot was concerned with something more or other than
presenting social aimlessness. And at any rate he thought, with Croce, that
it is "the intensity of the artistic process",[4] not the "greatness" or originality
of the emotions and ideas, that counts most.

I think neither Professor Cleanth Brooks nor Mr. Norman Nicholson
have interpreted *The Waste Land* satisfactorily. Both these critics find it
a poem of faith rather than of despair.[5] Miss Helen Gardner has a more
adequate understanding of it.[6] And Miss Bradbrook, F. O. Matthiessen and
Stephen Spender have all given valuable commentaries on it.[7]

---

[1] NPB.   [2] Cf. "Thoughts after Lambeth", SE p. 358.   [3] *Eng. Lit. & I. in
20th C.*, p. 164.   [4] TIT, SE p. 19.   [5] Cf. F3 pp. 31, 35 and Nicholson: *Man
& Lit.*, p. 196.   [6] Cf. F3 p. 60.   [7] Cf. F3 p. 126; ATSE pp. 98—9, 106—7;
and SELCR pp. 263—4.

One of the critics who has best understood Eliot is E. M. Forster. Concerning *The Waste Land* he wrote in 1929:

If I have its hang, it has nothing to do with the English tradition in literature, or law or order, nor, except incidentally, has the rest of his work anything to do with them either. It is just a personal comment on the universe, as individual and as isolated as Shelley's *Prometheus*.

In respect to the horror that they find in life, men can be divided into three classes. — — those who have not suffered often or acutely; — — those who have escaped through horror into a further vision; — — those who continue to suffer. Most of us belong to the first class, and to the elect outside it our comments may sound shallow. — — Mr. Eliot — — belongs to the third. He is not a mystic. His last volume contains many well-turned compliments to religion and Divine Grace, but no trace of religious emotion. — — what he seeks is not revelation, but stability.[1]

Mr. Forster's awareness of suffering enables him, if nothing else does, to understand something fundamental in Eliot's outlook. He may have become more inclined, since 1929, to place Eliot in his second class of sufferers and to recognise the genuineness of his religious and mystical emotions.[2] But in spite of Forster's original failure in appreciation here we would do well to keep his criticism in mind, if only to counteract a too superficial reading of Eliot's poetry.

[*The Waste Land* certainly expresses disgust with modern civilisation and with post-war society. What else could one expect of an American who wrote as early as 1909 of "the failure of American life" and of the many Americans whose "hearts were always in Europe": he could hardly fail to be disappointed on a closer acquaintance with European civilisation] We must also take into account the feelings expressed in the quotation from Hesse's *Blick ins Chaos* in the Notes to *The Waste Land*. But it is much nearer the mark to call the poem "a personal comment on the universe". The "waste land", in one of its aspects, is the wilderness of thought into which Eliot's studies and speculations had led him, a wilderness unenlivened by a vital faith. He is himself the Fisher King, who has only fragments of ideas to shore against his ruins. And at the same time the Fisher King, who is conspicuously absent from most of the poem, is the God whom he cannot find. The poet is unable to surrender to belief. This inability was hinted at already in "The Love Song". It is notable that throughout Eliot's poetry the themes of human union and divine union are accompanied by feelings both of ecstasy and of *fear*. [The despair of *The Waste Land* is a despair of metaphysics,[3] and the horror of life has its source in this despair.] The scorn of humanity is really a loathing of anything that reminds the poet

---

[1] "T. S. E. & his Diff.", *Life & Letters*.　　[2] In a note to a reprint of his article in SELCR, he declares: "In view of Mr. Eliot's later work (not here considered) I would modify these remarks."　　[3] Cp. Eliot's opinion of *In Memoriam*: "*In Memoriam* is a poem of despair, but of despair of a religious kind." (EAM p. 187.)

of the meaninglessness of existence. The Waste Land is determined by its religious attitude. It is a criticism of life from a Christian and Hindu and Buddhist point of view, but without the faith of any of these religions, or rather with the faith of them all but with a still more powerful scepticism.

There is plain personal suffering too, caused by the buffetings of life, and especially by the feeling of isolation which neo-Kantian philosophy helped to make vividly conscious. There is no doubt much purely personal matter that the reader cannot trace. But it is all made to contribute to the *pessimisme absolu* which is caused by the absence of the Absolute.

The personal emotions of the poet, however, have been objectified in accordance with his theory and usual practice. The poet's tiredness of life has become the death-gravitation of a society. The objective images of a sterile civilisation have been seized upon to express the poet's sense of sterility in his soul. In comparison, "Gerontion", with its "thoughts of a dry brain in a dry season", presents itself much more directly as a personal confession. The objectification of The Waste Land is obviously justified, because the poet felt strongly about the aspects of modern life that he used for his objective correlatives as well as about the states of his own soul. And he successfully transposed the poem, as he had often transposed poems before, from being lyrical in intention to being descriptive, narrative and dramatic. In doing this he availed himself of his technical skill, and he was carried along, no doubt, by his technical interest, which in turn helped to shape his thought in many places. Ezra Pound's poems and other modern poetry besides were also there to exercise their suggestive influence. The result was a broken sequence in which the order and unity were not of technique, as Dr. Richards contends, but of mood, of negative belief, of doubt. The fragments of the poem are not just aspects of modern civilisation, but images of the desires, pains, thoughts and misgivings of the poet, who had crammed his mind with metaphysical ideas which had no meaning, and in his "natural wakeful life" incessantly "perceived" objects and events which had no meaning either.

This being the case, and given the unaccustomed technique of the poem, it was perhaps inevitable that readers should be content if they found the disillusionment of a generation to be its meaning. Otherwise they might have found nothing and the poem would have had no appeal. This meaning is the poet's "bit of nice meat" for the house-dog of the premises he is breaking into.[1] What is more, it has made the poem useful to the generation it is assumed to satirise by making it conscious of its shortcomings. The Waste Land may well be regarded as "a cry from the wilderness, a call to repentance".[2] When a poem arouses suitable emotions in the reader, it is already justified as poetry. We will be reminded here of Eliot's recognition of the fact that a sensitive reader is as well qualified to determine the meaning of a poem as is the poet himself.

---

[1] Cf. UPC p. 151.   [2] H. R. Williamson: *Poetry of T. S. E.*, p. 87.

With this we have no quarrel. What we object to is the canonisation of one definite interpretation, which gets in the way of the reader who wishes to think and judge for himself. We are at liberty to interpret *The Waste Land* as the expression of the disillusion of a generation, if we wish. But it must be because we personally find this significance, not because we have been told to find it. The danger is that of sensibility being ousted by habit, a danger that Eliot has always fought to obviate. That the danger is very real is testified by so acute a critic as Cecil Day Lewis. "It is my own experience", he wrote in *A Hope for Poetry,* "that, when I have expressed some private experience in a poem, I have frequently discovered it to contain a 'political' significance of which I was quite unconscious while writing it. A year or two ago I wrote a sequence called 'From Feathers to Iron' which for me expressed simply my thoughts and feelings during the nine months before the birth of my first child: the critics, almost to a man, took it for a political allegory; the simple, personal meaning evaded them".[1]

We may admit, then, the social satire of *The Waste Land,* and the generation which has survived the Second World War will find it as urgently topical as their fathers — and perhaps as salutary. But much of the poem cannot find its true perspective or become properly intelligible unless we regard it as the experiences of a mind looking into itself. And certainly, if the poem continues to captivate our great-grandchildren, it will not be because it describes a particular historical situation but because it describes a human soul tormented by eternal problems which the historical situation only served to actualise.

V.

Philosophy.

Our examination of vision and mood in Eliot's poetry was mainly concerned with his early works, because there the expression of these things is most conspicuous. While Eliot still had a negative relation to metaphysical questions, a relation which itself might be defined as a mood, definite ideas did not play a large part in his poems. But when metaphysics reasserted itself as a positive interest, a number of philosophical and religious ideas were vitalised and employed imaginatively, whether by a deliberate or an unconscious process. Consequently we must pay rather more attention to the poet's later work in our examination of these ideas.

It matters little how consciously Eliot used them. The main thing is that they do inform his poetry. He may have been consciously interested primarily in the technique of composition. But years of philosophical and theological studies are not sloughed off for the sake of pure poetry. He had too much on his mind, and too much *in* his mind to be able to abstain from ideas.

---

[1] Op. cit. p. 38.

For the convenience of our analysis, we may make a division between general philosophical ideas and the emotions and ideas of a more specifically religious character ("faith"). This does not mean, however, that we recognise any clear distinction between these domains in Eliot's outlook, any more than we find a distinction between his vision and his ideas. They are all intimately bound up one with the other. But as a preliminary to understanding them in their wholeness, we must examine them in their parts.

Reality.

It is interesting to study the development of Eliot's imagery, and to see how it reflects the development of his thought.

The image of the sea, in the *Prufrock* and 1920 poems, suggests all the phenomena and events of life which impinge upon the individual without his being able to order or relate them in his mind, or utilise them (cp. Hamlet's "sea of troubles"); he is choked, and the sensation is one of drowning. His individuality is dissolved, and his bones are picked, as in the case of *Phlébas, le Phénicien,* and his counterpart, *le garçon délabré,* who is unable to cope with *his* reality. A precarious existence can be led among all the unco-ordinated phenomena by means of dreams, and thus the sea itself can come to represent dreaming and unreality, as in "The Love Song" ("I should have been a pair of ragged claws / Scuttling across the floors of silent seas"; "We have lingered in the chambers of the sea / By sea-girls wreathed with sea-weed red and brown / Till human voices wake us, and we drown").

Because the phenomena of life have their existence within our consciousness, the sea, too, is within us. And the idea of the sea as a confusion of unrelated matter contained in the mind is seen clearly in "Rhapsody on a Windy Night":

> The memory throws up high and dry
> A crowd of twisted things;
> A twisted branch upon the beach
> Eaten smooth, and polished
> As if the world gave up
> The secret of its skeleton,
> Stiff and white.

Connected with the sea and drowning are the symbols of fog and smoke. "Morning at the Window" joins the two sets of symbols by speaking of "the brown waves of fog". More directly than the sea, the fog suggests ignorance and bewilderment, the sense of being lost and of not knowing where to go.

Music also, like the sea in one of its aspects, seems to represent illusion and delusion, especially the delusion provided by art. It betrays itself by its false notes, by the instruments being broken and cracked and out of tune. The titles of some of the poems suggest music: "Love Song", "Preludes",

"Rhapsody", but the poems — except in their mere formal aspects — do not give us the harmony of music; in fact they are — conceptually — parodies of what we usually understand by harmony. In "The Love Song", the "music from a farther room" is part of the conventional and meaningless atmosphere. In "Portrait of a Lady", Chopin's Preludes echo at first "among velleities and carefully caught regrets / Through attenuated tones of violins / Mingled with remote cornets". And soon it is this:

> Among the windings of the violins
> And the ariettes
> Of cracked cornets
> Inside my brain a dull tom-tom begins
> Absurdly hammering a prelude of its own,
> Capricious monotone
> That is at least one definite "false note".

In "Conversation Galante" the man remarks:

> — — "Someone frames upon the keys
> That exquisite nocturne, with which we explain
> The night and moonshine; music which we seize
> To body forth our own vacuity."

"To body forth our own vacuity" — that is what music stands for in these poems: illusion, hypocrisy even. A similar significance seems to attach to the moon, in "Rhapsody" and "Conversation Galante".

In *The Waste Land,* the sea is "oed' und leer". We again meet Phlebas the Phoenician. "The king my brother's wreck" — death at the bottom of the sea — means no more than death in the earth: "White bodies naked on the low damp ground / And bones cast in a little low dry garret." And yet — it is not for nothing that Madame Sosostris warns against death by water, for there is the chance of a sea-change ("Those are pearls that were his eyes. Look!"), of a resurrection, just as the body buried in the earth may be dug up again by "the Dog — — that's friend to men," — or it may begin to sprout! Thus the sea becomes the symbol of a mysterious transformation "into something rich and strange": bewilderment and confusion may turn into knowledge.

The music symbol has also acquired a different significance in *The Waste Land*. Music and singing now stand for purity, which also may have a magical potency ("this music crept by me upon the waters"). The nightingale's song is something in the nature of a revelation of the spirit: it fills "all the desert with inviolable voice". Then there are the "voix d'enfants, chantant dans la coupole", which is the "singing in the dome heard at the ceremony of the foot-washing which precedes the restoration of the wounded Anfortas (the Fisher King) by Parzival and the taking away of the curse from the waste land".[1] Finally, there is the "pleasant whining of a mandoline" among the fishmen. But music, too, is vitiated and turns into

---

[1] C. Brooks, F3 p. 20.

gramophone records, the cries of crickets and bats, and the singing of the
dry grass. In "What the Thunder Said", a woman fiddles "whisper music"
on her hair — ghostly, unreal music — a symbol of unreality joined to a
symbol of life (the hair).

By the time we come to the *Four Quartets,* the transformation is complete. The sea is no longer within us, "the sea is all about us". It still
tosses up curious things on its beaches, but they no longer confuse, they
are merely hints of something beyond our present understanding. The sea
is now eternity. And music is used as a symbol of absolute Reality. It is
no longer noisy and out of tune, but something "heard so deeply / That it is
not heard at all."

The development of these images marks a development in the poet's
mind from a feeling of helplessness in a world of appearances and illusions
to a sense of a transcendent reality which human beings may not be able
to grasp but of which they can receive intuitive glimpses.

The world of Prufrock and Sweeney is, on the whole, the familiar,
material world of every day. And yet it is bewildering enough, because,
as we saw in the previous chapter, there appears to be no necessary relation
between its phenomena and no ultimate meaning. And then there is the
obtrusive and disturbing fact of death. It may be accounted for by means
of "whispers of immortality", but the young man in "Portrait of a Lady"
is entirely baffled by it. "What if she should die some afternoon," he asks —

> Should die and leave me sitting pen in hand
> With the smoke coming down above the housetops;
> Doubtful, for a while
> Not knowing what to feel or if I understand

More and more the poet becomes aware that there are two worlds,
two planes of existence They are both unreal, both "death's kingdoms", as
in *The Hollow Men.* But this life, the "life" of the crowds flowing into
the City, is "death's dream kingdom", is more definitely unreal than "death's
other kingdom" which we do not know, and which only flashes past our
awareness like "sunlight on a broken column". Through "Marina" and
Ash-Wednesday the certainty of an immaterial, transcendent world beyond
this deepens towards the mystic conviction of the *Four Quartets,* in which
the two planes of existence are seen to be really connected:

> Garlic and sapphires in the mud
> Clot the bedded axle-tree.
> The trilling wire in the blood
> Sings below inveterate scars
> Appeasing long forgotten wars.
> The dance along the artery
> The circulation of the lymph
> Are figured in the drift of stars
> Ascend to summer in the tree

> We move above the moving tree
> In light upon the figured leaf
> And hear upon the sodden floor
> Below, the boarhound and the boar
> Pursue their pattern as before
> But reconciled among the stars.

The "vision and nightmare of the material world, and the vision and nightmare of the immaterial" have here lost their element of terror and have become "reconciled among the stars".

The "material world" was the rational world, the world of waking. It is Eliot's distrust of rationalism that makes him ironically call it "death's dream kingdom". The "immaterial world" is the irrational world, the world of sleep, but it was not to be apprehended except by a peculiar wakefulness. Everything depends upon the awareness of the individual. We are accustomed to the distinction between the spiritual and the material, but that is of little use to us in "explaining" Eliot's poetry. The difference goes deeper than that, and at the same time it is more indefinable. It springs from different kinds or degrees of consciousness from those we are accustomed to.

"The poet", says Eliot, "is occupied with frontiers of consciousness beyond which words fail, though meanings still exist".[1] And privately he has said that, though poetry has no direct ontological significance, it can help one to approach the understanding of an ultimate reality which includes both the religious and the aesthetic. A sensitive reader can gain from poetry the assurance that there is this kind of reality. But it is something to be experienced, not explained. Our explanation of Eliot's philosophical and religious premises cannot, of course, provide this experience, but it may be able to facilitate it.

We are not surprised to find that the philosophy which seems to have exercised the strongest influence on Eliot's poetry is that which he studied with the greatest application, namely that of Francis Herbert Bradley, particularly Bradley's theory of knowledge. His entire poetical output may be regarded, if one chooses, as a quest for knowledge — not necessarily of a rational kind — and one frequently recognises in it Bradley's ideas in poetic costume. They are often indistinguishable from those of Royce and other Idealists, but, recognising the importance of Bradley to Eliot, we may let his name stand for them all where they are in general agreement.

In this quest for knowledge, the nature of Reality is a main objective. The phrase "Unreal City" in *The Waste Land* has far-echoing philosophical implications to a person who has studied Bradley's *Appearance and Reality*. And in *The Hollow Men* "the Shadow" falls, accompanied by similar echoes, "Between the idea / And the reality". The child of "Animula" is

---

[1] MUS p. 15.

offended and perplexed "With the imperatives of 'is and seems'", and learns to fear "the warm reality". *The Family Reunion* also works on the problem of Reality. But it is not till the *Four Quartets* that it becomes a major theme and is faced directly. The recurrent phrase "human kind cannot bear very much reality", a repetition of Becket's words in *Murder in the Cathedral*,[1] indicates the trend of the poet's speculations.

In Bradley's theory of knowledge, the senses play an important part. "To be real", he declares, "is to be indissolubly one thing with sentience".[2] This assertion, which is more or less a restatement of an old Aristotelian idea, seems to be the starting-point of Eliot's poetry as well. Like Webster and Donne of his "Whispers of Immortality", he finds "no substitute for sense, / To seize and clutch and penetrate". As we saw when dealing with his vision, it is awareness of individual phenomena, his direct perception by means of the various senses, from which he fashions images and ideas. Imagination is never far from experience. Sentience with Bradley, however, is not enough for reality, nor does Eliot feel anything to be real merely because he perceives it.

Actuality in Eliot's view is fragmentary and inconsistent. The world as it appears to the senses is divided, not united, by the qualities perceived in it. And imperfection is painfully apparent. Evil and error, on comparison with any ideal, immediately jump into prominence. All this means that actuality, i. e. the sensuous universe, has in Eliot's view precisely those properties which Bradley attributes to the unreal. The universe is just appearance.

The self as visualised in Eliot's early poetry is no more integrated than anything else. What is commonly regarded as a criterion of the self, the memory, dissolves on a close scrutiny. In Bradley's words: "Memory is plainly a construction from the ground of the present. It is throughout inferential, and is certainly fallible."[3] In Eliot's words:

> Dissolve the floors of memory
> And all its clear relations,
> Its divisions and precisions,
> — — — —
> And through the spaces of the dark
> Midnight shakes the memory
> As a madman shakes a dead geranium.[4]

The petals of the dead geranium are scattered far and wide, and the images bunched together in the memory cling no closer. It is of little avail for the young man in "Portrait of a Lady" to assure himself that he remains self-possessed. His mind is not his own. He recalls "things that other people have desired". And he is completely trapped by the question whether his ideas are right or wrong.

---

[1] MC p. 69.   [2] A&R p. 146.   [3] A&R p. 257.   [4] "Rhapsody".

˪ Prufrock feels concern about his age, and the idea of the ravages of time constantly crops up in Eliot's poetry from first to last. The stranger of "Little Gidding" discloses "the gifts reserved for age":

> First, the cold friction of expiring sense
> Without enchantment, offering no promise
> But bitter tastelessness of shadow fruit
> As body and soul begin to fall asunder.
> Second, the conscious impotence of rage
> At human folly, and the laceration
> Of laughter at what ceases to amuse.
> And last, the rending pain of re-enactment
> Of all that you have done, and been; —

Eliot's obsession with age can best be explained by his horror at the idea of the dissolution of the personality, so carefully hedged about by its owner. "What is this essence of the self which is never altered?" asks Bradley. "Infancy and old age, disease and madness, bring new features, while others are borne away."[1]

Age and change break continuity and identity. "You cannot face it steadily, but this thing is sure, / That time is no healer: the patient is no longer here."[2] The travellers voyaging over the sea of life do not remain the same:

> "Fare forward, you who think you are voyaging;
> You are not those who saw the harbour
> Receding, or those who will disembark".[3]

For Bradley, too, change — in time, space or circumstances — alters the identity and proves the unreality of whatever is subject to it, whether it be ideas, persons or objects.[4]

Bradley is led to deny the reality of the soul, and Eliot follows him until his conversion to Christianity. He depicts us as automatic creatures, whose "souls" are nothing — "I could see nothing behind that child's eye".[5] The symbol of this nothingness is the wind. In the first "Prelude" the wind rustles among "newspapers from vacant lots". In "Gerontion" we see

> — De Bailhache, Fresca, Mrs. Cammel, whirled
> Beyond the circuit of the shuddering Bear
> In fractured atoms. — —

And a gull fights vainly against the wind, to disappear completely: "White feathers in the snow." The dialogue of "A Game of Chess", which partly echoes a poem by Thomas Hardy, is very illuminating:

---

[1] A&R p. 80.   [2] DS III.   [3] DS III.   [4] Cf. A&R p. 45 and *Princ. of Logic*, p. 143.   [5] "Rhapsody".

"What is that noise?"
                    The wind under the door.
"What is that noise now? What is the wind doing?"
                    Nothing again nothing.
                                        "Do
"You know nothing? Do you see nothing? Do you remember
"Nothing?"
    I remember
Those are pearls that were his eyes.
"Are you alive, or not? Is there nothing in your head?"

In "Marina", the various categories of the vain and wicked "are
become unsubstantial, reduced by a wind". And the wind retains the same
significance in the *Four Quartets,* where it sweeps the gloomy hills of a
London which knows only

> Tumid apathy with no concentration
> Men and bits of paper, whirled by the cold wind
> That blows before and after time.[1]

In the *Four Quartets* the wind is not the only effective power in human
lives. In the early poems, however, especially "Gerontion", scepticism is
complete, as complete as it is in Bradley's enquiries in the first part of
his main work, that which is entitled merely "Appearance".

But Eliot followed Bradley beyond this stage, even while he himself
was still in his first phase of scepticism. In his very vision, as we have
seen, there was an awareness of connectedness and wholeness co-existing
with the prevalent awareness of dissolution. The fact that Eliot's objects
and fragments are so often broken, in itself points to an ideal, complete
existence in which they are whole, or, in Bradley's terms, to a transcendence
of the parts in the individuality of total experience. In *The Hollow Men*
sunlight falls on a broken column as if to continue it in a world beyond,
just as the dry pool of "Burnt Norton" is "filled with water out of sunlight". Things only *appear* to be incomplete and imperfect because we have
usually no awareness of totality.

As early as in the *Prufrock* poems Eliot reaches out for an experience
of totality. Distinctions between objects are suppressed. They are made
to represent wholes of feeling:

> The winter evening settles down
> With smell of steaks in passageways.
> Six o'clock.
> The burnt-out ends of smoky days.[2]

It is characteristic that metaphors, in which disparate elements are
seen as identical, are much more common in Eliot's poetry than similes.

---

[1] BN III.   [2] "Prelude" I.

He excels in metaphors of a daring and delightfully surprising kind, such as "all the works and days of hands / That lift and drop a question on your plate", "His laughter tinkled among the tea-cups", "the last fingers of leaf / Clutch and sink", "footfalls echo in the memory", "the future is a faded song".

We have already dealt with these and similar devices (p. 102), and decided that they can only give the illusion of unity, not the real sense of it. Possibly many readers of Eliot are of another opinion, and we must admit that our conclusion is not obvious or easy. The poet often imparts to us a sense of wholeness which almost convinces us that he must have really felt this wholeness in things. But there is a feeling of unfulfilment besides, which perhaps may be accounted for on reflection: the wholeness is not a wholeness perceived in outer things and received as an impression. There is no essential unity between these things, for instance between a suburban evening and the smell of steaks in passageways, but only one of habitual togetherness. The unity which we feel is one of mood, which the actual perceptions only serve to express. There are unifying moods, but no unifying ideas to support them. In the *Quartets* it is different. The smell of wild thyme and the sight of winter lightning have no spatial or temporal connection, but an ideal unity nevertheless. And in the beginning of "East Coker" the objects mentioned have no unity of mood, but an essential oneness of substance and significance:

> Old stone to new building, old timber to new fires,
> Old fires to ashes, and ashes to the earth
> Which is already flesh, fur, faeces,
> Bone of man and beast, cornstalk and leaf.

The "deep lane" does not exist in its own right, but "insists on the direction / Into the village", and "the sultry light / Is absorbed, not refracted, by grey stone", making itself one with it.

I do not mean that poetry must necessarily render the kind of impression of unity that we find in the *Four Quartets*, or even that it is better poetry if it does. There is wonderful poetry which relies on a merely picturesque harmony, or in which the unity is only that of the poet's mood. I simply contend that we must not mistake mood for philosophy, so as to miss the vision of disconnectedness which may be at the bottom of a uniform mood of despondency.

If there had been a real unity of perception in the *Prufrock* poems, this would have presupposed the unity of a central perceiving organ, i. e. the mind or soul. This was argued by Aristotle, and the argument still applies. But no such central perceiving organ is recognised in Eliot's early poetry, as we have seen. On the contrary, the self, or the soul, is considered to be no separate entity. This being the case, it is able to mingle with its environment. In "Hysteria", the man is "aware of becoming involved in" the woman's laughter "and being part of it". In "Morning at the Window" we have found a kind of interpenetration between the passer-by and the poet who observes her smile. And the fourth "Prelude" begins with the lines:

> His soul stretched tight across the skies
> That fade behind a city block,

What happens in these cases, however, is a dissolution of individualities rather than an integration of anything. It may suggest, but it is really different from, the merging of one's self in a monistic Absolute.

There is absolute integration, but there is also individual dissolution in the kind of unified perception that Bradley describes in *Appearance and Reality*:

If, seeking for reality, we go to experience, what we certainly do *not* find is a subject or an object, or indeed any other thing whatever, standing separate and on its own bottom. What we discover rather is a whole in which distinctions can be made, but in which divisions do not exist. — — — to be real — — is to be something which, except as an integral element of such sentience, has no meaning at all.[1]

The last remark here might be discussed. If "meaning" means something more than "existence", then objects and individuals only have meaning in so far as they are known as distinct one from another. If "meaning" signifies "existence", however, then it is true that it is undifferentiated: everything that we perceive simultaneously exists for us in "one whole of feeling". In Eliot's early poetry there is this kind of perception. Things exist in one whole of feeling, but they have no significance. Instead, meaning is lost in the general dissolution of individual differences; and that which might have justified this process, namely the ecstatic knowledge of pure existence, the sense of an absolute reality, is absent.

Bradley does not think that direct communication between one soul and another is possible.[2] We have seen that he regards human beings as isolated from each other as finite persons. But the self is not isolated from the objects it perceives, nor is it isolated from "the Absolute" of which it is a part. In this Absolute everything finite is transcended and completed. And by a kind of intuition, which is more than both thought and feeling, or perhaps a Hegelian synthesis of thought and feeling, the finite mind is able to gain a faint realisation of the totality.[3] This realisation is what Eliot aims at in a number of his later poems, particularly the *Four Quartets*. And in so far as he consciously strives to catch a glimpse of the Absolute, he is modelling his efforts on those of Bradley:

---

[1] A&R p. 146.   [2] Cf. A&R p. 343.   [3] Cf. A&R p. 172; also pp. 159—160.

> Old men ought to be explorers
> Here and there does not matter
> We must be still and still moving
> Into another intensity
> For a further union, a deeper communion [1]

Every part of Bradley's Absolute contains within itself the whole, and to grasp a part means to grasp the whole. It is only a slight exaggeration to say that, to Eliot, to grasp a word is to grasp the entire language to which it belongs, and the entire past of that language. In his criticism as in his poetry, he sees the sum of tradition and history as being actual in the present: "History is now and England".[2]

Generally, however, we grasp nothing completely, which is why some things seem bad to us. For not only truth and goodness are contained in the Absolute, but error and evil as well. Bradley, like Meinong, recognises falsehood and fiction as equally real with "fact". The important thing is that they exist in experience, an experience which is not purely rational. But such things as error, evil and pain are altered when they are transcended,[3] i. e. when they are made to fit into the pattern of the whole; and Bradley is convinced that there will ultimately be a balance of goodness, beauty and pleasure. It is some such idea as this that is at the bottom of Eliot's assurance that "Sin is Behovely",[4] and that

> — all shall be well and
> All manner of thing shall be well
> When the tongues of flame are in-folded
> Into the crowned knot of fire
> And the fire and the rose are one.[5]

It matters little to our contention that Bradley's main reason for believing in these things seems to be an urgent desire that they should be so.

With regard to morality, Bradley thinks that "the moral man is the man who tries to do the best which he knows". "That man is to be judged by his inner will", he says, "seems in the end undeniable".[6] "To make perfect the will" is Eliot's supreme moral commandment in all his completed plays, as well as in the *Four Quartets*. The correspondence with Bradley's ideas is reinforced by the fact that both men reject the notion of an "inner Morality", as Bradley has it, or an "inner light", as Eliot puts it.

We come now to an important point: Bradley's views on religion. "Like morality", he says, "religion is not ultimate. It is a mere appearance, and is therefore inconsistent with itself". "Religion", he goes on, "naturally implies a relation between Man and God. Now a relation always — — is

---

[1] EC V.   [2] LG V.   [3] Cf. A&R pp. 192, 199, 440.   [4] LG III. Cp. MC p. 68: "These things had to come to you and you to accept them."   [5] LG V.   [6] A&R pp. 159, 247.

self-contradictory". Man, on the one hand, is a finite subject, yet, on the other hand, apart from God, he is merely an abstraction. "And religion perceives this truth, and it affirms that man is good and real only through grace, or that again, attempting to be independent, he perishes through wrath." "God again is a finite object. But sundered from relations God is emptiness." God, therefore, "finds his reality and self-consciousness in union with man". Religion consists in a practical oscillation between the monistic and dualistic views. But "short of the Absolute, God cannot rest, and, having reached that goal, he is lost and religion with him".[1]

Eliot, in his adherence to Christian theology, is bound to repudiate such views, though, being a Catholic, he has approached them as closely as orthodoxy allows. Far from him the fixing of such gulfs between God and man as are indicated in the theology of Karl Barth.

In his poetry the Bradleyan idea of the Absolute asserts itself in many places. Thus the fulfilment envisaged from time to time in the *Four Quartets* is thought of as a completion of the incompleteness which is now, as a filling of the concrete pool "with water out of sunlight", as a reconciliation among the stars. This means an eschatology based on the belief that this world is to be transfigured, not destroyed or left behind, that the earthly paradise is to be rediscovered:

> — the end of all our exploring
> Will be to arrive where we started
> And know the place for the first time.
> Through the unknown, remembered gate
> When· the last of earth left to discover
> Is that which was the beginning;[2]

> — — — See, now they vanish,
> The faces and the places, with the self which, as it could, loved them,
> To become renewed, transfigured, in another pattern.[3]

The very word "pattern", which recurs so frequently in Eliot's later poetry, is reminiscent of Bradley, who thought that the broken pattern of the life which we perceive is completed in the Reality which transcends it. And so we find

> — — — both a new world
> And the old made explicit, understood
> In the completion of its partial ecstasy,
> The resolution of its partial horror.[4]

A statement of Eliot's which has previously been quoted may now be regarded in a new light. "Poetry", he said in effect, "points to a reality that includes the aesthetic, the ethical and the religious. The religious way

---

[1] A&R pp. 444—7.   [2] LG V.   [3] LG III.   [4] BN II.

and the poetic way lead to the same thing, which is wider than both.] But religion itself takes no account of the aesthetic". This pronouncement may seem puzzling unless connected with Bradley's philosophy. According to Bradley, of course, both religion and art are equally transcended and swallowed up in the Absolute. I do not know whether Eliot's statement on this occasion was well considered, but it appears to substantiate the general impression derived from the reading of his poetry: that the consummation which he aims at is a state of existence in which everything, faith, love, reason, action, contemplation, beauty, is of equally great (or equally small) value.

Eliot criticised Bradley's conception of the Absolute in an early philosophical essay[1] in which his religious scepticism is apparent. Yet it can hardly be denied that Bradley's ideas continued to hold sway in his poetic world. And if they were not altogether acceptable to him when he became a Christian poet, there was always Royce's variety of Idealism to fall back upon, so that the belief in God and in the individual soul might be preserved. It should be pointed out, perhaps, that his recognition of the behoveliness of sin and evil owes still more to Royce (who regarded these things as being willed by God, in order that greater good might ensue) than to Bradley.

The fact that Bradley's philosophy has been so important to Eliot means that his poetry is indirectly, but profoundly, influenced by Hegel's philosophy as well. One might almost say that Eliot uses Bradley (and Hegel) in the same way that, according to him, Lucretius used Epicurus or Dante used St. Thomas: as a groundwork on which to construct the edifices of his poems. It is remarkable that the main line of development of Eliot's poetry follows the main trend of Bradley's philosophy: the early poems roughly correspond to the demonstration of everything as appearance, and the later poems correspond to the phase, or aspect, of reality.

It would be foolish to suggest that Eliot tries to illustrate Bradley's philosophy. Nor is this philosophy the only groundwork of his poetry; it is not even the main influence in his recent work. There are many other things besides. Thus the correspondence to the two phases of appearance and reality has a parallel in the correspondence to Dante's *Inferno* (if evil is only appearance) and *Paradiso*. Christianity, Oriental mysticism and modern scientific thought have all powerfully contributed to the meaning of the poems. Kant is nowhere far to seek in them. And one is often reminded of Spinoza's "amor intellectualis Dei". But for many of these influences it is likely that Bradley paved the way. To take only one example: there is a clear basis for religious mysticism in the idea that the object of thought is inherent in the thinking of it.[2]

---

[1] "Devel. of L's Monadism", *Monist*, Oct. 1916.   [2] Cp. A&R p. 146.

The philosopher who, after Bradley and to a great extent in conjunction with Bradley, seems to have affected Eliot's poetry most deeply, is Aristotle. Thus the ideas of everything striving towards perfection ("Everything tends towards reconciliation"[1]) and of everything being essentially good or necessary, are Aristotelian as well as Bradleyan. The same applies to the importance attributed to sentience, and to the idea that what is sensed is actually *in* the sensation. There is even a tentative monism in Aristotle's suggestion that "the soul is in a way all existing things",[2] but he leaves this suggestion hanging in the air.

Aristotle's conception of form is particularly interesting. In the terms of his philosophy, the form of an object is its actuality, or entelechy. It is tempting to relate Eliot's idea of pattern to this conception of form. As form is the principle both of individuation, of realisation and of fulfilment in the one case, so pattern is the principle of fulfilment in the other: "Only by the form, the pattern, / Can words or music reach / The stillness".[3] Eliot speaks constantly of pattern, not only of the pattern of words, or pattern in art, but pattern in history, pattern in the life of individuals, etc. And it seems clear that what he partly means by this word is potentiality, and vocation: a latent purpose in the lives of communities and individuals, as well as in the existence of objects, which demands to be fulfilled, i. e. to become real.

The form of an animate object Aristotle calls its soul. As such the soul is an ordering principle of the matter of which the body is constituted. The soul of a human being is manifested in his activities, which in turn can give form to inanimate matter, stamping it with an idea. Our poet takes a similar view:

> Out of the formless stone, when the artist united himself with stone,
> Spring always new forms of life, from the soul of man that is joined
>   to the soul of stone;

— — —

> Out of the slimy mud of words, out of the sleet and hail of verbal
>   imprecisions,
> Approximate thoughts and feelings, words that have taken the place
>   of thoughts and feelings,
> There spring the perfect order of speech, and the beauty of
>   incantation.[4]

The powers which characterise the human soul are those of self-nutrition, sensation, thinking and motivity. Sensation again comprises sight, hearing, smell, taste and touch, and it is only by means of these five senses, says Aristotle, that the outer world, and also, of course, other persons, can be apprehended by us. If we bear this in mind, an added force will be given to such lines as these in "Gerontion":

---

[1] FR p. 104. Cp. MC p. 70.   [2] *De Anima* III, 8.   [3] BN V.   [4] *Rock, Chorus IX.*

> I have lost my sight, smell, hearing, taste and touch:
> How should I use them for your closer contact?

This is an emphatic way of saying that Gerontion has lost all possibilities of contact with anything or anybody outside his own mind.

The mind in Aristotle's philosophy is the power of thinking, and only man is endowed with it. Thus there is a distinction between soul and mind, as between the more and the less comprehensive, a distinction which may or may not be alluded to in Eliot's use of the terms soul and mind in "La Figlia Che Piange". The mind, unlike the sense-perceptions, can be in error; it is also conceivable apart from the body which it inhabits. The body without the soul, on the other hand, would be nothing but brute matter. And so Eliot strives, in all his poetry, to feed thought (mind) from the senses, and to experience reality with the fullness of the soul.

The mind, says Aristotle, is one, and yet it is able to discriminate: consequently it must be both divisible and indivisible. He explains this somewhat darkly by imagining it as a point "which twice over uses the same dot at one and the same time".[1] Now "the point" is an image particularly favoured by Eliot. He uses it frequently to suggest that which is both still and moving, and it is likely that some of the mysterious meaning that he tries to put into it derives from Aristotle's conception of the mind.

I think we may safely assert that the feature of Greek philosophy which has had the most telling and enduring influence on Eliot's thought is its concern with the typically human rather than with individual differences.[2] The mind to Aristotle was a type-mind, not a personality. Heraclitus emphasised the common reason, and frowned on peculiar insights.[3] In "Tradition and the Individual Talent", in which he denies the individual personality, Eliot has an epigraph, which is a quotation from Aristotle, meaning: "mind is, no doubt, something more divine and impassible", scilicet, than the personality. The poet believed in "the metaphysical theory of the substantial unity of the soul",[4] but not in individuality. Or perhaps we should say that he *tried* to believe in the substantial unity of the soul, in the sense of a spiritual life common to all. The lack of spiritual individuality that we have noticed in his poetry may also be a reflection of this belief:

> His soul stretched tight across the skies
> That fade behind a city block,
> Or trampled by insistent feet
> At four and five and six o'clock;[5]

No individual has a soul to call his own, though there is a kind of integration in an over-soul, or collective consciousness. The part played

---

[1] *De Anima*, III, 2.   [2] Cp. "Devel. of L's Monadism", *Monist*, Oct. 1916, p. 544.
[3] Cp. epigraph to 4Q.   [4] TIT, SE p. 19.   [5] "Prelude" IV.

by Tiresias, the man who is everybody, in *The Waste Land* suggests such
a view of the soul. This view, of course, need not be ascribed to Greek
philosophy. It may have been nourished by modern Idealists, as well as
by psychology and ethnology. But the substratum of Greek thought must
not be underestimated.

Eliot's adherence to Bradley and Aristotle makes it fair to assume that
at first he believed in a kind of collective consciousness, but without believing in individuality. His poetry, however, seems to show that he suffered
acutely by reason of his disbelief in the spiritual oneness of the individual.
At one time he probably disbelieved both in the substantial unity of the
soul and in its individual unity, and then he was in the most abysmal
depths of his metaphysical depair — till he found that in Christianity, and
perhaps only in Christianity, belief in the supreme worth of the particular
soul could be reconciled with belief in a supreme super-human spirit. Royce
and many others might have told him this before, but he had to find out
for himself, and perhaps he had to find his own soul through suffering.

An all-mind which is both one and all things, which is also both a
unity and a trinity, is the conception of the Absolute which answers best
to Christian dogma. It also has many points of contact with Aristotle's
first mover, a divine mind, or νοῦς, which ceaselessly thinks itself, and
which causes all activity by the love which it inspires:[1]

> Love is itself unmoving,
> Only the cause and end of movement[2]

This is straight from Aristotle, and similar passages occur elsewhere
in Eliot, for instance:

> Here the past and future
> Are conquered, and reconciled,
> Where action were otherwise movement
> Of that which is only moved
> And has in it no source of movement —
> Driven by dæmonic, chthonic
> Powers.[3]

Eliot thinks we must accustom ourselves to "find meaning in *final
causes* rather than in origins. — — The final cause is the attraction towards
God".[4] He applies this particularly to our notions of sex, and it is obvious,
as we have already touched upon, that much of the sexual imagery of his
poetry is meant to convey the idea of "the attraction towards God" as the
mover of all things, the end of all activity. This end cannot ever be actually
attained, according to Aristotle, but here Eliot parts company with the

---

[1] *Metaphysica*, XII, 7, 9.   [2] BN V.   [3] DS V.   [4] "Dante", SE p. 274.

Greek sage. The latter's philosophy is on the whole optimistic, but Eliot, despite his general pessimism, has become more optimistic than Aristotle in his view of the end of man.

Mind and soul, to Aristotle, are activity, and nothing in themselves. They are the turning of potentiality into actuality (a doctrine, by the way, which helps to set Eliot's lines in *The Hollow Men* in their true perspective: "Between the potency / And the existence / — — Falls the Shadow."). To Aristotle, as Eliot says,[1] the soul is to the body as cutting is to the axe, it is only operation. Thus soul is present in the simplest sensation as well as in rational speculation. From this point of view suffering might also be regarded as action, since it involves sensation. It is a manifestation of soul and of divine purpose:

> — — — action is suffering
> And suffering action. Neither does the agent suffer
> Nor the patient act. But both are fixed
> In an eternal action, an eternal patience
> To which all must consent that it may be willed
> And which all must suffer that they may will it,
> That the pattern may subsist, for the pattern is the action
> And the suffering, that the wheel may turn and still
> Be forever still.[2]

This identification of action and suffering and the view of both as the movement of consent to an eternal purpose make a central theme in *Murder in the Cathedral*. It owes most, no doubt, to Christian and Eastern mystics, but it would not have been what it is in Eliot's poetry without Aristotle's contribution.

Since reality, to Aristotle, is in activity, we may infer that reality is new in every moment. This again means that what matters most is the "here and now".[3] The latter idea is important to Eliot. It probably helped to direct his poetic vision. And it is present in much of his thought. He emphasises it in *Murder in the Cathedral:*

> Every day is the day we should fear from or hope from.
>   One moment
> Weighs like another. Only in retrospection, selection,
> We say, that was the day. The critical moment
> That is always now, and here. Even now, in sordid
>   particulars
> The eternal design may appear.[4]

Eliot is here also dealing with the time concept in the light of modern, scientifically determined thought. It is a long step from Aristotle to Ein-

---

[1] *Monist*, Oct. 1916, p. 554.   [2] MC pp. 21, 40.   [3] *Monist*, Oct. 1916, p. 554.
[4] MC p. 57; cf. also p. 62.

stein, but Eliot nevertheless takes it. I do not know how thoroughly he has studied any particular modern philosophy, but one recognises in his poetry a number of the modern ideas, especially relating to time, which most people have met in a popularised form.

In his early poetry, he had a tendency to express time as something concrete ("the smoky candle-end of time", "devoured the afternoon", "fragments of the afternoon", "time's ruins", etc.). No doubt concrete imagery was here a poetic aim in itself, and there may have been no further significance in the phrases than there is when we speak of "a wet after-noon" or "a sunny day", which are such common expressions that we do not think of them as metaphors. But from a very youthful age it seems that Eliot was intrigued by philosophical speculations about time. In a poem which originally appeared as "A Lyric" in the *Smith Academy Record* for April 1905 (Eliot was then sixteen and a half), and was reprinted with slight alterations as "Song" in the *Harvard Advocate* for 3 June 1907, the young poet disagrees with the sages:

> If space and time, as sages say,
>   Are things that cannot be,
> The fly that lives a single day
>   Has lived as long as we.
> But let us live while yet we may,
>   While love and life are free,
> For time is time and runs away,
>   Though sages disagree.

At the other end of a long career, we find the following lines in "Little Gidding":

> The moment of the rose and the moment of the yew-tree
> Are of equal duration. A people without history
> Is not redeemed from time, for history is a pattern
> Of timeless moments.

It seems that "the sages" have conquered.

From first to last the sense of time is almost obtrusive in Eliot's poetry. Even in his young days he was constantly preoccupied with the passing of years, the withering of flowers, the coming of age. Looking back into the past, there was the interminable sequence of history, looking into the future, there was a measureless void. But for many years the time concept seemed to engage mainly his feelings:

> History has many cunning passages, contrived corridors
> And issues, deceives with whispering ambitions,
> Guides us by vanities.[1]

---

[1] "Gerontion".

It is not till *The Waste Land* that time definitely becomes two things, or rather that a distinction is made between the commonsensical notion of a "time of chronometers"[1] and the mystical intuition of a "time not our time". The two conceptions are symbolised by the fortune-teller Madame Sosostris and the "hyacinth girl" respectively, figures whom we do not meet for the last time. One looks into the past and future, the other represents a vision of "the heart of light, the silence". Perhaps we should make a further distinction between the "time of chronometers" and the view of time as an inconsequent flux in which forwards and backwards are one movement. In that case we get three different conceptions of time (they might be called history, eternity and timelessness).

The Waste Land depends on these different conceptions in its whole lay-out. Golgotha and the voice of the Thunder are brought into the present, and we already see the rain which may fall in the future, and which therefore falls and does not fall. ("What might have been" is also included, and the whole poem may be elucidated by the first lines of the later "Burnt Norton".) The past and the future are merged in different ways, and by means of different symbols. April, we hear, "is the cruellest month — — mixing memory and desire". And under a rock, red with the noonday sun of the "present moment of pointed light",[2] there is timeless shadow where you may be shown

> — — — something different from either
> Your shadow at morning striding behind you
> Or your shadow at evening rising to meet you;

The shadow at morning is the past, and the shadow at evening the future — excellent visual images both. The "reminiscent bells" of Part V, tolling upside down, toll for the future as well as for the past. Time is all one ("HURRY UP PLEASE ITS TIME") — a continual flux as of humanity over a bridge, to be engulfed in a stone wilderness with a dead sound on the stroke of nine; or a "perpetual revolution"[3] as in "Death by Water", to be remembered by those "who turn the wheel". "What shall I do now?" asks the lady of the toilet, "What shall we do tomorrow? What shall we ever do?" The seasons follow each other "year to year". Only now and again, as under the red rock, is there a moment of pause:

> At the violet hour, when the eyes and back
> Turn upward from the desk, when the human engine waits
> Like a taxi throbbing waiting,

History, which was prominent in "Gerontion", now only becomes part of the great Heraclitean flux. It is referred to in one place, with an ex-

---

[1] DS I.   [2] FR p. 103.   [3] *Rock*, Chorus I.

pression that reminds one of similar phrases in the *Prufrock* and 1920 *Poems,* as "withered stumps of time".

We will leave aside, for the moment, the mystical implications of these conceptions of time, and glance at them in their connection with the modern scientific and philosophical outlook. This outlook has crystallised in certain general ideas, which may not be altogether palatable to the experts, but which seem to be pretty widely accepted outside their circles. In the formation of these ideas Bergson has played an important role; and though Eliot partly objected to Bergson's teaching, the very interest that he took in it made it part of his mental furniture.

Space and time, the sages are supposed to say, are dimensions in a common continuum. Time is not like a carpet that is being woven, or a carpet that is being unrolled. It is rather like a huge carpet that is for ever spread out, and what we see of it depends on where we stand and which way we are facing. "All time is eternally present".[1] This may mean that everything that has happened is eternally happening (and what only might have been is for ever impossible), while "the things that are going to happen / Have already happened"[2]. Or, to put it in another way, "History is now and England". But it need not mean this, which, in so far as it involves the future, comes very near determinism. Time may be present in the future without actions and events being predetermined, because time, as such, is not dependent on actions or events, or they on it. Neither in our memory of the past nor in our expectations of the future are events linked to measured or measurable time.

Eliot seems to accept the conception of time as eternally present. But this, because it excludes "what might have been" and fixes what actually was, the wrong things with the right, would appear to make time "unredeemable". It is true that Harry, in *The Family Reunion,* says that "what did not happen is as true as what did happen"[3] (an idea possibly inspired by Meinong), but this seems to be a flight of fancy away from the main path of speculation that the poet pursues. Time, then, considered merely as time, whether it be a sequence (as Bradley would say) or a development ("the latter a partial fallacy / Encouraged by superficial notions of evolution"[4]) or a fourth dimension, is unredeemable. But there is also such a thing as timelessness, and in timelessness the poet finds hope.

Much of what we think, remember and feel seems to us to occupy no time. And, philosophically, it is possible to make a good case for the total independence of time of psychic events, and possibly of other events. Just as figures, images, etc., can exist theoretically and to all practical purposes in only two spatial dimensions, and a point in one, so the fourth dimension of time may also be eliminated. "There are hours", says Agatha, "when

---

    [1] BN I.   [2] FR p. 74.   [3] FR p. 108.   [4] DS II.

there seems to be no past or future, / Only a present moment of pointed light".[1] But "East Coker" takes us a step further:

> — — — Not the intense moment
> Isolated, with no before and after,
> But a lifetime burning in every moment
> And not the lifetime of one man only
> But of old stones that cannot be deciphered.

If History is a pattern of such timeless moments, we are no longer imprisoned in time.

The individual can be liberated by heightening his consciousness of timelessness. In the ordinary enchainment of the years, the future, like the past, has no destination. In "The Dry Salvages" the poet gives us the image of fishermen "forever bailing, / Setting out and hauling, while the North East lowers" — they sail out and return in ceaseless repetition. And the first section of "East Coker" conjures up the eternal cycle of fertility and destruction in nature. But because there is such a cycle, we may be brought round again, as Harry is brought round, and as the protagonist in *Ash-Wednesday* is brought round, to previous states and conditions, so that a kind of "loop in time" is formed, in which those who have sufficient awareness are given a new opportunity. The explanation seems to be roughly this: the time, if time it may be called, of memory, of history, of the subconscious, lets nothing vanish that once has been, and it contains the materials that go to the making of the future. The present and the future, in other words, are determined by the past. And because our consciousness of the past is modified by subsequent events ("every moment is a new and shocking / Valuation of all we have been"[2]), the future also, in a sense, determines the past. Thus we cannot in the ordinary course of things rid ourselves of anything that is, has been or will be; we cannot leave anything behind. But in *The Family Reunion* the poet shows how, by going back to face the past, or rather by recognising the past in the present, the imprisoning cycle of time may yet be broken. We are really required to be conscious of ourselves, of our own minds and complexes and the influences which have worked upon them to make them what they are. We cannot fully succeed in this life, for "to be conscious is not to be in time",[3] but we can achieve a measure of success. And if we thus manage to heighten our awareness, we contrive to live, as Harry does, on several planes at once. As Bergson thinks we can take cognisance of *durée* by an act of intuition, and Bradley thinks that the "finite centre", which is our perceiving self, is outside of time,[4] so Eliot would lead us to perception of timelessness through contemplation and awareness. There is the gratuitous moment of illumination, too, but that has rather a religious than a philosophical significance.

---

[1] FR p. 102.   [2] EC II.   [3] BN II.   [4] Cp. "L's M. & B's Fin. Cen.", *Monist*, 1916, p. 574.

Freud and Frazer.

Not being either a physicist or a philosopher, I dare no more than indicate Eliot's debt to modern scientifically-inspired conceptions of time. In the same way I can only briefly indicate his debt to the philosophical sciences of psycho-analysis and anthropology.

Without the work of Freud it may be reasonably doubted whether modern poetry would have been what it is, either in technique or inspiration. The work of William James, especially his theory of associations, probably meant a great deal to Eliot and others before Freud became famous. But even in Eliot and his contemporaries the method of associations in poetry, the recognition of the subconscious and of the importance of dreams, all derive to a great extent from psycho-analysis. No doubt the facts which Freud studied existed long before his time and were vaguely known to thinkers and artists from the beginnings of civilisation. Poets employed dreams and symbols before they were systematically examined, and in recent times the Symbolist school of poetry may even have provided Freud with useful suggestions. But not till the reports of clinical studies of the psyche became known did literature receive a real impetus to avail itself of knowledge and theories of the subconscious. Freud may be dated now, but his influence is still marked in poetry and fiction.

It would be easy to exaggerate Eliot's debt to the Freudian ideas of association. The broken sequence, for instance of *The Waste Land*, is due to conscious construction and more or less accidental juxtaposition as much as to "free association". But I do not dispute the fact that the latter plays a large part in most of Eliot's poetry. What is more important, however, is the general use of symbols, and the prominence of sexual themes in many poems. The symbols are sometimes ancient ones, which anthropology knows as well as psycho-analysis, such as the lance and the grail, the hair, the sea and the rain, the fish and the fire. Sometimes they are such as modern *Traumdeutung* would give a new or added significance, for instance the eye (the father-complex), drowning (alternatively the herd-instinct or coition) etc. In addition, of course, there are the private symbols, like the wild thyme and the thrush, often of a more intellectual character than the "standard" ones.

The sexual urge can be traced in many stages of sublimation: "the transition from Beatrice living to Beatrice dead, rising to the Cult of the Virgin",[1] to use Eliot's own words about Dante. We rise from the rose of the *Rubáiyát* to the rose of the *Paradiso*. The little girl of "Dans le Restaurant" rings the changes through "la Figlia", Marie and the hyacinth girl of *The Waste Land*, and Marina to the Lady of *Ash-Wednesday* and *Four Quartets*. We have seen that Eliot himself is more or less aware of this development and of its Freudian significance.

---

[1] "Dante", SE p. 275.

It seems obvious that psycho-analysis gave him the material for much of his character-drawing, such as it is. It helped him to "look into the cerebral cortex, the nervous system, and the digestive tracts".[1] We need only think of the inhibited Prufrock, the neurotics of "Gerontion", *The Waste Land* and "Sweeney Agonistes", and above all, perhaps, of the figures of *The Family Reunion*. Harry complains that "Of the past you can only see what is past, / Not what is always present. That is what matters".[2] "What is always present" may be taken to mean the subconscious impressions of past events. Mr. C. L. Barber sees the Eumenides as "the *voyeurs* in the typical nightmare of nakedness", and finds the same exhibitionistic motive in the beginning of "Burnt Norton".[3] Harry at any rate suffers from a guilt-complex[4] which we can trace from one of Eliot's earliest poems in the *Harvard Advocate*, "Nocturne", in which the hero smiles to see the effect of his mistress's blood on the moonlit ground. The story of the play is a complicated mixture of psycho-analytical patterns, including incest-urge, with, of course, many things besides that cannot be covered by such formulae. In the early poetry, the death-wish, or the disguised wish to return to the womb, is clearly apparent. In the later poetry it is sublimated as religious self-annihilation.

The influence of anthropology makes itself felt particularly in *The Waste Land*. Says Stephen Spender:

Instead of a basis of accepted belief, the whole structure of Eliot's poem is based on certain primitive rituals and myths, which, he seems to feel, must be psychological certainties, being a part of what psychologists call our "race memory". He is appealing to scientific legend, where Yeats appeals to poetic legend. The authority behind *The Waste Land* is not the Catholic Church, nor romantic lore, but anthropology from the volumes of Sir James Frazer's *The Golden Bough*. Eliot has tried to indicate, beneath the very ephemeral and violent movements of our own civilization, the gradual and magical contours of man's earliest religious beliefs. The effect he sets out to achieve is illustrated by Freud's remark in *Civilization and its Discontents* that the growth of the individual mind resembles the growth of Rome, supposing that modern Rome, as it is to-day, were coexistent with the buildings of Rome at every period in her history; and that beneath the modern architecture was found the architecture of every earlier period, in a perfect state of preservation.[5]

I have quoted the whole of this paragraph because I think it is essentially right, though definitely exaggerated in the importance it assigns to anthropology. We need not hesitate to say that Eliot's awareness of the whole past of religion and culture is as distinct as his consciousness of the past of words. And this awareness informs not only *The Waste Land*,

---

[1] SE p. 290.   [2] FR p. 29.   [3] SELCR pp. 418, 440.   [4] Cp. Ibsen's *Rosmersholm*.   [5] From Spender: *The Destructive Element*, SELCR p. 273.

but practically his entire production. In one of the *Rock* Choruses (VII) he summarises the history of religion from its cradle among early savages. And even in the *Four Quartets* the connection is recognised between religion and the "primitive terror":

> — the past experience revived in the meaning
> Is not the experience of one life only
> But of many generations — not forgetting
> Something that is probably quite ineffable:
> The backward look behind the assurance
> Of recorded history, the backward half-look
> Over the shoulder, towards the primitive terror.[1]

Anthropological lore gives its meaning to the dance around and through the bonfire in the first section of "East Coker". And anthropology provides the background for the poetic vision of the river as "a strong brown god" in the beginning of "The Dry Salvages". The child whose growth the poet follows in "Animula" takes pleasure "In the fragrant brilliance of the Christmas tree"; and there is a correspondence between the pleasure of the child and the cult of fertility symbols in the childhood of the race; while the "running stags around a silver tray" remind one of the magic drawings of primitive hunters. "The wind, the sunlight and the sea" in the same poem are favourite symbols of Eliot's, and are also well known to anthropology (they are connected, of course, with the "elements" of air, fire and water, which, with the fourth element, earth, are also dear to the poet). Fire is one of the most frequent symbols in Eliot's poetry. It has been used extensively by religions and philosophies (Catholicism, Zoroastrianism, Heraclitus), and is one of the most ancient in the history of the human race.

Thus the whole history of religion is behind Eliot's Christianity. I think it is right to say, nevertheless, that anthropological learning only plays a subordinate part in his poetry, and that he uses it entirely as he thinks fit. In *The Waste Land* it certainly helped to fashion his general outlook, but in the rest of his poetry it has little influence on his ultimate views. His later poetry, in particular, is mainly determined by religious faith, and not by a special way of explaining such faith.

VI.

Faith.

Christian ideas are almost ubiquitous in Eliot's poetry, but the emphasis on various parts of dogma and different aspects of faith is very uneven.

We need not dwell upon the many satirical references to Christian doctrines in the 1920 *Poems,* or the apparently blasphemous comparison of Sweeney in his bath with Christ in the Jordan. But the early poems also

---

[1] DS II.

show the poet frequently puzzling over the problem of immortality, for instance in "The Love Song" and "Portrait of a Lady"; and they are pervaded, as I have pointed out before, by a sense of guilt and sinfulness, clearly voiced in "Gerontion".

The sense of sin, increasingly attached to the doctrine of Original Sin, remains strong throughout, though it is countered in the more recent poems by the trust in human effort and divine grace. In *The Waste Land* it is continually implied that sin and guilt are shared by everybody. And this is stated directly in *Sweeney Agonistes:*

> I knew a man once did a girl in
> Any man might do a girl in
> Any man has to, needs to, wants to
> Once in a lifetime, do a girl in.

In *The Hollow Men* there is "the Shadow" which falls

> Between the idea
> And the reality
> Between the motion
> And the act

In *Ash-Wednesday* we hear of those who "affirm before the world and deny between the rocks", "spitting from the mouth the withered appleseed". *The Family Reunion* is described by Agatha as a story "of sin and expiation", and Harry declares:

> I can clean my skin,
> Purify my life, void my mind,
> But always the filthiness, that lies a little deeper.

He feels that there must be "some origin of wretchedness".[1]   "East Coker" has a highly "metaphysical" image of the Church as a "dying nurse"

> Whose constant care is not to please
> But to remind of our, and Adam's curse,
> And that, to be restored, our sickness must grow worse.

And the Fall is again alluded to in "The Dry Salvages" — "The bitter apple and the bite in the apple".

The doctrine of Original Sin was at first welcomed, perhaps, chiefly because it lent a semi-mythical support to Eliot's opposition to the romantic-humanistic view of life. But this opposition was inspired in turn by a deep realisation of human imperfection, the causes of which we dealt with in connection with the poet's moods. We remember that Eliot was so de-

---

[1] FR pp. 104, 93, 100.

pressed by the spectacle of modern civilisation that he regarded the possibility
of damnation as in itself a relief. And in one way, if evil was regarded as
the common human lot, it was easier to bear: one might make the comforting
reflection that *I* am no worse than others, and none of us can help being
what we are. I am not saying that we find this reflection in Eliot's poetry,
but nor do we find the opposite thought, that *I* am the "chief of sinners".
The conviction of sin is objectified, and generally experienced in a sort of
communion of either wretchedness or hope. We are at least companions
in misfortune, even though we have no real contact with each other.

The weight of literary tradition was also behind the view of evil as sin,
not only because most European writers before our century were genuinely
or conventionally Christian, but equally perhaps because the doctrine of sin
had dramatic and picturesque associations which were valuable to poetry.
Eliot has benefited by these associations, which is another reason why the
doctrine is so constantly alluded to in his work. It is true that his satiric
purpose would run counter to the use of it. Satire cannot be effective if
it assumes that those who are satirised cannot be blamed for their faults.
This fact, and the poet's disbelief in Christianity at the beginning of his
career, help to explain why the doctrine of Original Sin is so often camouflaged in the poems before *Ash-Wednesday.*

It was natural that the poet, in his pre-Christian phase, should stress
the efficacy of human effort in the working-out of salvation, that is, if he
envisaged the possibility of salvation at all. More and more, however, the
striving for perfection came to be seen as an effort of expiation on the
one hand and towards a mystical penetration on the other.

The Waste Land, after leading us through all the rigour and nausea
of a modern wilderness, shows us in the last section that it has all been
part of a journey to a definite goal, the Chapel Perilous, where the Holy
Grail is to be found. In other words, by braving dangers, looking evil in
the face and toiling onwards, a regeneration may perhaps be attained. Life
must be an ascetic discipline, akin to the mystic disciplines of the East.
There is no question yet of grace. The "awful daring of a moment's surrender" must refer to a surrender to a deity without attributes, such as
Huxley worships in *The Perennial Philosophy.* But in "Journey of the Magi"
and "A Song for Simeon" we hear of the cost of seeking Christ: "A cold
coming we had of it" — "They shall praise thee and suffer in every generation." And the little poem "Usk" directs us to "the hermit's chapel, the
pilgrim's prayer".

In the third section of *Ash-Wednesday,* the protagonist labours up the
stairs of spiritual life, "Struggling with the devil of the stairs who wears /
The deceitful face of hope and despair". Ugliness, darkness and terror are
there to deter him. He is also tempted by a view of life as an enchanting
pastoral scene. But he goes on climbing. And in *The Family Reunion* a

way to salvation is pointed out "across a whole Thibet of broken stones / That lie, fang up, a lifetime's march".[1]

The effort and the action may consist in suffering.[2] Many Christian mystics, especially perhaps Meister Eckhart, have found a virtue in suffering. And the Church has always tried to find a place for suffering in the scheme of things, regarding it as meritorious if accepted in the right spirit. In Eliot's mind this idea finds a strong response because he was predisposed, as an artist, to regard suffering as a source of something valuable. In Eliot's historical play, Becket declares several times that "action is suffering / And suffering is action". In this case it is a question of martyrdom, and martyrdom, we are made to understand, is as necessary to the Church in our age as in the twelfth century. *The Rock* actually contains a call to martyrdom. But all cannot be martyrs. Obviously, then, suffering must be significant in lesser degrees or in other ways besides, though we are not told precisely how.

"Right action" may be an internal as well as an external affair, in fact it is chiefly a matter of making "perfect the will". There is something of Ibsen's Brand, though without his ruthlessness, in Thomas Becket forcing his will to perfection and completion in a single purpose. What Harry has to perform, what the *Quartets* hold up before us, is the same task of gathering our personality in a determination which leads so directly to action that it is indistinguishable from it. In this task lies a main obligation, and in the fulfilment of this task the efficacy of our effort. It demands renunciation. Becket has to resist the temptations of youth, popularity, temporal and spiritual power. In *Ash-Wednesday,* too, there is much to forego:

> — the lost heart stiffens and rejoices
> In the lost lilac and the lost sea voices
> And the weak spirit quickens to rebel
> For the bent golden-rod and the lost sea smell
> Quickens to recover
> The cry of quail and the whirling plover
> And the blind eye creates
> The empty forms between the ivory gates
> And smell renews the salt flavour of the sandy earth

Life may be an exile, but it has its compensations, and the consciousness of having to lose cherished, familiar things increases the doubt and incertitude. We stand "Wavering between the profit and the loss / In this brief transit where the dreams cross". But, says St. John of the Cross, "the soul cannot be possessed of the divine union, until it has divested itself of the love of created beings". Eliot used these words as an epigraph to *Sweeney Agonistes.*

---

[1] FR p. 103.   [2] Cp. p. 141.

If renunciation is to be complete, it must involve the self. Each individual self has to be annihilated if life is to be won. This is the eternal paradox of nature: *si le grain ne meurt* —. And it is the paradox at the heart of Christianity. Renunciation and askesis have always played an important part in Christianity, and they have obviously appealed strongly to Eliot. The note of renunciation is heard in practically all of his poems from "The Love Song" onwards. The more definite note of askesis is struck in "Whispers of Immortality" and continues down to "Little Gidding". It is partly that Eliot was attracted to what is difficult, partly that the corruption of mankind has made him see the need of a spiritual discipline, and partly that he has found askesis the best way of integrating the personality. These motives are clearly exemplified in his two complete dramas and his latest poems. But in his earlier poetry there is another motive as well that draws him to an annihilation of the personality: the fear of judgment, the fear of Reality, the very fear of losing his individuality. Prufrock is prompted by such a fear.[1] But it is best illustrated in a poem in which it has already been overcome: *Ash-Wednesday*. In the magnificent vision of the scattered bones, "Forgetting themselves and each other, united / In the quiet of the desert", we have an image of the human desire for escape and oblivion.

The alternative to escape is the way which Harry discovers: to "turn again" and face the ministers of vengeance, to accept renunciation and suffering as a penance. In the purpose of penance both action and suffering find their chief importance. This is the "lifetime's death in love" of "The Dry Salvages". Its symbol is usually that of voluntary isolation in a desert, which because of its association with the story of Christ in the wilderness, includes the idea of a gain in spiritual power as the result of renunciation and the victory over temptations. Eliot was also inspired by the lives of saintly men and women. Thus he was greatly struck by Bazin's biography of Charles de Foucauld, and wrote that "there is no higher glory of a Christian empire than that which was here brought into being by a death in the desert".[2] Like Charles de Foucauld, Harry chooses to go "to the worship in the desert, the thirst and deprivation".[3] His way is the way of solitude, of

> Internal darkness, deprivation
> And destitution of all property,
> Dessiccation of the world of sense,
> Evacuation of the world of fancy,
> Inoperancy of the world of spirit.[4]

---

[1] Prufrock's fear may quite well be interpreted as a fear of the decision that must have been the most momentous one in the poet's life: to surrender himself to God.
[2] "Towards a Chr. Britain", *Church Looks Ahead*, p. 117.   [3] FR p. 114.
[4] BN III.

His purpose is one of expiation. It is also clear that the ascent of the stairs in *Ash-Wednesday* is an effort of penance, ending with the cry, "Lord, I am not worthy". The whole of this poem, of course, is a poem of penitence, as is suggested, among other things, by its use of the liturgical colour of penitence, violet.

Harry chooses something that very much resembles a Purgatory on earth. We have mentioned the frequency of the Purgatory theme in Eliot's works. So constantly does he revert to it and so much significance does he attach to it that it may safely be called a central, if not *the* central, motif of his poetry. He sees man as hovering in a twilight between salvation and damnation. It is impossible for most people, because of their weakness, their nothingness, to cross "With direct eyes, to death's other Kingdom". So our only hope, if we are to avoid damnation, and if we realise that it is useless to dissemble, is in the purgation of that which weakens us:

> The only hope, or else despair
> Lies in the choice of pyre or pyre —
> To be redeemed from fire by fire.[1]

It is perhaps characteristic that Ibsen, a writer with a Protestant background, found the only hope for his Peer Gynt in a sort of poetic figuration of divine grace, whilst Eliot, a Catholic writer, is more disposed to think of a real purification of human nature.

It is mainly Dante's visions of Purgatory that have appealed to Eliot. There is one episode that he seems to have found particularly striking: that in which Arnaut Daniel asks that his pain may be remembered, and then dives back into the purifying fire:

> "Ara vos prec, per aquella valor
> que vos guida al som de l'escalina,
> sovegna vos a temps de ma dolor."
> POI S'ASCOSE NEL FOCO CHE GLI AFFINA.[2]

These few lines have given Eliot the title for one of his collections of poems (the 1920 *Poems* were first called *Ara Vos Prec*), and for one of the sections of *Ash-Wednesday* ("Al som de l'escalina"); they have provided a quotation at the end of *The Waste Land* ("Poi s'ascose nel foco che gli affina"); a quotation in *Ash-Wednesday* IV ("Sovegna vos"); a reference in "Little Gidding" ("that refining fire") and other references besides. What Eliot chiefly found striking in the episode, conceptually, was no doubt the voluntary acceptance of the "refining fire" by the spirits who were bent on attaining salvation.

The images and ideas of Purgatory are fairly constant throughout, mixed in the beginning with images of Hell and later with those of Paradise.

---

[1] LG IV.   [2] Cf. SE p. 256.

The epigraph of "The Love Song" has the hopelessness of the *Inferno,* and *The Waste Land* alludes to all those in Hell (or Limbo) whom Death has undone. The poems of the *Ash-Wednesday* phase are more exclusively associated with Purgatory. Purgatory is definitely suggested by the allusion to the three steps leading to Dante's Purgatorio, or the three stages of ascent through the Purgatorio. In the recent poems there are such allusions to the *Paradiso* as the "heart of light" (in "Burnt Norton") and the Rose of "Little Gidding". But there is no clear progression from one stage to another. The "heart of light" occurs in *The Waste Land,* and the images of Purgatory are as dominant in *The Family Reunion* and the *Quartets* as are those of Heaven. The vision of earth as an immense hospital, which occurs in both the latter works, is akin to that of Purgatory. And Harry is regarded as the consciousness of his unhappy family, "Its bird sent flying through the purgatorial flame".[1]

Heaven "which flesh cannot endure", is in the hereafter. Hell is felt to be both in this life and the next. We are also put in mind of a Purgatory after this life by the frequent allusions to Dante. But on the whole the poet tends to see Purgatory as a state of life on this earth, as in the image of the hospital. It is a self-imposed discipline in "death's dream kingdom". The explanation lies partly in the fact that the distinction between physical life and physical death means very little to Eliot — much less than the distinction between the different planes of life which may be visualised as Hell, Purgatory and Heaven. Life and death fight for the upper hand both in "this life" and "the next", in "death's dream kingdom" and in "death's other Kingdom". And partly the earthly Purgatory is explained by the need for poetic concentration: the state of Purgatory is identified with the life of askesis inaugurated by the saint or the penitent here on earth. Also it gives significance to the suffering which one cannot avoid seeing in life, and which often seems so unprovoked and meaningless. If it is accepted as purgatorial it may work towards our spiritual health.

We saw that Eliot thinks with the Catholic Church that human beings may strive effectively towards their salvation by their actions. But this belief is countered and complemented by another, which is almost Molinistic. For the poet also thinks that action is useless and that we must submit passively to the will of God, or rather make his will our will and our peace: *la sua voluntate é nostra pace.* Even the action that is required of the protagonist of *Ash-Wednesday,* of Becket and of Harry is very much like inaction. And in the *Quartets* the poet now tells us to "fare forward",[2] and now to "be still, and wait without hope".[3] In one of his striking phrases, he joins the two ideas indissolubly: "We must be still and still moving."[4] We are reminded of the two ways of liberation indicated by Agatha in *The Family Reunion:* the "present moment of pointed light" and

[1] FR p. 105.   [2] DS III.   [3] EC III.   [4] EC V.

the "lifetime's march" "across a whole Thibet of broken stones". And here we come nearer to a full understanding of the purpose of askesis and purgation. Their ultimate purpose is to consummate a union of the spirit with God. It is to achieve this end that St. John of the Cross preaches a divesting oneself of the love of created beings and destitution of property. It is for this purpose that he exhorts us to descend into the "dark night of the soul".

Eliot's debt to St. John and other Christian mystics is well known. Mr. Raymond Preston brings it out clearly in his commentary on the *Four Quartets*. In St. John of the Cross Eliot chiefly found support for the idea (derived first, I suppose, from Indian philosophy) of a way of contemplation by voiding the mind of everything save faith:

I said to my soul, be still, and wait without hope
For hope would be hope for the wrong thing; wait without love
For love would be love of the wrong thing; there is yet faith
But the faith and the love and the hope are all in the waiting.
Wait without thought, for you are not ready for thought:
So the darkness shall be the light, and the stillness the dancing.[1]

St. John provided Eliot with much of the imagery of darkness in the sense of evacuation of the mind and ignorance of God and his ways; with paradoxical statements such as "the way up is the way down",[2] to denote the humility that is necessary if the soul is to be exalted; and with the image of the stairs by which the soul ascends to God, and which are glimpsed in *Ash-Wednesday* (joined with reminiscences from Dante), in "A Song for Simeon" and in the *Quartets*. A metaphor very like St. John's metaphor of the "dark night" is "the cloud of unknowing", which is the title of a work by an anomymous English mystic of the fourteenth century, and is alluded to both in *The Family Reunion*[3] and "Little Gidding". And then there is Dame Julian of Norwich, who "was much troubled by the thought of the origin of sin in a world created by infinite Goodness" but heard a voice saying to her: "Sin is behovable, but all shall be well, and all shall be well, and all manner of things shall be well."[4] Eliot has used these words and this thought to excellent purpose in "Little Gidding".

The way of mysticism leads to divine union; or, to put it differently, it prepares the mystic for a divine revelation. One feels that Eliot is personally engaged in the mystic experiences which he describes. I am not satisfied that Mr. Preston is right in saying that the *Four Quartets* are merely the writings of a poet, and not of a mystic, and that "there is no claim to *share* the experience of the saint".[5] I asked Mr. Eliot if he was seeking a revelation in these poems. He replied that he was not seeking a revelation when writing them, but that he was "seeking the verbal equivalents for small

---

[1] EC III.   [2] Also suggested by Heraclitus.   [2] FR p. 110.   [4] Helen Gardner, F3 p. 76.   [5] 4QR p. 22.

experiences he had had, and for knowledge derived from reading". The "small experiences" he referred to were no doubt such as the moments of revelation mentioned in "Eeldrop and Appleplex",[1] the "rare moments of inattention and detachment" mentioned in the essay on Marston,[2] and the "kind of unexplainable experience which many of us have had, once or twice in our lives, and been unable to put into words", which Eliot spoke about in a broadcast talk on Charles Williams.[3] In this case poetry is not simply "une prière qui ne prie pas et qui fait prier", to use Brémond's words. It *is* prayer "qui prie", in the mystical sense, or at least the memory of such prayer, in so far as it can be rendered by means of words. And it shows, I think, not only "the distraction fit, lost in a shaft of sunlight",[4] but also a conscious straining to achieve a revelation. The words of E. M. Forster — "what he seeks is not revelation, but stability" — are no longer valid, if they ever were.

According to Christian doctrine, a divine revelation is an act of grace. Eliot recognises this — most of the time. The climbing of the stairs in *Ash-Wednesday* would not have brought the protagonist *"al som de l'esca-lina"* if he had not been invested with "strength beyond hope and despair". Grace, symbolised by the colour blue, is one of the leading themes of section IV of *Ash-Wednesday*. And in "The Dry Salvages" the poet sees our only hope in the "Prayer of the one Annunciation", the message of grace to humanity. It is because divine grace is necessary in the last resort that the soul must wait even without hope — so that no thought of our ability to earn salvation shall supervene.

In our dependence on revelation for our knowledge of the Absolute, we have come to a position opposed to that of Bradley. Bradley, like Hegel, found the idea of the Absolute by rational induction based on common sensuous experience. In "East Coker" Eliot rejects the inadequate ideas arrived at in this way:

> — — — There is, it seems to us,
> At best, only a limited value
> In the knowledge derived from experience.
> The knowledge imposes a pattern, and falsifies,
> For the pattern is new in every moment
> And every moment a new and shocking
> Valuation of all we have been. — —
>
> — — —
>
> The only wisdom we can hope to acquire
> Is the wisdom of humility: humility is endless.

Humility is the only state in which one is fit to receive a revelation. The emphasis that he lays on this Christian virtue may be a sign of his

---

[1] *Little Review*, May 1917, p. 8.   [2] SE p. 232.   [3] LIS, 19 Dec. 1946.
[4] DS V.

pride; but it also shows that his pride has been challenged and virtually overcome. With doubts and pride to block his way, his fight to accept a divine revelation has not been an easy one. In this fact we may find an earnest of his good faith: his moments of illumination are not, to his best knowledge, just an exploitation of his own immanent resources of spirit. They have nothing to do with Emerson's "inner light", but possibly represent actual intuitions of divine Reality.

It seems to me that there is something like a closing of accounts with Bradley and Absolute Idealism in the *Quartets*. The human reason, which "was believed in as the most reliable" has failed. For a while there had been "the failing / Pride or resentment at failing powers, / The unattached devotion which might pass for devotionless". But now things look different. Life is not just a sequence of appearances as for Bradley, nor just a development. It has another pattern, in which it is the moments of "sudden illumination" that count. Things no longer merely *happen* to one, but there is the hope that something may *come* to one from above. The second section of "The Dry Salvages", in which all these ideas are reflected among momentous images, is extremely interesting in its conflict of philosophies. One might pursue this train of thought further and discover a final reckoning with many of the ideas of ancient Greece as well. Instead of Aristotle's cyclic movement which never quite brings life to perfection, there is, in *The Family Reunion* and the *Quartets,* the idea of a stillness in which a sudden union with the divine may be effected. Instead of Lucretius's mechanistic regularity combined with blind accident, there is a far from accidental element of the wonderful, a "disturbance of the seasons" which indicates a higher law than that of mechanical atoms. But to develop this further would soon lead us on to thin ice. Let it suffice to say that Eliot has become more and more convinced of the supernatural character of Christian life.[1]

However, we must look more closely at the significance of the moments of illumination which he tries to suggest to us by means of so many paradoxes and images.

First, then, these moments reveal "the point of intersection of the timeless with time". They may occur at any time in the life of an individual, but historically and theologically the point of intersection is that of the Incarnation:

There came, at a predetermined moment, a moment in time and of time,
A moment not out of time, but in time, in what we call history: transecting,
   bisecting the world of time, a moment in time but not like a moment
   of time,
A moment in time but time was made through that moment [2]

---

[1] Cp. "Mod. Dilemma", *Chr. Register,* 19 Oct. 1933.   [2] *Rock,* Chorus VII.

It is this moment that shatters the lives of the Magi and brings to completion the life of Simeon. Becket speaks of the Incarnation in his Christmas Day sermon. In "The Dry Salvages" we hear of the Annunciation, and the poet states explicitly:

> The hint half guessed, the gift half understood, is Incarnation.
> Here the impossible union
> Of spheres of existence is actual,

Mr. H. R. Williamson regards Eliot's early scepticism concerning man as a necessary iconoclasm: he turned against the hero-worship and deification of man and embraced instead the belief in God become human, i. e. Incarnation. Mr. Williamson approves of the Catholic emphasis on the doctrine of the Incarnation, and thinks the Protestants stress the Atonement to a dangerous extent.[1] As far as Eliot is concerned, there is, of course, no exclusion of the Atonement either from his opinions or from his poetry. It has significance, for instance, in the Good Friday poem "East Coker". But it is true that the Incarnation seems to mean much more to him. This is partly, we may suppose, for the usual reason, that the doctrine of the Incarnation attaches a greater value to human nature and human life than does that of the Atonement. But it is also because the former doctrine lends itself much more easily than the latter to Eliot's speculations about the nature of Reality and of Time. His revelations, then, are associated with The Revelation; and his moments of illumination seem to give him, however remotely and vaguely, an integral experience of God.

Yet it is not God in his historical Incarnation that he sees. Eliot's supreme visions are different from those of Dante and from those of a number of medieval mystics to whom it seemed that Christ or the Virgin Mary appeared. St. Francis, it is said, had a vision of a six-winged seraph carrying a crucifix. In comparison with such experiences, Eliot's are indeterminate. This is not because Francis of Assisi was a saint and Eliot probably is not. Dante was no saint but a poet, yet his visions were definite enough. And there must have been many poets in the Middle Ages and later who were far from saintly and still described heavenly sights with the utmost confidence. The reason why Eliot experiences the Absolute as a timeless inexpressible something, while Dante saw a host of the blessed gathered as the petals of a bright rose, is rather a matter of cultural and religious environment. We have learnt to-day to be sceptical of allegories. And we have learnt to look for ultimate Reality in something outside both time and eternity. And a poet of our time, as Eliot would be the first to acknowledge, must start from the assumptions of our time. He cannot make a show of knowledge "by any concitation of the backward devils".

---

[1] *Poetry of T.S.E.*, p. 161.

Eliot has frequent images of a garden bathed in sunlight:

> I only looked through the little door
> When the sun was shining on the rose-garden;
> And heard in the distance tiny voices [1]

> There, the eyes are
> Sunlight on a broken column
> There, is a tree swinging
> And voices are
> In the wind's singing [2]

> Quick, said the bird, find them, find them,
> Round the corner. Through the first gate,
> Into our first world, — — [3]

The examples might be multiplied. The rose-garden obviously stands for a vision of ultimate Reality. But it only stands for the vision; it is not the vision itself. And the fact that it occurs so frequently is due to its representing something else besides, namely the poet's nostalgia for Paradise and happiness. As a symbol of reality it falls into line with the many tentative metaphors which are rejected as inadequate almost as soon as they are conceived:

> The wild thyme unseen, or the winter lightning
> Or the waterfall, or music heard so deeply
> That it is not heard at all, but you are the music
> While the music lasts. These are only hints and guesses [4]

And so Eliot, in the fashion of the true mystic rather than in that of the poet, stands powerless to describe what he has experienced.

It might be objected to what I said above about Eliot's indeterminate vision as compared with the almost physical apparitions reported in the lives of many saints that it is in the nature of true mystic experience to be indeterminate. This, of course, cannot be denied. Huxley has demonstrated the striking similarity between mystic experiences in all great religions in his *Perennial Philosophy*. And the fact that Eliot's intimations resemble so many others in this respect is as much a sign of their genuineness as of imitation on Eliot's part. He has not deliberately tried to conjure up or copy states of ecstasy to exploit them for poetic purposes (a behaviour which he reprehends in *After Strange Gods*). He has had experiences, differing in degree quite probably, but not in kind, from those of St. John of the Cross and Julian of Norwich. There may be a more intimate sense of a Presence in the visions of most mystics than in Eliot's. In the latter one is more impressed by the Absence of everything. But perhaps the difference between Presence and Absence becomes meaningless when we are speaking of these things.

---

[1] FR p. 107.   [2] HM.   [3] BN I.   [4] DS V.

I merely contend, then, that Eliot's supreme visions are not concretely and specifically Christian. They are as closely akin to those of Oriental as to those of European mystics. We will return to this subject in a moment.

In his instants of illumination, the poet's "awareness" (op. p. 97) is stretched as far as it will go. He is aware of timelessness, which no logical explanation can make us understand effectively. We can have some sort of idea of a time that goes on and on into eternity. But a time that *is not* cannot be grasped by our ordinary understanding. St. Augustine asks in his *Confessions:*

> Who will hold [the heart of man], and so fix it, that it may stand a while, and a little catch at a beam of light from that everfixed eternity, to compare it with the times which are never fixed, that he may thereby perceive how there is no comparison between them ...... and that all both past and to come, is made up, and flows out of that which is always present? Who now shall so hold fast this heart of man, that it may stand, and see, how that eternity ever still standing, gives the word of command to the times past or to come, itself being neither past nor to come? Can my hand do this, or can the hand of my mouth by speech, bring about so important a business?[1]

We cannot pry into all mysteries, says St. Augustine. And we must agree that speech cannot convey any adequate concept of timelessness. If timelessness is experienced it must be in an ecstasy (and ecstasy is not the same as nervous exaltation) in which everything that exists in time is seen to be transfigured, or redeemed.

Such a vision would naturally give one a strong sense of spirituality, of possessing an immortal soul. Eliot's doubts concerning the soul have vanished in his recent poetry. Even in *The Hollow Men* immortality appears to be real. And in *Murder in the Cathedral* it enters decisively into the very catastrophe of the drama, turning it into what Eliot terms a comedy.[2] In the *Quartets* the soul is a unifying principle of the personality, holding together even the individual memory. In his new conception of the memory, Eliot takes his stand with Aristotle against Bradley:

> — — — This is the use of memory:
> For liberation — not less of love but expanding
> Of love beyond desire, and so liberation
> From the future as well as the past.[3]

Eliot's references to and images of the Divine Persons generally do not occur in these moments of ecstasy. They elude his supreme visions just as the hooded figure in "What the Thunder Said" elude his sight:

---

[1] Op. cit. Book XI, ch. XI. Also quoted by Martz, SELCR p. 451. He rightly draws our attention to the whole section on time from which this passage is taken.
[2] According to Rolf Lamborn, *Stockholms-Tidningen,* 5 Nov. 1948.   [3] LG III.

> Who is the third who walks always beside you?
> When I count, there are only you and I together

The Divine Persons, when they appear, which is not so very often
if one considers Eliot's later poetry as religious poetry, are seen through
the window of dogma, and in a more matter-of-fact mood than that which
envelops "the wild thyme unseen, or the winter lightning". *More* matter-of-
fact, but not entirely so. There is still the vision in the sense of the "higher
dream", which Eliot found in so much medieval poetry and misses in
our own.[1]

The "higher dream", as I interpret it, is a vision of the sublime and
the divine which is aesthetic rather than mystical. In this vision, the Father
and the Holy Spirit appear under such ancient symbols as the eye and the
dove. The eye (or eyes) from being entirely human in "The Love Song"
become semi-divine in *The Hollow Men,* and finally completely divine in
The Family Reunion, "Burnt Norton" and elsewhere. Christ appears as
"the tiger" of "Gerontion" and "the wounded surgeon" of "East Coker".
And the Virgin, to whom prayers are addressed, is "the rose" of many
poems.[2] She is also the mysterious Lady of *Ash-Wednesday,* as well as
the Lady of "The Dry Salvages". There further seems to be a Beatrice
in a number of the poems, who tends on the one hand to be identified
with la Figlia, and on the other hand with the Virgin. The role which is
played by this figure suggests the importance of the intercession of saints
in Catholic devotions.

Let us return to the symbol of the garden or orchard. It is a direct
reference to the Garden of Eden (and occasionally to the Garden of Geth-
semane), but also represents a persistent longing of humanity, for perfection
here and now, and for a heaven of bliss to come. This longing is one
that Eliot feels acutely. But I think it would be wrong to present it merely
as a nostalgic mood. It is something more: a mood of adoration, in which
the object of adoration is a beautiful dream and at the same time an article
of faith. Even before it became an article of faith, the dream was there.
It is noticeable in "The Love Song", which contains not only *spleen* but also
idéal, in the vision of a garden which is there submarine. It is visible in
the fourth "Prelude", in "La Figlia", and in the gardens of *The Waste
Land.* In the preceding chapter we chiefly considered Eliot's negative mood
of doubt and despondency. But we must not forget that right from the
beginning there were also this positive mood and this positive vision, even
if they were almost submerged for a long time, partly because of the poet's
literary prejudices.[3] It can hardly be doubted that the longing for a Paradise
and the adoration of ideal perfection have been powerful inspirations in

---

[1] Cf. "Dante", SE p. 262; and cp. *Ash-Wednesday* IV.   [2] E. g. HM IV, *Ash-
Wednesday* II and all the *Quartets.* Of course, the rose symbolises other things besides
the BVM.   [3] Cf. "Dante", SE p. 262.

Eliot's poetry. However they were symbolised, in ancient myths or his own, in the beauty of roses in a sunlit garden or the blissful innocence of children in an apple-tree, by a return to past ages, or to childhood, or an advance into mysticism, this longing and this adoration have nourished the vital flame in his work.

The Biblical conception of heaven is as that of a feast, in other words a beatitude that is shared by all. And one of the chief things that Eliot sought in the Church and in its doctrine of a state of immortal bliss, was clearly a sense of communion. Among the seven Catholic sacraments, that of the Penance is most frequently alluded to in his poems; but next comes that of the Holy Communion. We find it most conspicuously in "Gerontion" and "East Coker". And, characteristically, the poet says in the ninth Chorus of *The Rock:*

> Let us mourn in a private chamber, learning the way of penitence,
> And then let us learn the joyful communion of saints.

In the second Chorus the need of community is emphasised very strongly:

> What life have you if you have not life together?
> There is no life that is not in community,
> And no community not lived in praise of GOD.
> Even the anchorite who meditates alone,
> For whom the days and nights repeat the praise of GOD,
> Prays for the Church, the Body of Christ incarnate.
> And now you live dispersed on ribbon roads,
> And no man knows or cares who is his neighbour

The life of the Church is still the solution of the problem of isolation, intensified in modern civilisation. In the Church, tradition is a living thing, which can make Communion actual. Here, by annihilation of the self, one's isolation can be broken and even God can be communed with. God first, human beings afterwards. There is still a sense of frustration in the poet's attempts to achieve fellowship with human beings. There is still a lack of warmth in the description of human relations. Even in the moments of ecstasy which he tells us of, there is nothing comparable to the experience of the two souls who are completely united in Donne's poem "The Ecstasy".[1] But Eliot's efforts to break down the spiritual barriers between himself and others are energetic, and do not seem altogether vain. We may find some significance in the growing use of the pronouns "we" and "us" in a real plural sense where earlier the first person singular was used or at least intended. An intermediate stage may be discovered in *Ash-Wednesday,* where "I" alternates with "we", and where, "at its peaks and climaxes the poetry passes into the anonymous language of the Church".[2] In the Monchen-

---

[1] There are reminiscences of this poem in "Burnt Norton", and I would hazard the conjecture that Donne's "Ecstasy" must often have seemed to Eliot to be mocking him and yet goading him on in his search for spiritual communion.   [2] Mrs. Duncan Jones, F3 p. 37.

sey family there is no real "reunion", but Harry and Agatha really contact
each other, and Harry and Mary almost do. Harry seeks the life of the
desert, not only for his own sake, but to find God, and so vicariously to
benefit his whole family.

In one way, then, we see a development in Eliot's poetry, as in his
prose, from individualism by way of Christianity to a search for social unity
and an acceptance of social obligations. But from an irreligious point of
view he probably appears to be as individualistic as ever. He tends to make
Christianity a religion of spiritual discipline, which to a great extent means
a religion of ethics. The nature of his Christian ethics, however, regarded as
ethics, is not social and practical, but rather asocial and impractical (regarded
as religious devotion it becomes a different matter; but the social benefits
which accrue from perfecting the individual in a life of devotion would
obviously be denied by the irreligious). A passage in "The Dry Salvages"
seems to me to sum up Eliot's position quite well:

> —— — "on whatever sphere of being
> The mind of man may be intent
> At the time of death" — that is the one action
> (And the time of death is every moment)
> Which shall fructify in the lives of others:

Only from a religious point of view can such a statement be appreciated.
In this case I do not think that any amount of poetic imagination alone
can help one to believe.

Catholic individualism and Protestant individualism are two different
things. Catholicism, in spite of (or perhaps because of) the importance it
attaches to the Church and the community, stresses the need and the right
of the individual to perfect his own soul, even if this entails physical isolation from the society of men and devotion to a seemingly inactive life of
contemplation. Protestantism tends to reject such religious cloistering.
Eliot here takes the Catholic position. But Protestant individualism teaches
the need and right of the individual to receive and understand the word of
God direct in his own heart and in his own way (though I do not deny
that heterodoxy may be tolerated less in many Protestant Churches than
in the Catholic Churches). Catholicism, on the other hand, is *a priori*
sceptical of personal revelations, though historically it has accepted a great
number of mystics. It might look as if Eliot here inclines to the Protestant
attitude; so that in either case he opts for individualism. But this view is
contradicted by one of his epigraphs to the *Quartets*, a quotation from
Heraclitus, which in Diels's German translation runs thus: "Aber obschon
das Wort allein gemein ist, leben die meisten doch so, als ob sie eine eigene
Einsicht hätten." According to Miss E. M. Stephenson, Eliot has commented
upon this translation as follows: "I should say that Herakleitos meant a
great deal more than simply 'the word is in common use'. I think he meant
rather that the reason, the Logos, or the rational understanding of the nature

of things is common or available to all men. *'Most people live as if they had a peculiar and individual insight'.*[1] Thus the poet's use and interpretation of the fragment from Heraclitus show that he regards his mystical insight as something that is available to all men. It may be practised individually, but it is in the nature of things that the knowledge thus gained will be the same for all. In other words, if meditation is rightly practised it will not really be an individual affair and there will be no really separate and particular ways of understanding divine truths. If we agree with this assumption, we shall recognise that Eliot is completely true to Catholicism (and to Greek thought) in this matter. If we disagree, we shall tend to find greater significance in his Protestant independence and individualism.

To determine Eliot's poetry as Catholic or Protestant is of no denominational interest, at least to the present writer. But it may be useful as indicating which aspects of Christianity he is particularly occupied with, and which aspects he more or less ignores. He stresses the dogma of Incarnation rather than that of Atonement; the perfection of the will and religious discipline rather than the intensity of faith; penance, confession and purgation rather than judgment; communal rather than private worship. Such things as the adoration of the Virgin and the belief in the intercession of saints are more superficial Catholic elements of his poetry.

It is remarkable that it is only in his Christian poetry that certain hedonistic tendencies have manifested themselves, as if Omar and Lucretius had to wait for a Catholic acceptance of asceticism to come into their own. In many ways there is more variety in Catholic than in Protestant feeling, the former encouraging both austerity and pleasure in greater extremes than the latter. As a matter of fact Eliot's asceticism is not so much that of austere practices as that of severe thought. "You must not deny the body", he reminds us in the ninth Chorus of *The Rock*. He has not the Protestant distrust of pleasure. He has, however, the Protestant sense of the corruption of the world. And it may be worth remarking that the doctrine of Original Sin would hardly have received so central a place in his poetry without the emphasis given to it by generations of Protestants.

On the more definitely Puritan traits in his make-up there is no need to dwell. They consist rather in emotional attitudes than in points of doctrine. Perhaps the pull which a conventional and environmental Puritanism may have exerted helps to account for a certain latitude of doctrine, which, in spite of everything, we find in his poetry. Eliot's eschatology, too, is much concerned with the need to be constantly prepared for the end, a need which Puritans are fond of stressing. "The time of death is every moment", says the poet, and this idea underlies much of his vision. On the other hand, we rarely meet the idea of a general conclusion of all things. The apocalyptic phantasmagoria so beloved of many poets has little appeal

---

[1] *T.S.E. & the Lay Reader*, p. 80.

to Eliot. It is "a worn-out poetical fashion".[1] And so the common Puritan eschatology of a final destruction and judgment in connection with the second coming of Christ, gives place in his poetry to an individual eschatology, in which, as I have shown, the states of Heaven, Hell and Purgatory play an important part.

Eliot's Christianity is strongly tinged with a monist philosophy. We have seen how Bradleyan ideas constantly occur in his poetry. He seems to regard time and timelessness as distinct spheres, but he does not recognise any essential difference between the human and the divine. And good and evil are both subsumed under a higher purpose. No doubt his monism, from a religious point of view, is as much an extension of the Unitarianism in which he was brought up, as it is a remnant of his purely philosophical enthusiasms. He traced his mother's spiritual descent from Schleiermacher, by way of Channing, Emerson and Herbert Spencer.[2] And the philosophy of Schleiermacher is a meeting-ground of Absolute Idealism and Unitarianism, just as Harvard University in the last century was a meeting-ground of these two closely-related schools of thought.

It may quite well have been in reaction against Unitarianism that he has insisted so urgently on such doctrines as the Incarnation of God in Jesus Christ and the sacramental nature of the Eucharist. But other Christian doctrines he has left in abeyance. We saw that he tends to ignore the doctrine of Atonement in favour of that of Incarnation. It is a concomitant tendency to see salvation for human beings in attaining to the divine union, rather than in a divine Atonement and forgiveness. And in such tendencies his old Unitarianism, supported by a monistic Idealism, may be seen to be still alive.

Monism can be many things, and it is not necessarily hostile to perfectly orthodox Christianity. But on the whole it tends to regard the Christian conception of God as falling short of the Absolute, and the teachings of Christianity as failing to give a final interpretation of the universe. It is natural that Catholics should regard it with a certain amount of suspicion. In *The Catholic Encyclopedia*[3] we read:

Reality eludes our attempt to compress it within the categories which we frame for it. Consequently, Dualism is often the final answer in philosophy; and Monism, which is not content with the partial synthesis of Dualism, but aims at an ideal completeness, often results in failure. Dualism leaves room for faith, and hands over to faith many of the problems which philosophy cannot solve. Monism leaves no room for faith. The only mysticism which is compatible with it is rationalistic, and very different from that "vision" in which, for the Christian mystic, all the limitations, imperfections, and other shortcomings of our feeble efforts are removed by the light of faith.

---

[1] EC II.   [2] Cf. Introd. to *Savonarola*.   [3] New York, 1911.

Eliot accepted faith and the Christian vision, and consequently had to
relinquish many of his monistc ideas. But he could not entirely give up
former loyalties, and it seems that he found in his poetry (in which, as we
have seen, he does not ask to be "believed") an outlet for Unitarian and
monistic ideas which Catholicism closed to him in the ordinary way. So
that, while his course might have been expected to lead from monism to
Catholic dualism, even pluralism, he has retained, in his poetry, a fundamentally monist conception of the universe.

Oriental Mysticism.

Just as Eliot's interest in Western philosophy can still be clearly traced
in his poetry, so his study of Oriental philosophies and religions have left
indelible marks. It is not always easy to distinguish these marks from those
left by Christian mysticism, and one risks attaching too much importance
to concrete references, such as the quotation from the *Bhagavad-Gita* in
"The Dry Salvages". There are obvious points of contact between Eastern
and Western thought: The two currents meet in the New Testament, while
in the Old Testament, which has become part of the basis of Western culture,
we really meet a tributary of the Oriental tradition. Thus *Ecclesiastes,* which
Eliot draws upon extensively, presents a view of life related to that of
Buddhism. If, however, the distinctions between Eastern and Western
mysticism are not always easy to draw, Eliot's allusions show at least that
he has often had the Oriental mystics in mind; and occasionally he introduces the peculiarities of Oriental thought into his poetry.

The more obvious references to Oriental religions and mysticism are
to be found in "Gerontion", *The Waste Land* and the *Quartets*. In "Gerontion" we meet "Hakagawa, bowing among the Titians", a representative of
an Eastern religion as eviscerated as Christianity, unable to distinguish the
pictures of gods or apotheosised ancestors from those of mortals. In *The
Waste Land,* the Buddha, as a representative of Eastern asceticism, is
"collocated" with St. Augustine, a representative of Western asceticism.
And in the final section of the same poem the ethical and mystic teachings
of the *Upanishads* are drawn upon. "Burnt Norton" pictures a lotos floating
on the water of the empty pool, and in a later section speaks of "a Chinese
jar" (of the kind, I take it, with mythological decorations upon it) to rein-
force the impression of a designed allusion to Buddhism. "The Dry Salvages" reminds us in section II of Vishnu and Siva in the Hindu Trinity
by the notion that "Time the destroyer is time the preserver", and in section
III quotes from Krishna's admonitions to Arjuna in the *Bhagavad-Gita*.

These allusions call our attention to a far profounder saturation of
Eliot's poetry with Hindu and Buddhist thought than they immediately
indicate.

The ancient Indian philosophers, especially Śaṁkara, stand very close to the Absolute Idealists in their interpretation of reality. Reality, they thought, was one and spiritual, Brahman. And the world of sense-perception was relative and deceptive (māyā). But there were various degrees of unreality. In the *Bhagavad-Gita*, Krishna discourses thus:

> — — — They do not know my nature
> That is one with Brahman, changeless, superhuman.
>
> Veiled in my Maya, I am not shown to many.
> How shall this world, bewildered by delusion,
> Recognize me, who am not born and change not?

I know all beings, Arjuna: past, present and to come. But no one knows me.

All living creatures are led astray as soon as they are born, by the delusion that this relative world is real. This delusion arises from their own desire and hatred. But the doers of good deeds, whose bad karma is exhausted, are freed from this delusion about the relative world. They hold firmly to their vows, and worship me.

Men take refuge in me, to escape from their fear of old age and death. Thus they come to know Brahman, and the entire nature of the Atman, and the creative energy which is in Brahman. Knowing me, they understand the nature of the relative world and the individual man, and of God who presides over all action. Even at the hour of death, they continue to know me thus. In that hour, their whole consciousness is made one with mine.[1]

Eliot calls the *Bhagavad-Gita* "the next greatest philosophical poem to the *Divine Comedy* within my experience".[2] This passage from the *Gita* not only expounds one of the most fundamental ideas in Eliot's philosophy, that of one absolute Reality, but might also quite well have been his own expression of many more incidental attitudes, for instance the fear of old age and death. There is no need to repeat what we have said before concerning Absolute Idealism in the poet's work. It is enough if we see clearly that it has been inspired by ancient Indian philosophy as well as by Western thinkers of more recent times. The differences between the ideas of the old Hindus and those of the modern Europeans can hardly be gauged in poetry. The imagery by means of which the poet conveys his ideas and intimations is mostly modern, it is true, but this is no indication of the age or origin of the ideas. There is a better indication in such rare Oriental images as that of the lotos, which is strangely incongruous in its context. Its import may be phallic, but its Buddhist associations are far closer.[3]

---

[1] GITA p. 93.   [2] "Dante", SE p. 258.   [3] In "Burnt Norton" it appears to be a symbol of the complete Reality of which sensible things (the concrete pool) are only a part. This, of course, would attach it to Hinduism rather than to Buddhism.

A basic belief in Oriental religions is the belief in metempsychosis. This belief was used as a motif by James Joyce in his *Ulysses*. And it would seem that some such idea is at the bottom of Eliot's constant visions of human beings metamorphosed in the most curious ways:

> And I must borrow every changing shape
> To find expression .... dance, dance
> Like a dancing bear,
> Cry like a parrot, chatter like an ape.[1]

Prufrock imagines himself as a crab, Tiresias assumes an unlimited number of different identities, and in *The Hollow Men* human beings are reduced to the state of scarecrows. In the *Quartets* the "travellers" who start on a journey are not the same when they arrive at their destination. However, they are asked to meditate during their journey upon Krishna's words to Arjuna concerning re-incarnation:

> On whatever sphere of being the mind of man may be intent at the time of death, to that he goes .... having been used to ponder on it.[2]

Thus their change will still be a part of their spiritual progress. And the final goal of all changes is liberation, and the divine union.

The doctrine of metempsychosis never appears very clearly on the surface in Eliot's poetry. But another doctrine, very closely connected with it, is worked upon far more overtly, namely that of the universal cycle. The *Gita* uses the old symbol of the wheel, "the terrible wheel of rebirth and death".[3] This terrible wheel may be an illusion, but it nevertheless imprisons us:

> Maya makes all things: what moves, what is unmoving.
> O son of Kunti, that is why the world spins,
> Turning its wheel through birth
> And through destruction.[4]

The wheel, we must repeat here, is one of the most frequent symbols in Eliot's work from his first poems to the *Quartets*. And generally it has a significance more or less as in the *Bhagavad-Gita*. I assume that in the Tarot pack of cards alluded to in *The Waste Land*, the Wheel originally symbolised the cycle of life and seasons. It appears significantly in "Death by Water", where Phlebas the Phoenician enters "the whirlpool". And in an earlier section, Madame Sosostris sees "crowds of people, walking round in a ring". In *Murder in the Cathedral* the wheel is again a major symbol. Only the fool, says Becket on one occasion, "may think / He can turn the wheel on

---

[1] "Portrait of a Lady".   [2] Quoted after Preston, 4QR p. 44. Cp. GITA p. 95.
[3] GITA p. 44.   [4] GITA p. 102.

which he turns". And Harry in *The Family Reunion* speaks of "the burning wheel", or simply "the human wheel".[1]

By successful re-incarnations, the wheel of Hinduism and Buddhism can be turned into an ascending spiral. This idea also enters into Eliot's poetry, especially in the image of the winding stairs in *Ash-Wednesday*.

So long as we are climbing the stairs, however, or turning on the wheel, we are bound to suffer. Eliot's conception of life as suffering found its most consistent philosophical support in Oriental mysticism. The Buddha's Fire Sermon, alluded to in *The Waste Land,* is an account of the sterile and painful burning of the senses, of desires and thoughts, and of all their objects. We found that the poet's pessimism had nourished itself on these ideas.[2] Without their background it is hard to explain what I can only call the thoughtfulness of Eliot's *Weltschmerz,* or to account adequately for the death-wish expressed in such poems as *The Waste Land, Ash-Wednesday* and "A Song for Simeon".

Only by the practice of disaffection, by spiritual discipline and askesis, can release from the circle of suffering be attained. Krishna explains the "Karma Yoga" to Arjuna, and declares that "even a little practice of this yoga will save you from the terrible wheel of rebirth and death".[3]

Eliot's study of Patanjali left him, he says, in a "state of enlightened mystification". But his knowledge of Yoga, even if imperfect, has nevertheless been extremely fruitful to his poetry. In the self-mortification and austerities enjoined by Patanjali he found not only the answer to a religious need, but also the matter for a poetry of contemplation which should be both intense and dramatic. In the repetitive muttering of Vedic hymns he may have found the idea for some of his own hypnotic effects.

The practice of Yoga tends to consist in renunciation and in abstention from movement, physical and mental. Bearing this in mind, we can approach such passages as the following from "Burnt Norton" with an increased sensibility to their range of suggestion:

> Descend lower, descend only
> Into the world of perpetual solitude,
> World not world, but that which is not world,
> Internal darkness, deprivation
> And destitution of all property,
> Desiccation of the world of sense,
> Evacuation of the world of fancy,
> Inoperancy of the world of spirit;
> This is the one way, and the other
> Is the same, not in movement
> But abstention from movement; while the world moves
> In appetency, on its metalled ways
> Of time past and time future.

---

[1] FR pp. 30, 101.   [2] Cf. pp. 116—7.   [3] GITA p. 44.

The symbol of darkness is a Hindu as well as a Christian symbol, as Raymond Preston has pointed out. He quotes from the *Bhagavad-Gita:*

In that which is night to all things, therein the self-subjugated remains awake; but where all else is awake, that is night for the knower of self.[1]

Purification by fire is also a Hindu symbol:

> The blazing fire can turn wood to ashes:
> The fire of knowledge turns all karmas to ashes.
> On earth there is no purifier
> As great as this knowledge,
> When a man is made perfect in yoga,
> He knows its truth within his heart.[2]

Patanjali's "Eightfold Path" aims at the suppression of mental activity (and similarly the Buddha's "Aryan Eightfold Path", which otherwise differs considerably from it, consists chiefly in abstentions). But all Yoga is not passivity. Krishna urges Arjuna to pursue the course of right action, for "freedom from activity is never achieved by abstaining from action"[3]:

> The wise see knowledge and action as one:
> They see truly.
> Take either path
> And tread it to the end:
> The end is the same.
> There the followers of action
> Meet the seekers after knowledge
> In equal freedom.[4]

This passage reminds one strikingly of a number of passages from Eliot. There is a special yoga of action which Eliot no doubt has in mind when he urges us to be "still moving", to "fare forward". And by reference to Hindu mysticism we see how Eliot's insistence on inaction can be reconciled with his insistence on activity. The action must be that which we are destined to fulfil, and there must be no thought of its fruits. "You have the right to work, but for the work's sake only. You have no right to the fruits of work", says Krishna.[5] And further, "You must perform every action sacramentally, and be free from all attachment to results".[6] And similarly Eliot, "For us, there is only the trying. The rest is not our business";[7] "And do not think of the fruit of action".[8] Krishna: "Action rightly performed brings freedom".[9] And Eliot: "And right action is freedom / From past and future also".[10]

There is a certain contrast between "Burnt Norton" and "East Coker" on the one hand and "The Dry Salvages" on the other: the two former deal

---

[1] 4QR p. 103. Cp. the fragment from the *Isa Upanishad* quoted by J. J. Sweeney, SELCR p. 406.   [2] GITA p. 66.   [3] GITA p. 51.   [4] GITA p. 70.   [5] GITA p. 46. Contrast Christ's "the labourer is worthy of his hire".   [6] GITA p. 52. [7] EC V.   [8] DS III.   [9] GITA p. 69.   [10] DS V.

mainly with the dark night of the soul, while the latter has right action for
its theme. But the opposite themes are combined in the poem of reconciliation, "Little Gidding", in which all the activity of history is seen to be
a pattern of timeless, motionless moments, and all our exploration to lead
us only back to our starting-point.

If we turn to the *Upanishads,* we find a kind of "right action" indicated
by "what the Thunder said": "datta, dayadhvam, damyata" — "give, sympa-
thise, control". The main significance of these words is that one should
subdue oneself and give oneself to others, and to the Brahman, who is in
all things; and this is how Eliot uses them in *The Waste Land.* If the
voice of God in the thunder is obeyed, it means a breaking out of the
isolation which prevents a fruitful intercourse, and the consummation of
a final union.

The end of Yoga is liberation —

> The inner freedom from the practical desire,
> The release from action and suffering, release from the inner
> And the outer compulsion, — —[1]

Liberation is divine union and the annihilation of the individual; not
divine union so much to Patanjali, and not to the Buddha, but to the authors
of the *Upanishads* and the *Gita* (the word yoga is derived from the Sanskrit
yuj = join). And the divine union may be best described by the word
"shantih", which concludes *The Waste Land,* and which Eliot makes
equivalent to our phrase, "the Peace which passeth understanding".

Only in the divine union is there true existence:

> The awful daring of a moment's surrender
> Which an age of prudence can never retract
> By this, and this only, we have existed

In the union with Brahman only intuitional knowledge is of any avail,
for Brahman is "the negative of everything that is positively known",[2] and
knowledge as we commonly understand it must therefore be eliminated
(this, of course, is the idea of "the darkness of the soul" again)., The
Brahman is "the unmoved and the moving".[3] One of this aspects is ubiquitous presence, the Atman.

> Not subject to change
> Is the infinite Atman,
> Without beginning,
> Beyond the gunas:[a]

Brahman is timeless; therefore those who seek illumination must become oblivious to the passing of time, just as those who seek Nirvana
must detach themselves from temporal relations. Such detachment cannot

[1] BN II.   [2] *Enc. Brit.,* article on Indian Philosophy.   [3] GITA p. 125.
[a] GITA p. 138.

be dependent on a "distraction fit" or accidental illuminations, but must be practised deliberately and wholemindedly. Our karma follows us always, but it can be controlled by a disciplined observance of the yogas. If this is to be successful, humility is required. The insistence of this virtue in Hinduism and still more in Buddhism reminds us that Eliot does not see it exclusively as a Christian virtue.

The Yoga of Patanjali counts on an irresistible will in its addicts to see them through their spiritual discipline. And in spite of an admixture of fatalism in Hindu belief, it would seem that the idea of the perfect efficaciousness of human effort rightly applied is implicit in all Oriental asceticism. Yoga leads to union with the Brahman without divine interference. Eliot is strongly attracted to this idea, as we have already seen. But at the same time his Christian orthodoxy prevents him from accepting it completely. His dilemma resembles that of his own spiritual hero, Thomas Becket, who is tempted to win saintliness by deliberate martyrdom, but who realises that only divine grace can bestow it. Eliot seems to stop half-way, from either point of view, or even to contradict himself. He believes strongly in human effort, and yet he denies its efficacy. In the same breath, almost, as he tells us to "be still, and wait without hope", he declares, not only with hope but with seeming confidence, "So the darkness shall be the light, and the stillness the dancing".[1] The apparent opposition between human passivity and human activity can be reconciled. But it is harder to reconcile the reliance on divine grace with the reliance on human effort. That Eliot is fully conscious of the difficulty we can tell from his essay on "The *Pensées* of Pascal".[2] A mysterious reconciliation is effected in Catholic theology, where the will is considered to be really free only if its acts under grace. But this part of Catholic theology has not been drawn upon to any extent in Eliot's poetry. The result is that the Oriental view of spiritual discipline has been given great prominence and is juxtaposed with the Christian view of grace. There is an unresolved conflict in these ideas, which we can only feel as a conflict in the poetry, though it does not necessarily impair the value of the poetry.

The foregoing chapters have shown us that the conceptual structure of Eliot's poetry is so intricate and his themes so diverse that if homogeneity were to be demanded of art, his would be doomed by that very fact. Fortunately poetry, by its emotional quality, has a power of gathering even logically inconsistent elements in a wide synthesis.[3] In so doing it directs our attention to what the elements have in common. And if there is no important inconsistency, the poetic synthesis may suggest a rational synthesis.

---

[1] EC III.   [2] EAM p. 153.   [3] Cp. Santayana: "it is an old maxim with me that many ideas may be convergent as poetry which would be divergent as dogmas." ("Brief Hist. of My Opinions", *Philos. of Santayana,* p. 18).

VII.
Eliot's Synthesis.
In which the three preceding chapters find their conclusion.

If we view the attitudes and ideas of Eliot's poetry as a whole, we find a striking correspondence between them in many points. And where there are discrepancies, they have mostly been overcome in various ways.

His pessimism, in the first place, finds its complement in the historical disillusion of our epoch. It further unites itself with a congenial aspect of Christianity, and finds a still more suitable atmosphere in the philosophies of Hinduism and Buddhism. His acceptance of suffering and belief in askesis as ways to perfection and bliss find support in both Protestant and Catholic Christianity and in the religions of the East.

The poet endeavours to *feel* in a Christian way, as well as to adopt a Christian mode of thought; or rather to grasp this mode of thought with his sensibility. "The trouble of the modern age", he wrote in 1943, "is not merely the inability to believe certain things about God and man which our forefathers believed, but the inability to *feel* towards God and man as they did".[1] Eliot would like to make religion a matter not of sentiment or emotionalism, that is to say, not of emotional effervescence, but of emotional response. And in so doing he compasses in addition to Christianity other religions to which he has responded emotionally, especially Hinduism.

By trying to describe in poetry what it felt like to believe in something, rather than to make statements of beliefs, he has managed to integrate belief with art to an amazing extent, persuading each to fulfil the conditions of the other. Thus Christianity becomes vision, a certain way of seeing and feeling things, a "higher dream" as with Dante.

His idea of divine union might be that of either Christian or Oriental mysticism. In fact it belongs to both. That the difference between them can be made negligible, is shown by the following passage from St. Thomas Aquinas:

By means of the ordering of all things, which has been as it were projected out of Him and which bears certain images and likenesses of its divine patterning, we ascend in ordered degrees so far as we are able to that which is above all things, by the ways of negation and transcendence, and the conception of a universal cause.

Thus God is known in all things and yet apart from all things; and He is known through knowledge and through ignorance. On the one hand, He is apprehended by intuition, reason, understanding, touch, sense, opinion, imagination, name, and so on; while on the other hand He cannot be grasped by intuition nor can He be uttered or named, and He is not anything in the world, nor is He known in any existent thing.[2]

---

[1] "Social Function of Poetry", *Norseman*, Nov. 1943. [2] Quoted by Preston. 4QR p. 16.

Apart from the style in which it is couched this passage might have been an excerpt from the *Bhagavad-Gita*. Hegel and Bradley, Schleiermacher and Emerson would sanction most of it too. Even Aristotle would recognise some of his own principles, which is not surprising, seeing that his philosophy was very influential in shaping patristic thought.

Eliot's conception of divine union also appears to have borrowed more than one would think at first from higher Nature cults and esoteric mysteries. The identification of the "I" with the Fisher King of *The Waste Land* is more than an accident, and Christ is deliberately associated with the Vegetation God. We have only to notice the part played by the seasons in most of Eliot's poetry — *the Four Quartets,* for instance, are appropriated each to one of the four seasons — and the importance of the ideas of fertility, to gain a better understanding of the poet's vision of the relation between God and man. Eliot can truly say

> That the past experience revived in the meaning
> Is not the experience of one life only
> But of many generations —

Not only in literature does he take account of the legacy of the past, but in religion too. In many respects his position is that of the Gnostics of early Christian times, of whom G. R. S. Mead wrote: "The claim of these Gnostics was practically that Christianity, or rather the Good News of the Christ, was precisely the consummation of the inner doctrine of the Mystery-institutions of all the nations: the end of them all was the revelation of the Mystery of Man".[1]

Among the elements of Eliot's poetry that derive from "the primitive terror", it can hardly be denied that there is one of pagan superstition pure and simple. He resorts from time to time to magic and incantation, despite his contempt for Madame Sosostris[2] and her sisterhood, and his condemnation of magic practices in the fifth section of "The Dry Salvages". This element appears clearly in Agatha's conjuring in *The Family Reunion*:

> Round and round the circle
> Completing the charm
> So the knot be unknotted
> The crossed be uncrossed
> The crooked be made straight
> And the curse be ended[3]

It would be impossible to tell to what extent magic is woven into the poetry as a whole. In one way, of course, all poetry has an incantatory

---

[1] Quoted by Jessie Weston, *Fr. Rit. to Rom.*, p. 145.   [2] Madame Sosostris prophesies rightly, even if she turns things upside down. And there is an obvious similarity between her, Doris in *Sweeney Ag.* and Agatha in FR.   [3] FR p. 136.

purpose, or at least an incantatory effect, even at its "freest"; otherwise it would not be poetry. But Eliot frequently seems to emphasise both the purpose and the effect, for instance in the close of *The Waste Land* and *The Hollow Men,* and the beginning of *Ash-Wednesday:*

> Because I do not hope to turn again
> Because I do not hope
> Because I do not hope to turn

He even avails himself of something very like magic formulae in his attempts to disclose the nature of Reality. Of this, and of its legitimacy, we shall have something more to say in our chapter on "Technique and Thought".

The nature of Reality is generally approached by the poet both from a Christian point of view and from the point of view of a rationalistic monist philosophy. Both points of view may be simultaneously present:

For all things exist only as seen by Thee, only as known by Thee, all things exist
Only in Thy light, and Thy glory is declared even in that which denies Thee; the darkness declares the glory of light.
Those who deny Thee could not deny, if Thou didst not exist; and their denial is never complete, for if it were so, they would not exist.[1]

"Those who deny Thee could not deny, if Thou didst not exist." We have here an argument taken straight out of the phenomenology of Meinong and Bradley. Another close reminder of Bradley, this time in a statement about Christian grace, is found in "Marina". When the hero of the poem rejoices that those who sinned in various ways have become "By this grace dissolved in place", one cannot avoid thinking of Bradley's dissolution of the elements of evil to be re-grouped in a wider synthesis and thus turned into good.

The view of history which corresponds to such a view of Reality is that of a sequence of timeless moments, in Bradleyan terms, or "a pattern of timeless moments" in Eliot's words from "Little Gidding". There is a feeling of the Absolute, or alternatively of God, in history, vivifying tradition, which would otherwise have been dead and waste, and providing a teleology for all development. Time and timelessness are dealt with according to the hypotheses and indications of modern science and philosophy combined with the intimations of mystics of various religions, and memories of personal experiences.

Both Freud and Frazer with other pioneers in the sciences of the human mind and human conduct are accepted in Eliot's poetry. And since they are united there with the teachers of religion, it is demonstrated — as emphatically as poetry can demonstrate anything — that neither psycho-

[1] MC p. 86.

analysis nor anthropology invalidates Christianity. Rather the points of contact between them come to the fore: the psycho-analyst's demonstration of the imperfection, or the sinfulness, of human nature; the anthropologist's demonstration of the perennial urge towards religious belief and community in life and tradition.

Politics also contribute to the general "ideology", though I have not thought it necessary to mention the political element before: it is not so important as some critics of Eliot would have it. In "Coriolan", the aristo-cratic ideal is held up to reflect unfavourably on the bureaucratic clumsiness of a falsely democratic society, and on the mob mentality which Eliot so detests. His political and social ideals are not those of American, or French, or Russian equalitarianism, but spring in the last analysis from Plato, Aristotle, Brahmanism, Confucianism and the Schoolmen. In *The Rock,* the author turns equally against redshirts, blackshirts and plutocrats:

> There is no help in parties, none in interests,
> There is no help in those whose souls are choked and swaddled
> In the old winding-sheets of place and power
> Or the new winding-sheets of mass-made thought.
> O world! forget your glories and your quarrels,
> Forget your groups and your misplaced ambitions,
> We speak to you as individual men;
> As individuals alone with GOD.[1]

Eliot does not give his allegiance to any party, but envisages a state of things in which the Church, "the Rock", shall be our guide in temporal as well as in spiritual affairs. His interest in King Charles I in "Little Gidding" is dictated by Anglican as much as by royalist sympathies, and he sees Charles with his opponents "folded in a single party" by the recon-ciliation of history. In the same way, it is suggested, present controversies will be reconciled. Meanwhile he advises us to take sensible policies where we can find them. In *The Rock* he advocates the principles of Credit Reform and the economic theories of J. M. Keynes. *The Rock,* however, is a pageant, and at the same time almost a propaganda play, so that its preoccupation with practical questions of politics and economics cannot be regarded as typical of Eliot's poetry as a whole.

Out of all the various concepts that he utilises in his poetry, he makes a synthesis, which may be regarded as the exponent of a typically modern conception of the universe. If we wish to examine it as such, it is enough to consider the more or less *popularised* ideas of our age, because it is the current ideas that determine the mentality and atmosphere of a period. As Arnold wrote in "The Function of Criticism":

---

[1] *Rock,* after Chorus VI.

In literature — — the elements with which the creative power works are ideas; the best ideas on every matter which literature touches, current at the time. — — — And I say *current* at the time, not merely accessible at the time; for creative literary genius does not principally show itself in discovering new ideas, that is rather the business of the philosopher. The grand work of literary genius is a work of synthesis and exposition, not of analysis and discovery.[1]

The deprecation of new ideas in poetry is familiar in Eliot's criticism. And the rest of this passage can easily be applied to his poetic achievements, whether or no he took the cue from Arnold (his debt to Arnold is so extensive that it doesn't much matter). Eliot employs current ideas rather than special and recondite theories; a good reason for our not entering into philosophical and scientific subtleties in our analysis of his concepts and attitudes.

Speculations regarding the nature of time have been very common in English literature for more than two decades. Often they are little more than a game. Priestley, for instance, may have taken J. W. Dunne's ideas seriously. But he serves us his "Split Time, Serial Time, and Circular Time" as so many fancy dishes. Wells and Shaw, in their experiments with time, are only half in earnest; but Joyce, Huxley and Virginia Woolf all have a background of real thinking for their imaginative treatment of time. H. V. Routh mentions a number of other authors who have struggled with the same problem.[2] That Eliot himself regards a vague awareness of modern ideas on this subject as common property, is shown amusingly in *The Rock*, in which one of the workmen is made to declare: "There's some new notion about time, what says that the past — what's be'ind you — is what's goin' to 'appen in the future, bein' as the future 'as already 'appened. I 'aven't 'ad time to get the 'ang of it yet; but — ."

Though novel time concepts have been handled by many writers, however, it is doubtful whether they have often been made part of such a comprehensive view of existence as in Eliot's poetry, a view which comprises rationalism, mysticism and religious dogma.

Mysticism — Christian and Oriental — has also become quite fashionable among writers. When Somerset Maugham briefly introduced the thoughts of St. John of the Cross into *Of Human Bondage*, he was probably acting on an original impulse. But when, in *The Razor's Edge*, he introduced yoga it seemed a tribute to the fashion of the moment. Aldous Huxley's has probably been the strongest influence in our time in popularising the mysticism of the East. But Eliot's influence has been far from negligible, and one must recognise that his interest in mysticism is at least as original and deep-seated as Huxley's.

---

[1] *Essays in Criticism, Works*, III, p. 5.   [2] *Eng. Lit. & I. in 20th C.*, pp. 144—5.

Here again Eliot has achieved a more comprehensive synthesis than most writers. His mysticism is not merely of the same colourless variety as Huxley's. Huxley rejects historical Christianity because it interferes with his idea of a God without attributes and without a Church. Eliot comes near freeing himself from Chrstian dogma at times. But his synthesis of ideas is yet dominated by Christianity. And, what is more, it is *ordered* by Christianity, so that it has a core, and is no longer the mere conglomeration of notions which with most of our contemporaries passes for a view of life.

Eliot achieves his synthesis without doing violence to Christian orthodoxy. But he does take up Christian positions which in many respects are extreme, whilst he leaves other positions undefended. And in so doing he has helped to change Christianity, if ever so slightly. We remember his words about Christianity having to be constantly adapted into something that can be believed in (which, he said, had nothing to do with liberal theology). By his own work he has contributed to the adaption of Christianity to the consciousness of our own age. To illustrate this we need only remember the way in which he repeatedly suggests the Redemption of mankind, not by "the blood of the Lamb", but through the realisation of timelessness. Miss Helen Gardner objects to the introduction of Krishna in "The Dry Salvages" on the ground that "there is an unbridgeable gap between a religion that despairs of the material world and a religion that is built upon faith in an event by which the material world was not condemned but saved. It is in their view of history and the time-process that Christianity and Hinduism are most irreconcilably opposed; the incarnations of Vishnu give no significance to history, as does the unique Incarnation of Christian belief".[1] Miss Gardner's objection is valid, but unnecessary. Eliot envisages redemption *from* history *and* redemption *of* history; and there are two opinions among Christians as to whether the material world is or is not included in the work of Salvation. By clinging to the doctrine of the Incarnation ("the intersection of the timeless with time") rather than to that of the Atonement, Eliot finds it possible to believe in Redemption through the realisation of timelessness without alienating himself from Christianity. In this way, and in spite of Miss Gardner's objection, he manages to reconcile Christianity and Hinduism. For this kind of reconciliation I think there is a growing understanding among religious-minded people to-day. There is even a growing tendency to recognise the partial validity of primitive cults — or, on the other hand, to include both Christianity and primitive worship in the rejection of all religious belief whatsoever.

It is curious to see that Eliot registered concern at the interest taken by I. A. Richards, Irving Babbitt and Ezra Pound in Chinese philosophy.

---

[1] F3 p. 69, note.

This interest indicated, he feared, "a deracination from the Christian tradition".[1] If this were true, Eliot, with his similar interests, would be equally uprooted from Christianity. Like most poet-critics, he often comments on himself in commenting on others. But perhaps he did not mean that the interest in Chinese philosophy actually *caused* the deracination from the religion of the West, in which case of course he is on perfectly safe ground. And I think it may be said that in his own poetry an interest in Eastern mysticism neither indicates nor causes a deracination from Christianity. The latter is big enough to comprise many tendencies. The Christian God is both an impersonal principle and our Heavenly Father, and though it may be dangerous in the long run to stress only one of his aspects, as Eliot does, yet it cannot be said to be wrong to do so temporarily, least of all in poetry.

Whether or not the poet's later works can be called "religious poetry", is a matter of definition. *The Rock* and *Murder in the Cathedral,* which were written for special Church occasions, have a more direct devotional character than most of the other compositions, and this character is shared to some extent by the Good Friday poem "East Coker". In the remainder of his poetry he strives, generally — but not always — with great success, to avoid a didactic attitude and to voice merely his personal religious feelings. But he cannot altogether avoid making his poetry the vehicle of a Christian message; and in any case he is commonly understood to do so, which again must affect his attitude. In this respect he is perhaps less fortunate than W. H Auden. The latter's Christmas Oratorio *For the Time Being* is not held to be more than tentatively, "poetically" Christian, judging by the critiques that have come to my notice.

However, if Eliot's is not religious poetry in the sense of devotional verse, it is certainly not just lyrical effusiveness into which religion enters as more or less fortuitous material. In Donne's poetry he found only "a vast jumble of incoherent erudition on which he [Donne] drew for purely poetic effects". A malicious critic might say the same of Eliot's poetry. But he would be wrong, and I think Eliot was wrong about Donne. In our discussion of poetic belief, we decided that belief was emotional attachment, and such attachment cannot be absent from poetry if the latter is at all moving. The conceptual suggestions of Eliot's poetry (as of Donne's) call for belief. And not only must the reader believe, strongly or less strongly, in order to enjoy, but the poet himself must believe, intensely or less intensely, in order to create. Eliot's synthesis, in my opinion, appeals very strongly to the belief of our age.

It is a synthesis which may not be very original in its details, as Dr. Routh and others have pointed out. But it is original and great in the final combination which it effects, a combination which welds otherwise

[1] UPC p. 132, note.

disparate elements of the outlook of our time in an organised whole: there
are inconsistencies, but they appear rather as different facets of one body
of philosophy than as contradictory fragments of various philosophies.
This combination has been possible because the thoughts of the age have
been deeply experienced by a personality which has not been deterred by
doctrines or prejudices (I am speaking of the poet) from creating a unity
of its experiences. Perhaps it was a boon that Eliot came late to Christianity:
he assimilated more ideas than he might have done if he had come to anchor
at an earlier date.

"A great poet, in writing himself, writes his time", said Eliot. He
himself not only writes his time, or he no longer does only that. If he
did, it would mean confusion, because our time is confused in many ways.
He is also instrumental in *creating* the outlook of his time by amalgamating
its scattered ideas: Eliot praised Joyce for trying to do something like this.
The structure of *Ulysses,* he said, "is simply a way of controlling, of
ordering, of giving a shape and a significance to the immense panorama
of futility and anarchy which is contemporary history".[1] Joyce, however,
imposed an artificial significance on his world for the purposes of art
only. Eliot in some measure does the same thing, as when he uses the four
seasons and the four elements as a scaffolding for the *Quartets.* Poetry
can create a significance which isn't there. But both Joyce and Eliot, particularly the latter, are saved from artificiality by their awareness of and
their loyalty to the unifying experience. Eliot finds the union of scepticism
and faith, hedonism and asceticism significant because it has been significant to him. And his poetry is "the expression of a totality of unified
interests",[2] to use his description of Wordsworth's and Coleridge's work.

In Donne's cosmology, the geographical curiosity of his age played an
important part. To-day we witness explorations still more interesting and
astounding in their results than the discoveries of new continents. The
workings of the human mind, the history of "pre-historic" times, the nature
of the physical universe, are being revealed to us, in how permanent a light
we do not know. The general implications of these discoveries are related
in Eliot's poetry to the received truths of tradition. And they are more
significant as ideas than the maps and compasses which Donne used for
decoration.

Eliot, then, has not only given our age a poetic idiom, as has sufficiently been recognised, but has also shown the way to an integral philosophy. My calling it integral does not mean that it accepts all tendencies of
our time or takes cognisance of all its spiritual features. It repudiates

---

[1] "Ulysses, order, & myth", *Dial,* Nov. 1923. Also quoted by Matthiessen, ATSE
p. 40.   [2] UPC p. 81.

mechanism[1] and materialistic determinism. It repudiates equalitarianism and all sorts of mass loyalties. It also has little to do with the exact sciences and has not caught up with atomic physics. But there is enough left, as I have endeavoured to show. And what is left out is generally left out because is is incompatible with the *Primat des Spiritualen*. For Eliot's synthesis, human *ratio* and all, is based on the recognition of the supernatural. And "to believe in the supernatural", he said in an address to Unitarian clergymen, "is not simply to believe that after living a successful, material, and fairly virtuous life here one will continue to exist in the best-possible substitute for this world, or that after living a starved and stunted life there one will be compensated with all the good things one has gone without: it is to believe that the supernatural is the greatest reality here and now".[2] A supernatural, or call it an irrational, principle is at work in the combination of the very elements of Eliot's outlook: it is not for nothing that it is expressed in poetry and could hardly have been expressed otherwise without being mutilated. He has indicated a basis, perhaps the only basis, on which an integration of thought can take place to-day.

One final aspect of Eliot's philosophical outlook must be mentioned. Mr. Delmore Schwartz regards him as "a culture hero", chiefly because experience in the modern world has become international, "the true causes of many of the things in our lives are world-wide", and Eliot has been able to interpret this internationalism. "Since the future is bound to be international", concludes Mr Schwartz, "we are all the bankrupt heirs of the ages, and the moments of the crisis expressed in Eliot's work are a prophecy of the crises of our own future in regard to love, religious belief, good and evil, the good life and the nature of the just society. *The Waste Land* will soon be as good as new".[3]

Mr. Schwartz's arguments are sometimes fanciful, but his main conclusions stand. Eliot is a cosmopolitan, and apparently wants to be, for he addresses himself to those readers who have a cosmopolitan culture. I would add that if Eliot is to be regarded as an international prophet it is not only because he has stated the dilemmas of the modern *déraciné*, the international man, but because he has brought together in his work various cultures hitherto separated in time and space — Phrygian, Indian, Roman, nineteenth century American and modern European.

---

[1] Strangely enough, it has little to say of the outward mechanisation of life and still less of the value of country life. Mechanisation is reflected in the characters portrayed, and it is dealt with in *The Rock*, but otherwise these things do not seem to have interested Eliot very much as a poet.   [2] *Chr. Register*, 19 Oct. 1933.
[3] SELCR pp. 43—50.

Four Quartets.

The impression that we have gained of the attitudes and ideas which form the background of Eliot's poetry should help us to approach what are probably the most difficult poems from the conceptual point of view, the *Four Quartets*, with the right expectations. I mean expectations which help us to read without interrupting our enjoyment to puzzle out meanings. Just as *The Waste Land* is often misinterpreted, or understood in a stereotyped fashion, so we find that the *Quartets*, too, are often read very superficially.

A common conception of the *Four Quartets* is that they are "religious poetry", implying something dogmatically narrow, and that their "subject" is religious ecstasy. This conception, though not far from the truth, is sufficiently misleading to merit correction.

In the first place, there is nothing very dogmatic about the *Quartets*. Apart from "East Coker", perhaps, they are less specifically Christian than, for instance, *Ash-Wednesday* or *Murder in the Cathedral*. Richard Lea wrote a somewhat over-excited review of the *Quartets*, but was perfectly right when he found that, compared with *Murder in the Cathedral*, there was "greater depth, greater intensity, and greater beauty in these quartets, but less Christianity. Is it possible", he asked, "that the level reached here is beyond Christianity? A non-Christian mystic can feel just as much at home here as a Christian".[1]

The poems are the work of a man who has not only found a faith, but who has had to make a faith for himself, by integrating all that he has believed in or been attached to or even been strongly interested in. In *The Waste Land* there was still a conflict between religious faith and anthropological knowledge. Religion could hardly be ultimately true if it simply arose out of the need for food and safety. In the *Quartets* the strife has been resolved, the "primitive terror" and the primitive gods have been recognised in the modern world as something more than symbols. And Emerson, Bradley, Bergson, Patanjali, St. John of the Cross are all incorporated in an all-embracing Christianity. No voice is wholly lost if it has once sounded with authority or charm in Eliot's ears. He passes "the stages of his age and youth". Even Shelley was not drowned for good in his consciousness: there is much in his conception of an all-pervading love that is related to Shelley's idealism, only Christianised. Of a poet's development it may indeed be said that *il n'abandonne rien en route*. Thus we see that tradition, according to Eliot's early idea of it, operates on the level of individuals as well as on that of culture. The whole past history of a man composes an ideal order, and the sense of this order compels a man to write with his own past in his bones, to adapt the famous phrases from "Tradition and the Individual Talent". One's allegiance can change, as Eliot's

---

[1] *Adelphi*, July/Sept. 1945.

changed in respect of Babbitt or Bradley, but one's views and attitudes can hardly change so completely that the old ideas lose all their appeal and do not present themselves in moments of doubt as the only tenable ones. The hovering between two or more worlds is not only a personal affliction, but the affliction of our time, and we must be grateful to the poet who can help us to get a footing. I do not subscribe more than Eliot to the Arnold-Richards view that poetry can save us, ultimately, but at least it can help us over a difficult crossing. It is the difficulty to-day of integrating theories of life into a view of life that makes the work of poets so significant from an ideological point of view. And this applies eminently to the *Four Quartets*. It is by their ability to fuse various elements that poets can serve as prophets to the contemporary world.

Eliot has achieved his fusion, not only because he is a great poet, but also because of his education, and the different environments that he has become familiar with. Psychologically, how could it be otherwise? A great literary artist must needs write his spiritual autobiography.[1] And if, as Eliot sometimes suggests, the actual work of poetic composition is spontaneous, how could it avoid bringing out whatever contents of his mind were amenable to poetic treatment? How could it avoid cutting below surface loyalties to a substratum within himself where chronology holds no sway? Eliot's poetry is existentialist in that he recognises what actually comes into being. But it is essentialist in that an ideal unity is imposed on it by the oneness of his sensibility and the oneness of his conscious beliefs. Here is the explanation of the diversity and the unity of the *Four Quartets*.

In creating his philosophy in this way, Eliot is not entirely guiltless of the offence that he lays at the door of Blake and Goethe: he philosophises on his own. But it proves to be no offence. And in any case he was forced into speculation in order to save his mental and spiritual integrity. His despair in the *Waste Land* phase was a metaphysical despair, due in part to the disbelief in the personality which philosophy had inspired in him. He had to fight to remain self-possessed, and for this reason his poetry became a revolt against much that he never succeeded in freeing himself from entirely: against Bradleyan philosophy, with its sceptical, analytical tendencies, against psycho-analysis which dissolves the soul, against mass movements which obliterate the self. His dialogues with his self in the early poems are a sign of his Bradleyan stage. They disappear in the *Four Quartets,* where "I" and "you" really stand for I and you, and not just for "I". In section II of "Little Gidding", the poet says, "So I assumed a double part". But it is a double part different from Prufrock's duplication of himself. In "Little Gidding" the division, or doubling, of the personality is a deliberate fiction. In "The Love Song" it seems to cover a real division.

---

[1] Cp. "Pensées", EAM p. 145.

The deeper we go into the *Four Quartets* the more complicated do the strains and counter-strains which constitute it appear. They do form a unified outlook, but in any case it is an outlook which comprehends considerably more than the Christian view, and which at the same time is refined almost beyond Christianity.

As to the notion that religious ecstasy is the subject of the poems, it is far too restricted, as the foregoing reflections will already have made clear. It would be equally true to say that the poems deal with spiritual discipline. We remember the lines from "East Coker":

> To arrive where you are, to get from where you are not,
> You must go by a way wherein there is no ecstasy.

While it is yet true to say the poems are in part *about* ecstasy, they are also an exploration of the way of ecstasy, and an attempt to recapture and hold for contemplaton the feeling of insight that was given in moments of illumination. This leads the poet to turn over in his mind the central truths of religion to see if he can recognise in them any of his inspired certainties. What he is writing about is faith. And ecstasy is a means, not an end.

"Rational assent may arrive late, intellectual conviction may come slowly, but they come inevitably without violence to honesty and nature. To put the sentiments in order is a later, and an immensely difficult task".[1] This statement, which so much resembles a confession, is illustrated in the *Four Quartets*. They are personal and emotional, perhaps more than those people realise who like to call them intellectual. And the ideas which the emotions bring forward are probably not in the perfect order of orthodoxy which we find in Eliot's criticism. Moreover, we cannot expect, nor perhaps should we hope, that such intellectual order will ever be established in his poetry. But the emotions have an order of their own, and a synthesising power, which are equally valuable.

The Poet and the Critic.

If we now turn to Eliot's critical views and compare them with the attitudes and ideas of his poetry, we shall find, as is to be expected, a general correspondence in tendencies and in most important points of belief. (We need not here concern ourselves with his aesthetic ideas and his actual poetic technique, two domains between which a number of critics have found a wide divergence.) As far as the attitude to common problems of life and death are concerned, the poet and the critic are, on the whole, at one. But not entirely so. And the differences between them may be of some interest in their implications for his poetry.

---

[1] "Sec. Thoughts", SE p. 453.

In the *Prufrock* and *Waste Land* phase, Eliot's poetry and his prose share the disgust felt for modern civilisation based on technical achievements, mechanical pleasure, insular prejudices, a crumbling social order and a general corruption of values. So-called "progress" is regarded as a process of decay, characterised by self-indulgence and greediness, a process begun in the sixteenth century. Only the lower classes seem to have kept their vitality. Both the poet and the critic are sceptics in metaphysical questions, but recognise the need for a spiritual discipline. This is vividly brought out in *The Waste Land.*

The poetry, however, is at once more despondent, more facetious and more bewildered in mood than the prose, which is serious in a more or less uniform way (Eliot himself speaks of a certain "pontifical solemnity"[1]). This difference is natural enough, but there is more to it than the mere imaginative difference between poetry and prose. His *Weltschmerz,* his suggestions of Inferno, his continual sense of the loneliness of man, the sterility of love, the unfeelingness of nature, the unrelatedness of things, represent a definite attitude only found with difficulty in his prose. It seems that Bradley's disintegrating examination of the world and of the self has a good deal to do with this attitude. To his poetry also belongs a feeling of ubiquitous evil, and above all the view of Life (not only a particular aspect of life or a particular civilisation) as futile, meaningless and pointless. To his poetry further belong his sustained irony, and the grim, sardonic amusement he extracts from the contemplation of futility. Nor do we find in his prose the pervasive feeling of fear by which his early poetry is haunted, particularly the fear of facing a transcendent reality; or the culmination of fear and despondency in the death-wish. Such special ideas as the present-day corruption of sex and the baneful influence of the Jews seem to be peculiar to his poetry. But then again, though incertitude and doubt are found often enough in both his fields, his poetry is turned more towards the hope of religion and the search for connectedness and meaning than is his prose. There is a watching for the unique moment and the exceptional situation, as in "Eeldrop and Appleplex", to catch a glimpse of a possible something behind appearances. The poetry sometimes dwells on the intimations of immortality, of salvation, of the virtue of suffering. And, particularly in *The Waste Land,* it finds inspiration in Hindu and Buddhist asceticism.

The wider range of his poetry may be accounted for by the fact that a person who is shy or doubtful of his opinions more readily goes into the open under the camouflage of art than in full uniform. A writer often reveals more of his mind in imaginative writing than in straightforward exposition. But I think in this case another explanation is equally to the point. Eliot, judging by his prose writings, was at first much more inte-

---

[1] Pref. to SW 1928.

rested in literature *toute .simple* than in philosophy or politics or anything else. A young new poet himself, he was experimenting to sound his resources and to found his technique. Even G. M. Hopkins, that passionate poet, was more interested, according to his own statement, in "design, pattern, or what I am in the habit of calling *inscape*" than in the substance of his verses. No wonder Eliot was, who had been schooled by Laforgue and Pound.

The more we stress his preoccupation with technique, the less we can stress the earnestness of his poetic beliefs. To some extent the conceptions which we find in his poetry of this period and not in his prose are simply decorative material. His reliance on Dante and Jessie Weston and others points in the same direction. Presumably in his early poems he gave poetic assent to a number of ideas which meant relatively little to him in "real life". But then it must also be added that many of these ideas did come to mean more for him, and this may partly have been because once incorporated in his poetry they cast their spell over him and became part of himself. And of course we must not deprive the concepts and attitudes of his early poetry of all seriousness and urgency. (We shall attempt in our next chapter an estimation of the importance that Eliot attached to technique, compared with the importance he attached to ideas and purpose.)

A comparison of the underlying ideas of his poetry of the *Ash-Wednesday* period with the ideas of his prose writings of the same period shows a general correspondence in the movement away from cultural satire and towards religious affirmation. But, probably because the prose writings at least take so many Christian beliefs for granted, the total impression is that the poetry lags behind in the matter of faith, or rather that the faith it contains is more violently and persistently questioned than that of the essays. In a way this is very illuminating. It may be hard to write poetry or drama which moves undisturbedly either to affirmation or negation. A certain admixture of hesitation and doubt, a certain friction might seem to be necessary and fruitful to the creation of art. Thus there would not only be a category of "poetic assent", but also one of "poetic dissent". Perhaps lyric-dramatic poetry, reflecting the mind of the poet, especially needs doubt. Drama may rely on conflicting forces of a more external order. But it cannot be merely external. And, as Ronald Peacock observes,[1] Eliot's one attempt at strict drama from this earlier period, *Sweeney Agonistes*, remained a fragment because the main character was conceived as too passive. Later the author created figures with a positive purpose or energy (Becket, Harry), whose drama lay either in overcoming their own personal difficulties or in the fact that they were the battle-grounds of higher powers, or in both these things.

---

[1] Cf. *Poet in the Theatre*, pp. 9—10.

In Eliot's latest work the poetry is mystical, the prose logical, though the point of departure is the same.

In the *Quartets* mysticism joins hands with philosophical idealism. The positive side of Bradley's philosophy, his theory of the Absolute and of Reality, now has its turn. And together with Hinduism and what there is of Buddhism, it points to a position beyond Christianity, if it does not actually take us there. Aristotle's conception of form as meaning and teleology is recruited in support of the poet's mysticsim. All this, needless to say, is absent from the essays. The poetry is also concerned, far more than are the essays, with personal salvation.

The prose writings, on the other hand, have the political field to themselves. The statement of the politico-cultural alternatives before us, the propounding of the idea of a Christian Society with all its implications, the consideration of Catholic policies, all belong to the essays. They also deal with cultural and social questions, the derivation of morality from religion, and specific moral problems, especially economic ones. And the essays explicitly vindicate the intellectual way to Christianity and the intellectual relation to Christianity which the poetry only illustrates to a small degree.

To sum up, we may say that in spite of a general correspondence between the poetic concepts and the ideas expressed in the prose, a good deal enters into the poetry that finds little or no room in the essays.

That the poet should be more personal and more self-revelatory than the critic is not surprising. Nor is it strange that the poetry should make more of the emotional and picturesque elements of philosophy and religion than do the essays. But what about the theme of asceticism? Can it be said to have an emotional and picturesque character suitable to poetry? And what of such relatively abstract ideas as that of the perpetual cycle? Further, how can poetry breathe in the rarefied atmosphere of mysticism?

Now Eliot's leaning towards asceticism is undoubtedly connected in some way with his feeling for poetry. His poetic sensibility is not in the least restricted, but it is peculiarly responsive to bareness and dryness — of expression, of imagery and of thought. And here, perhaps, we may see an example of thought directed by sensibility.

But asceticism is also part of a philosophical complex in which the perpetual cycle and the groping towards transcendent Reality are other important factors. In his prose Eliot leaves ultimate questions well alone, and is content to accept Anglican orthodoxy. In his poetry, on the other hand, he is a metaphysical explorer. It is hard to avoid the conclusion that he regards poetry as the most adequate means of metaphysical exploration. It enables him to deal freely with beliefs which do not rest on logical demonstration, and which can only be justified poetically. And it gives him liberty to reach out beyond and beside Catholic belief without actually questioning the positions of the Church. Thus both individualism and obedience to authority are given their due, the former chiefly in his poetry, the latter mainly in his prose. As Dante in *The Divine Comedy* is crowned and mitred king and bishop over himself, so Eliot assumes the privilege of the poet to determine his own actions, and consequently he can do without the restrictions of political and ecclesiastical organisations.[1]

There is also another consideration, however. The ideas of the poetry form a pattern among themselves, which, for its extension, requires a wide field of reference. The synthesis which we have indicated constitutes such a pattern. The pattern comprises likenesses and contrasts. Likenesses, for instance, in the ideas of the cycle of determinism, the vanity of life, askesis and mystical illumination; contrasts in the opposition between such ideas and visions of temporal beauty, or between visions of temporal ugliness and divinations of timeless beauty.

The pattern of ideas, or "the music of ideas" to use Richards's phrase, depends largely on formal construction. And viewed in this light, the ideas lose some of their independent, philosophical significance. That they are actually ordered to some extent to formal requirements is beyond doubt. To *what* extent neither we nor the poet can exactly determine. But we may get some idea of it by an investigation of Eliot's technique. His synthesis of attitudes and concepts forms part of a still wider design, that of form and matter; and this we must now briefly consider.

VIII.

Technique and Thought.

An examination of the relative importance of the formal and conceptual factors of Eliot's poetry.

Having given our attention for so long to the philosophical background of Eliot's poetry, we begin to feel, perhaps, in spite of our precautionary reservations as to the partial and restricted nature of our investigations, that we are exaggerating the importance of this background. The time has come to relate Eliot's ideological material to his technique, and to remind ourselves of the claims of the latter. Which of these two factors, technique or thought, we may ask, has the final word in Eliot's composition? The importance which each of the two taken separately has already acquired in literature and popular opinion, makes such an enquiry a need literary criticism.

Most critics seem to look upon Eliot as "a philosopher whose thoughts must be expressed in poetry".[2] Mr. H. R. Williamson finds that his superiority over Pound was due to the fact that he "was all the time concerned chiefly with what he said, whereas Pound was more interested in how he said it".[3] And Dr. Richards, though he did think that Eliot in *The Waste*

---

[1] Cp. "Dante", SE p. 261.   [2] Routh: *Eng. Lit. & I. in 20th C.*, p. 161.
[3] *Poetry of T.S.E.*, p. 72.

Land divorced poetry from belief, regards all expression as being in some sense purposive,[1] and therefore meaningful. Against the emphasis on ideas and purpose may be mobilised many of Eliot's own statements in which he vindicates the primacy of form. But his general theoretical position, we have seen, is ambiguous,; and anyhow it would have to be compared with his practice. We have considered his critical views. We must now examine his poetry, to see if it can throw any light on this question.

There are one or two pitfalls that we must avoid. The first is one that better critics than the present writer have stumbled into, that of taking a too superficial view of the relation between form and matter, seeing, for instance, in the broken structure of a poem a way of expressing the broken appearance of our civilisation. This is a view which Eliot has encouraged by his much-abused words about poetry having to be difficult to-day because of the complexity of modern life.[2] If Eliot meant simply that the difficulty of living was to be symbolised by the difficulty of construing a poem, I think his opinion was rashly given and unmeditated. But he probably meant something more and different. Language, he said, had to be dislocated if necessary, to fit the poet's *meaning*. The difficulty, in other words, was one of thought, and the expression of thought, not one merely inherent in the environment and reflected mechanically by the poet from the environment to his poetic form. Yet we find so acute a critic as Paul Elmer More presenting Eliot as "a lyric prophet of chaos", by whom "the confusion of life" is "reflected in the disorganized flux of images; its lack of clear meaning in the obscurity of language"; in whom there is "something fundamentally amiss" since he can employ "for an experience born of Anglo-Catholic faith a metrical form and a freakishness of punctuation suitable for the presentation of life regarded as without form and void".[3] Mr. Yvor Winters, who is inclined to blame the influence of Henry Adams on Eliot, takes up the cry. Eliot, he says, "surrenders his form to his subject", making it chaotic in order to express chaos.[4]

Now there is obviously *some* justice in such accusations, though it is hard to see why they should be so accusatory. A confused or fragmentary reality will tend to produce a confused or fragmentary representation of it. An ordered reality will tend to produce a neat representation. Eliot's early poetry describes a fragmentary world and a fragmentary view of life. But there is an immense difference between the description of reality and the organisation of a poem. More and Winters, one feels, have not taken the mind of the poet and the poetic process into account. More's objection to the form of *Ash-Wednesday*, for instance, would be valid if the poem were intended to be an ordered exposition of Anglo-Catholic doctrines. But the mere idea is ridiculous. The poem is obviously something quite different:

---

[1] Cf. Richards: *Mencius on the Mind*, p. 91.　　[2] MP, SE p. 289.　　[3] "Cleft Eliot", *Sat. Rev. of Lit.*, vol. 9, 1932. Also in SELCR.　　[4] SELCR p. 110.

it is the moulding of the poet's mind into patterns of sound and meaning. And I can see no reason why even an unswerving Christian faith should not be expressed poetically in fragments. We may make allowance for a certain amount of direct imitation of the object in the form of the poetry, and suggestion *of* the object *by* the form of the poetry, but as an explanation of the relation between form and matter, this view is altogether inadequate.

The second pitfall we must avoid is the temptation to make sharp distinctions between the "prosy" parts of the poems and the "poetical" parts. In the *Quartets* and the plays there are passages in which the poet drops into the language of reasoning. Eliot's poetry certainly moves on many different levels, and the directness with which ideas are expressed varies considerably. We can recognise the prosy passages quite easily, but it would not do to tear them from their contexts, or, on the other hand, to read the lyrical passages alone. Since the general purpose is poetic, all the parts of the poems must be included in our examination of technique and thought. It was Coleridge, I think, who first declared that "a poem of any length neither can be, nor ought to be, all poetry. Yet", he goes on, "if an harmonious whole is to be produced, the remaining parts must be preserved in keeping with the poetry; and this can be no otherwise effected than by such a studied selection and artificial arrangement, as will partake of one, though not a peculiar property of poetry".[1]

Eliot's poetic development shows him struggling from the first out of the confines of romantic lyricism towards the conditions of drama on the one hand and music on the other. It was the possibilities of drama, including the dramatic monologue, that he chiefly explored in his early poetry. The theoretical side of this interest is exemplified by such essays as " 'Rhetoric' and Poetic Drama", "A Dialogue on Poetic Drama" and the *Elizabethan Essays*. The poetry of his "dramatic" phase has a strong descriptive element, usually combined with the critical expression of attitude or opinion. The dramatic presentation seems at first to have been employed chiefly to give objectivity to description and attitude, to allow the poet to escape from his own person and speak with the tongues of the old and experienced. Gradually he became interested in the opportunities which drama afforded to appeal to members of an audience at different levels of understanding; but his attempt to realise these opportunities (*Sweeney Agonistes*) was given up. He also came to see that "the most direct means of social 'usefulness' for poetry, is the theatre".[2] And though by this he did not mean that the theatre was the best means of "getting a message across", the plays that he wrote soon after he made this statement, namely *The Rock* and *Murder in the Cathedral* suggest that the idea of communicating a message was in his mind as well. At any rate, the dramatic form of poetry is the form that can least dispense with a sustained meaning.

---

[1] *Biographia Literaria*, Ch. XIV.   [2] UPC p. 153.

To teach, however, was never Eliot's desire, or at least never his success or his pleasure, unless he could teach by example. He was in a dilemma. He regarded the theatre as "the ideal medium for poetry",[1] he admired many of the Elizabethan and Jacobean playwrights, but he could not write drama himself without becoming didactic. It may have been the feeling that the dramatic form was leading him up a blind alley that made him turn more resolutely to the exploration of musical form. The *Four Quartets* and the lecture on *The Music of Poetry* are symptomatic of this new emphasis. It was intimately accompanied by a contemplative tendency, which is more marked in the *Quartets* than it ever was before. The *Quartets* are definitely musical in structure and quality rather than dramatic, and contemplative rather than descriptive: their themes are repeated, dropped and repeated again, and only the conclusion of "Little Gidding" shows tangible progression.

Eliot was long in two minds about musicality. It was proclaimed by the French Symbolists, echoing Poe. "De la musique avant toute chose", cried Verlaine. And Pound declared that "it is the musical phrase that matters". But there was Tennyson, there were the Pre-Raphaelites, there was Swinburne and there was the early Yeats to show that what could be done with music in English had been done, even to excess. So in his early compositions Eliot avoided, if not musicality, at least melodiousness as much as he was able without resorting to Whitmanesque prose-poetry. He was confirmed in this avoidance by such writers as Julien Benda, who, in his *Belphégor,* indignantly denounced the effeminate cult of music.[2]

There is no doubt, however, that Eliot has a fine ear for musical cadence and musical composition, though he says he is ignorant of the technical subtleties of music. A poem, he states, often begins in his mind as a fragment of rhythm. So it was not surprising that his sensibility and his poetic antecedents re-asserted themselves in a whole-hearted surrender to the music of poetry.

The influence of music, one might think, would make for a poetry as purified of ideas and conceptual meaning as possible. This probably holds good in many kinds of poetry inspired by music. But in the combination of music and contemplation which we find in the *Four Quartets,* there is, we have seen, a reaching out beyond the bounds of ordinary meaning to a transcendent reality which by its very existence implies a teleology even for the purest art.

> Words move, music moves
> Only in time; but that which is only living
> Can only die. Words, after speech, reach
> Into the silence. Only by the form, the pattern,
> Can words or music reach
> The stillness — —[3]

---

[1] UPC p. 153.   [2] Cf. *Belphégor,* p. 36.   [3] BN V.

Thus a relation between form and meaning, technique and thought, is re-established. It still remains for us to determine it. To do this with greater confidence, we must examine some of the main aspects of Eliot's technique.

Texture, Rhyme and Rhythm.

We will begin with the purely formal aspects. These, of course, are abstractions. There are no purely formal *elements* in poetry. Sound must be pitched and intoned according to its sense, and rhythm is rhythm of meaning as well as of stress, length and tone. This is probably why Eliot doubts "whether, from the point of view of *sound* alone, any word is more or less beautiful than any other — within its own language".[1] I nevertheless find it difficult to accept his view: as far as one can judge by the sound alone, the word "spiteful" is more pleasing than the word "gracious". But as one might expect from such a view, the words in Eliot's poems rarely seem to be chosen from any obvious consideration of phonetic harmony, such as variations of vowel and consonant sounds, assonance and alliteration. If we may illustrate from the art of painting, his texture rarely has the startling coloristic *naïveté* of a Rousseau, the lushness of a Rubens or the limpidity of a Reynolds. But it has something of the blurredness of a Turner, the sullenness of a Gauguin or the asceticism of a Manet. He can produce a beauty of texture that is something apart and relies more on effects of shading within a monochrome medium than on richness of contrast. For particular purposes he can create lush and limpid textures as well. But the general impression is one of sobriety, even of prosiness. I have verified this impression by careful comparisons of Eliot's poetry with passages from a number of other poets, ancient and modern: Spenser, Shakespeare, Keats, Tennyson, Browning, Lawrence, Auden. It would take up too much space to repeat these comparisons here. But a confrontation of a few typical lines by Eliot with a few of Shakespeare's may be useful as an example:

> — Yet I'll not shed her blood;
> Nor scar that whiter skin of hers than snow,
> And smooth as monumental alabaster. (*Othello*, V, 2, 3—6).

> So I would have had him leave,
> So I would have had her stand and grieve,
> So he would have left
> As the soul leaves the body torn and bruised,
> As the mind deserts the body it has used.
> I should find
> Some way incomparably light and deft,
> Some way we both should understand,
> Simple and faithless as a smile and shake of the hand.
>   ("La Figlia Che Piange".)

---

[1] MUS p. 17.

It is not Eliot's monotonous repetitions that mark the chief difference (I do not use the word "monotonous" in a disparaging sense). Shakespeare has similar repetitions (giving an all but monotonous effect) in the lines before and after those I have quoted. But there is a great difference in the patterns of sound. Shakespeare has especially an almost incomparable variety of vowels. In the above lines from *Othello* the stressed or half-stressed vowels are these:

[e], [ai], [ɔ], [e], [ə], [ʌ], [ɔ], [aː], [æ], [ai], [i], [əː], [ou], [uː], [ɔ], [e], [æ], [aː].

The consonants, too, show a fair variety, and when the complete words are read out the effect is marvellously melodious.

In Eliot's lines, there is a preponderance, at first, of unstressed and neutral vowels. The words "would have" are in each case unstressed, and the following "had" only weakly stressed. Full stress only occurs on the "so" and the last words of the first three lines. In the last four lines the vowel scheme (apart from the unstressed ones) is as follows:

[ai], [ai], [ʌ], [ei], [ɔ], [ai], [e], [ʌ], [ei], [ou], [ʌ], [æ], [i], [ei], [ai], [ei], [æ].

Thus in 27 syllables of Shakespeare's poem there are 11 different vowel sounds; out of 34 syllables in Eliot's poem there are 8 different vowel sounds (excluding unstressed vowels in both cases). But more important than this mathematical difference, which I do not take too seriously, for it is an inappropriate way of estimating poetry, is the difference of pattern obtained by the juxtaposition of the sounds, a difference which, I think, eludes exact description.

A comparison of Eliot's texture with that of leading poets of the seventeenth century proper and the eighteenth century, reveals a far greater similarity. This may be due to Eliot's conscious admiration of the Metaphysical poets and the classicists. But it may also be due to a certain consanguinity and parallelism of talent, temperament and purpose. In the matter of texture these poets have in common a general finish and in some cases polish, which makes the sound music reliable and serviceable but not very differentiated, and not very much exploited for particular effects. Both vowel and consonant sounds are neat and orderly, submitting to the sound patterns of the verse lines and allowing the words to run on unimpeded.

Milton is famed for his sonority, but the texture of his verse often closely resembles that of Eliot's:

> Come, come; no time for lamentation now,
> Nor much more cause. Samson hath quit himself
> Like Samson, and heroicly hath finished
> A life heroic, on his enemies
> Fully revenged — hath left them years of mourning
> Through all Philistian bounds; to Israel
> Honour hath left and freedom, let but them

Find courage to lay hold on this occasion;
To himself and father's house eternal fame;
And, which is best and happiest yet, all this
With God not parted from him, as was feared,
But favouring and assisting to the end.
Nothing is here for tears, nothing to wail
Or knock the breast; no weakness, no contempt,
Dispraise or blame; nothing but well and fair,
And what may quiet us in a death so noble.

(*Samson Agonistes,* 11. 1708 ff.)

No. For the Church is stronger for this action,
Triumphant in adversity. It is fortified
By persecution: supreme, so long as men will die for it.
Go, weak sad men, lost erring souls, homeless in earth or heaven.
Go where the sunset reddens the last grey rock
Of Brittany, or the Gates of Hercules.
Go venture shipwreck on the sullen coasts
Where blackamoors make captive Christian men;
Go to the northern seas confined with ice
Where the dead breath makes numb the hand, makes dull
      the brain;
Find an oasis in the desert sun,
Go seek alliance with the heathen Saracen,
To share his filthy rites, and try to snatch
Forgetfulness in his libidinous courts,
Oblivion in the fountain by the date-tree;
Or sit and bite your nails in Aquitaine.

(*Murder in the Cathedral,* p. 84)

It may be partly because *Samson Agonistes* has very free rhythms and because *Murder in the Cathedral* is deliberately archaic in some respects that the similarity of tone in these poems is often so striking. But, in spite of the coolness which Eliot felt for Milton for a long time, the two poets also seem to be united by a certain similarity of temperament, of acoustic sensibility — and of purpose.

That Eliot masters his sound effects is proved abundantly by the many passages in which the texture, for some reason, is specially rich or elaborate, for instance at the end of "The Love Song" and in the "Landscapes". A line in "Mr. Apollinax" contains what is probably the most concentrated word music that he has composed:

Where worried bodies of drowned men drift down in
   ·   the green silence

Do Eliot's natural genius and inclination lie in the direction of a musicality of sound pattern that he usually denies, or does he have to put himself out purposely to attend to the sound pattern? The truth probably lies somewhere between these explanations. But it seems to me that the poet's sense of phonetic values is critical rather than creative. His ear is generally (though not always) too fine to allow him to write anything so hideous, from a phonetic point of view, as Wordsworth's "Ode to Duty"; but on the other hand, his imagination does not work with individual sounds, so that they are often left to take care of themselves.

Eliot's use of rhyme follows no definite rules. Sometimes he uses very exacting rhyme schemes, but more often he renounces rhyme altogether. The most diverse schemes can jostle each other in one and the same poem. The characteristic device, however, is the apparently fortuitous rhymes, which occur sporadically, interspersed among unrhymed lines. We find them, for instance, in large parts of *The Waste Land,* in *The Hollow Men,* and in *Ash-Wednesday.* Everything considered, it seems that he employs ryhme opportunistically. But this is no sign of lack of ability or carelessness. It is his achievement to have liberated rhyme in such a way that it decorates suitable points of a poem, instead of having to conform to a mechanical arrangement. "Rhyme", he says, "is neither an essential nor a superfluity". Thus he restores to rhyme its aesthetic dignity. When it is desirable, he jingles, as in "A Cooking Egg" ("sitting—knitting, Sidney—kidney, instruct me—conduct me"). At other times he repeats words to rhyme with themselves, or he muffles the effect by using only half-rhymes and consonances.

In the matter of rhytm, he is no more dogmatic than in the questions of texture and rhyme. He thinks sensibility and practice are more important than theory and that the imitation of recognised models is the best schooling. His indebtedness to French poetry helps to explain his independence of English prosody and the fact that he was able to free himself from regular accentual rhythms.

All poetry can be scanned in two ways: according to the rhythm of natural speech, and according to a systematic metre. In poems of an artificial or solemn diction, one will tend to give preference to the systematic metre. In poems of a conversational style one will give preference to the natural speech rhythm. In both cases a contrapuntal effect is obtained by the simultaneous beat of both rhythms.

The style of Eliot's poems favours the natural speech rhythm. The systematic accompaniment tends to become very faint, and, besides, it constantly changes from iambic to dactylic, etc. But it is important that it is there, for poetry must have some regularity, however remote. Fortunately, our consciousness is able to act as an amplifier to whatever it is directed towards. If we look for redness in a mixture of paints, the colour red, if it is there at all, *saute aux yeux.* And if we are prepared to find rhythm in a poem, the rhythm will soon appear. A usual device for directing our attention to rhythm is the typographical arrangement. If you take a piece of prose and divide it into short lines, its rhythmical qualities will immediately become more marked. And, vice versa, much modern poetry will apparently lose its rhythmical distinction if printed as prose. The difference between

verse and prose can therefore be infinitesimally small. And in some of
Eliot's poetry it is almost negligible. His prose poem "Hysteria" might
well have been printed as follows:

> As she laughed I was aware
> Of becoming involved in her laughter
> And being part of it, until her teeth
> Were only accidental stars
> With a talent for squad-drill.

— — —

Conversely, some of the lines from "The Dry Salvages" would look perfectly
plausible as prose:

It seems, as one becomes older, that the past has another pattern, and
ceases to be a mere sequence — or even a development: the latter a partial
fallacy encouraged by superficial notions of evolution.

It is one of the criteria of verse as distinct from prose that the stressed
syllables are relatively frequent. The proportion of stressed syllables to weak
syllables we may call "stress frequency". Now a number of experiments,
which anyone may carry out for himself, have shown me that the stress
frequency in an average selection of Eliot's poetry is exactly intermediate
between the stress frequency in a representative selection of English poetry
of the kind tending towards prosodic regularity, and that of a representative
selection of English prose (mostly recent). The "free verse" of such as
Whitman, Lawrence, Edith Sitwell and Auden, on the other hand, has
a mean stress frequency which is exactly the same as that of prose, if the
latter is divided into verse lines before one counts the stresses. The highest
stress frequency, as is to be expected, is found in regular verse (43 % in my
analysis), then comes Eliot's verse (39 %), "free verse" and prose (both
36 %), and lastly Eliot's prose (29 %). (The low stress frequency of Eliot's
prose is probably due to its discursive nature.)

There would seem to be more variation (from poem to poem and
passage to passage) in the stress frequency of Eliot's verse than in the free
verse of most other poets. Eliot, it is evident, has a wide rhythmic range,
and great elasticity. But this again means that he does not once and for
all take up an extreme position in the neighbourhood of prose, as do the
thoroughgoing vers-libristes. His poems often seem prosy. He himself
thinks that "moments of prosiness" are necessary for contrast and variety
and because the poet cannot always stay on the lyrical plane. But rhythmi-
cally his verse generally comes somewhere between "Romantic" poetry and
prose, between Tennyson's "Song of the Lotos-Eaters" and Shaw's Candida.
Analysis confirms the impression that Eliot has restored the connection between the rhythm of poetry and the rhythm of ordinary speech. His task
has been analogous to that of Dryden and Wordsworth, with which he

expressly compares it in his essay on *Milton*. "It was one of our tenets", he says there, "that verse should have the virtues of prose, that diction should become assimilated to cultivated contemporary speech, before aspring to the elevation of poetry". He here speaks of diction, but his statement also has application to rhythm. And although he himself may have regarded his vocabulary work as the most important, the significance of his work with rhythm has been at least equally great.

Our examination of texture, rhyme and rhythm leaves us with a general impression of *moderation*. None of these formal factors would draw our attention from the contents and meaning of the poems; on the contrary, by their approach to prose they tend to reassure us as to the significance and the seriousness of the contents. From the poet's point of view these things may look rather different. Eliot may have worked hard to achieve precisely that effect of unelaborateness and moderation which we admire, and this concern may have completely overshadowed the concern for the thought he was expressing. He tells us, however, that rhythm must be learnt by imitation. The same, as we have seen, seems to apply to texture to some extent, while the similarity between Eliot and such a poet as Dryden would suggest a subordination of texture to sense. As for rhyme, we found it largely opportunistic. He would hardly, then, have given much systematic and conscious attention to these formal factors. Nor, if he had, does it seem likely that he would have achieved the kind of balanced, undogmatic free verse that is peculiarly his. Thus, if his attention to form has been his main concern, it is other aspects of it than the purely formal aspects of texture, rhyme and rhythm that have chiefly occupied him.

Structure.

Structure is obviously very important in the poetry we are studying. It is frequently determined by regular patterns of line and stanza and section; but more typically it resembles the accentual rhythm in being liberated from all rules. What interests us in our connection is whether the structure of Eliot's poems tends to conform to sense or to sound.

There is one thing that strikes us in the poet's technique of construction, both formal and logical: the abrupt breaks and veerings, both in the division of lines and in the longer sequences.

The division of lines is determined, I suppose, largely by rhythmical considerations. It has usually nothing to do with grammar, and frequently the meaning of a sentence is bitten off at the end of a line, to have its severed part dropped into the line below:

> Guides us by vanities. Think now
> She gives when our attention is distracted
> And what she gives, gives with such supple confusions
> That the giving famishes the craving. Gives too late
> What's not believed in, or if still believed,

> In memory only, reconsidered passion. Gives too soon
> Into weak hands, what's thought can be dispensed with
> Till the refusal propagates a fear. Think
> Neither fear nor courage saves us. Unnatural vices
> Are fathered by our heroism. Virtues
> Are forced upon us by our impudent crimes.[1]

The line division here seems to be determined by a kind of logical rhyming: "Think now" with "think", "gives too late" with "gives too soon", "vices" with "virtues". There is in this something belonging to Eliot's "music of ideas". Though the sense is served by the emphasis given to the words that "rhyme", the formal pattern is equally well served.

Mr. Eliot has told me that the division of lines in *The Family Reunion* was meant as a kind of punctuation, i. e. as a device to clarify or modify the meanings of the words. I assume that the line division has the same function in varying degrees in the remainder of his poetry. What usually happens, of course, is that a faint ambiguity is given to the meaning. When part of a sentence is retarded by a pause, this also means that part of the sense is withheld for a time while the reader's thought is engaged with the first part. When Harry says

> — — — — One thinks to escape
> By violence, but one is still alone [2]

the words "one thinks to escape" have at first a wider suggestiveness than when the qualification of the next line is added. However, the line division is often factitious from the point of view of sense, and there is a tendency to ignore it in reading, just as there is a tendency in the theatre to ignore the pauses between Shakespeare's blank verse lines in cases of enjambment. In a broadcast performance of *The Family Reunion* given by the BBC in the spring of 1948, the actors generally adhered to the grammatical rather than the prosodic pauses. But this was contrary to Eliot's intention. He means the line structure to serve both statement and cadence, sense and sound, and not merely the former.

Usually what look like stanzas in his poetry simply correspond to the paragraphs of prose in that a space is left when a break in meaning requires it; and the breaks in meaning come at irregular intervals. But they are often much more absolute than in prose. In *The Waste Land,* especially, the transitions from one "paragraph" to another are abrupt. Thus we skip direct from the hyacinth girl to Madame Sosostris, and only reflection shows us the connection and the contrast between them, as between timelessness and time, between the true and the false. Elsewhere, especially in the later works like *Ash-Wednesday* and *Four Quartets,* the transitions are easier. The prosy "commentaries" in the *Quartets* indicate the nature of the suppressed links in *The Waste Land:* in the latter poem, as well as in "The Love

---

[1] "Gerontion".   [2] FR p. 30.

Song", "Gerontion" and elsewhere, parts of the poet's trains of thought have been left out. But this very fact invites reflection on the reader's part. The broken sequence, then, so far from being a denial of thought and meaning may be regarded as a negative way of emphasising these things.

Sometimes the division into stanza-paragraphs is as surprising as the division into lines. In some cases the spacing has been altered in later editions of the poems to conform more closely to the logical sequence. Other examples of apparently unnatural spacing remain. In some of these the intention is obviously to create pleasing proportions in the formal composition. In other examples definite effects of sense and emotion are primarily aimed at. This, I think, applies to the following two lines from *Ash-Wednesday,* which belong to the same sentence, but to different stanza-paragraphs:

One who moves in the time between sleep and waking, wearing

White light folded, sheathed about her, folded.

The "white light", coming as it does in an initial position, becomes doubly impressive. The space in the middle of this sentence actually gives one the feeling of being dazzled.

The wish to create contrasts is at the bottom of much of the broken sequence, and here again it is both the formal and the ideal contrasts that count. Eliot's usual device is to set off passages that may be immediately recognised as poetry by passages which are close to prose. If we read his poems with the preconceived idea that everything must be equally "poetical" we are likely to be shocked. If, on the other hand, we read them in an unprejudiced frame of mind, we will be willing to accept both the poetical and the prosy parts for what they are: different movements of a symphony, and different approaches to thought apprehended in emotion.

Altogether, the salient features of structure point no more conclusively to the supremacy of either thought or technique taken singly than do the other formal elements that we have considered. We turn next to the verbal and pictorial elements of the poems, especially the imagery and symbols.

Imagery and Symbols.

The closeness of Eliot's poetic diction to prose was programmatical, as we know, and cannot be taken as an indication of his subjection of form to meaning, except perhaps in the prosy passages of his latest poetry. And form and meaning are served alike by his play on words, such as "World not world, but that which is not world".[1] The sound repetition here makes a formal impact, while the homonymy, though only phonetic, gives one that sense of secret, meaningful relationships which Émile Cailliet and Jean-

---

[1] BN III. Cp. SE p. 337, "Gerontion", *Ash-Wednesday* V.

Albert Bédé demonstrated in the use of "homonymes, onomatopées et calem-
bours" in the primitive conception of tabus.[1]

The imagery of many of the poems is at once precise and indefinite.
"L'Indécis au Précis se joint", so as actually to give the effect which Eliot
describes in "Marina":

> What is this face, less clear and clearer
> The pulse in the arm, less strong and stronger —
> Given or lent? more distant than stars and nearer than the eye

The precision of the images gives clearness of outline, and a formal,
objective beauty independent of the significance of the object:

> The showers beat
> On broken blinds and chimney-pots,
> And at the corner of the street
> A lonely cab-horse steams and stamps.[2]

But the precision of the images may also have something to do with
Royce's "law of mediation" which we have mentioned: the more distinctly
the poet can create an objective world, the more significant does his own
personality become, and the more meaning do his ideas acquire.

The complementary *im*precision of the imagery cannot be said to have
the same formal value. Where there is vagueness of outline in art, there may
be great beauty, but this is not due so much to the vagueness itself as to the
opportunities it gives to colour and tone and movement to assert themselves.
And much of the charm of indefiniteness in art lies in its spiritual effect;
or, as Poe said, "I *know* that indefiniteness is an element of the true music
[of poetry] — I mean of the true musical expression . . a suggestive indefiniteness of vague and therefore spiritual *effect*".[3] This suggestive indefiniteness I think we may find in the "Landscapes", especially if we compare them with the "Preludes":

> Children's voices in the orchard
> Between the blossom- and the fruit-time:
> Golden head, crimson head,
> Between the green tip and the root.

A landscape scene, with its soft contours, is better suited to convey an
effect of indefiniteness than the townscape with its more geometrical patterns.
But when the poet twice in four lines avails himself of "betweens", as he
does here, it means that he is purposely being oblique in his descriptions.

In one way the indefiniteness of poetic language corresponds more closely
to real thought than does a logically developed argument. As a psychic event,
a real thought (a) generally moves on to several new positions (b, c, d) simul-

---

[1] Cailliet et Bédé: *Le Symbolisme et l'âme primitive.*   [2] "Prelude" I.
[3] Quoted by Wilson, AC p. 13.

taneously, and keeps up inter-relations between them, then, perhaps, moving
a step further to a final main conclusion (e). An argument, however,
generally has to be set forth one stage at a time, so that many connections
are lost. A simple diagram will illustrate my meaning.

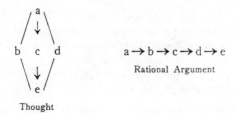

In a celebrated passage, Eliot declares that "in one's prose reflexions
one may be legitimately occupied with ideals, whereas in the writing of verse
one can only deal with actuality".[1] Thus poetry is seen to be the language
of actual thought, or actual ideas. Its actuality is not merely contingent, and
does not merely lie in its faithfulness to an external subject matter: it resides
far more in its faithfulness to the movements of the mind and spirit of the
poet. And this is manifested in the poetic use of imagery. For actual
thought also tends to move in images. "On pense au moyen d'images", said
Gourmont.

As one studies the poet's images, one seems to recognise a number of
basic scenes which in elaborated and differentiated forms constitute much of
his vision. There are the barren hills of New England, the sea mist, the
pines and thrushes of Cape Ann; things thrown up by the sea; a drowned
body; an orchard and children climbing in the trees in summer sunshine;
an arbour, flowers, and a girl in a shower of April rain; London fog and
filth; and the repeated experience of lying half awake towards morning.
Warfare has added little of direct imagery, but may be responsible for ideas
and states of feeling, and probably for the early ubiquity of death images
(bones) and for the frequent images of corruption and destruction (rat, fire).

The images are used at first in a comparatively naturalistic way. As
time goes on there is some shuffling and constant new assignments and differ-
entiation. Deception, we saw in an earlier chapter, is at first symbolised by
music, then music is used for other purposes, and the more apt image of
the thrush is used for deception (beautiful scenery and the spring may also
appear deceptive). The wind at first designates nothingness. In *The Waste
Land,* "the wind under the door" is "Nothing again nothing". Later the
wind acquires the additional significance of spiritual inspiration. The river
comes to denote life and the sea eternity. By the time he wrote the *Four
Quartets,* the poet had developed almost a complete code of symbols with
which one has to have some familiarity in order to understand and appreciate
these poems. It makes understanding more difficult to begin with, but it

---

[1] ASG p. 28.

enables the poet to operate very freely, exploring spiritual life by means of the evocative symbols he has evolved. It is something to the good that they are personal and elicit personal responses from us, for this makes them fields of force, of attraction and repulsion, which, combining both an emotional and an intellectual content, make it possible to throw an integral light forward in the direction of ultimate truths. Relevant thoughts are attracted and arranged in a pattern which the intellect alone would hardly have been able to achieve. And by grouping the symbols, the poet produces a similar effect to that of connecting several electric batteries to increase the power. All this at least gives poetic satisfaction. Whether it comes anywhere near sounding the deeps of spiritual reality, whether it is just a futile stretching out towards the impossible and illimitable, perhaps only a religious aesthetic dare answer. The poet may really have achieved an integral vision in which everything is caught up — or the many fragments may simply be a sign of confusion.

It is likely that much of the imagery which is used to suggest religious experiences may have its origin in purely personal and a-religious experiences. Thus the shaft of sunlight symbol, denoting religious illumination, is originally connected with la Figlia — it is the sunlight playing in her hair. And the aridity symbols may derive from the sight of the "barren New England hills". One might say that the later poetry is merely "emotion recollected in tranquility". It is not beliefs, one is tempted to think, that have made Eliot's poetry, but personal suffering. What is behind such a line as "looking into the heart of light, the silence"? Is it merely this: "J'éprouvais un instant de puissance et de délire"? Is this all the "distraction fit" amounts to? And what is the origin of the religious fear that is often felt, the fear of "reality", the "fear in a handful of dust"? Is it only some trivial experience such as that of having been scared by a dog?

It would be absurd to think the whole truth could be found in a reduction to childhood impressions and literary reminiscences. Nor, we must repeat, does it invalidate a religious experience to find its human roots in everyday adventures. If religion is true, all events must have some connection with it. And the Symbolist teaching that what we perceive conceals some inner reality, that the universe is all a mass of symbols, becomes perfectly right.

If we are to believe Eliot's words in *The Use of Poetry*,[1] he does not know quite why certain impressions assume a symbolical value. He has not arbitrarily chosen from his past life those memories which have been most violently dramatic and decided to turn them into symbols. The impressions have lent themselves unsolicited to symbolical interpretation. The scene with the six ruffians in a French tavern has been put bodily into "Journey of the Magi" because the poet felt it to be symbolical, i. e. that it might

---

[1] UPC p. 148.

disclose something about reality not only to himself, but objectively to others. It indicated a reality behind appearances. There is something in this. The scene, at least in the context of the poem, expresses an idea akin to that which Auden expressed in "Musée des Beaux Arts": the indifference of humanity at large to the great events which do not immediately concern them. And the dicing for pieces of silver inevitably puts us in mind of Judas, of the treachery that is already in waiting for the baby Christ, and of the soldiers at the Crucifixion. Thus we are prepared for the idea of Birth and Death coinciding. And a vaster idea is suggested, which may be Reality itself: that everything that is going to happen has already happened, and that time is nothing. This, at least, is what a happy use of a personal symbol *can* do. It points to something:

> Whisper of running streams, and winter lightning.
> The wild thyme unseen and the wild strawberry,
> The laughter in the garden, echoed ecstasy
> Not lost, but requiring, pointing to the agony
> Of death and birth.[1]

What may be called sublimation is thus wrongly used as an argument against the authenticity of faith. Dante, says Eliot, had experiences which seemed to him "important in themselves; and therefore they seemed to him to have some philosophical and impersonal value. I find in [the *Vita Nuova*] an account of a particular kind of experience: that is, of something which had actual experience (the experience of the 'confession' in the modern sense) *and* intellectual and imaginative experience (the experience of thought and the experience of dream) as its materials; and which became a third kind. — — If you have that sense of intellectual and spiritual realities that Dante had, then a form of expression like the *Vita Nuova* cannot be classed either as 'truth' or 'fiction' ".[2] (He concludes his essay on Dante by stating that we have to learn to accept Dante's "forms of imagination, phantasmagoria, and sensibility" — "and this *acceptance* is more important than anything that can be called belief. There is almost a definite moment of acceptance at which the New Life begins". This seems to me to be confusing things. Acceptance of *form* cannot be substituted for belief, and acceptance of the vision or matter or thought itself surely *is* belief, according to our previous discussion of these things.)

Thus we may recognise the philosophical or spiritual validity of the personal experiences, felt by the poet himself to have a higher significance. In many cases it looks as if a private memory becomes symbolical merely by the fact of its being incorporated in poetry. But we must remember that once the poet has used an image in a poem, he will see it in a new light. It will open itself up to him in its context, and he will be able to use it

---

[1] EC III.   [2] "Dante", SE p. 273.

later with greater significance. Actually I think a great deal of the imagery we are discussing has acquired its symbolical significance in this way.

There is something in what Mr. Middleton Murry says, that it is the highest function of imagery "to define indefinable spiritual qualities. All metaphor and simile can be described as the analogy by which the human mind explores the universe of quality and charts the non-measurable world". In these things, he says, "however much we struggle, we cannot avoid transcendentalism".[1] In fact, imagery is a means of approaching religious understanding, and it is used deliberately in this way in Eliot's later poetry. Speaking of the physical imagery of this poetry, Brother George Every says: "Religious feeling has to be translated in terms of physical sensation if it is to be made real again to those who are finding their way from a belief that only the physical is real to a renewed belief in the metaphysical. In their eyes the Christmas card stands for an old story, a kind of fiction, but El Greco gives a sense of interior experience, of something that tore at the very vitals of man".[2] And while we are again quoting we may include a statement by Cecil Day Lewis: "Animism lies surely at the very source of the poetic image. The image cannot, of course, reproduce the soul of things: what it can do is to persuade us, by the force of its own vitality, and our own answering sense of revelation, that soul there must be — or, if you dislike the word 'soul', to persuade us that there is beneath the appearance of things a life whose quality may not be apprehended in our everyday intercourse nor be gauged by the instruments of science".[3] "The poetic image", he says elsewhere, "is the human mind claiming kinship with everything that lives or has lived, and making good its claim".[4]

We have here a representative modern poet and critic speaking with the voice of the Symbolists. For Symbolism, though to a large extent a matter of form and technique, as witness Verlaine's "Art Poétique", was essentially a search for the mystic reality behind physical manifestations. So it was understood by Symons, who hardly interested himself in the technical aspect of French Symbolism at all. And this conception was no doubt passed on to Eliot, whose dependence on Symons right up to recent years appears clearly enough. Adequate philosophical support could be lent to this Symbolist doctrine by Bradley, who thought that "we should get a way of thinking in which the whole of reality was a system of its differences immanent in each difference. In this whole the analysis of any one element would, by nothing but the self-development of that element, produce the totality".[5] We remember Eliot's idea, expressed both in his poetry and his criticism, of the whole of history being immanent in one of its moments.

Symbolism, as understood by Symons, was eagerly embraced by Eliot, and I should not be surprised if it helped to actualise his spiritual dilemma

---

[1] *Countries of the Mind,* pp. 9, 15.   [2] Quoted by Preston, 4QR p. 26, n.
[3] *The Poetic Image,* p. 107.   [4] Ibid. p. 35.   [5] *Princ. of Logic,* p. 489.

and consequent despair. It pointed to final causes, to hidden meanings, to correspondences between phenomena, in fact to just those things which he wished to find and to communicate, but long failed to discover. In his recent work Eliot realises the Symbolist ideal. But he strove to realise it in his earlier work as well. His view of this life as unreal and of a transcendent existence as real owes much to the Symbolists as well as to more purely philosophical sources. In his Introduction to *The Symbolist Movement*, Symons wrote that "the literature of which I write in this volume [is] a literature in which the visible world is no longer a reality, and the unseen world no longer a dream". And it was this literature that he held up as the only hopeful model to his times.

In his first poetry Eliot often seems to be making deliberate efforts to fuse disparate experiences or impressions, the noise of the typewriter and the smell of cooking,[1] to force them to reveal their occult relationships. In his later poetry be convinces us quite often that he has actually found these relationships. Compare these two excerpts, one from "Rhapsody on a Windy Night", the other from "Journey of the Magi":

> The memory throws up high and dry
> A crowd of twisted things;
> A twisted branch upon the beach
> Eaten smooth and polished
> As if the world gave up
> The secret of its skeleton,
> Stiff and white,
> A broken spring in a factory yard,
> Rust that clings to the form that the strength has left
> Hard and curled and ready to snap.

> Then at dawn we came down to a temperate valley,
> Wet, below the snow line, smelling of vegetation;
> With a running stream and a water-mill beating the darkness,
> And three trees on the low sky,
> And an old white horse galloped away in the meadow.
> Then we came to a tavern with vine-leaves over the lintel,
> Six hands at an open door dicing for pieces of silver.

In both cases there are symbols, but the symbols of skeletons and broken springs are signs of nothingness: they are related by superficial similarities, but they reveal nothing — "I could see nothing behind that child's eye". The symbols in "Journey of the Magi", on the other hand, indicate a definite conception of man and a definite interpretation of history into which all visions of men and events readily fit themselves and thus show their inter-

---

[1] MP, SE p. 287.

connectedness. This is partly due to the traditional nature of the symbols
— running water, crosses, vine-leaves, pieces of silver. In contrast to these,
the early poetry gives evidence of what Stephen Spender calls "the crisis
of symbols" [1] experienced by modern Romantics and Symbolists: the lack
of a universal language of symbols to express "unreason" and anguish. But
Eliot has managed to create his own private signs as well, and to give them
a general validity by resting the symbolism of his later poetry on the imagery
of his earlier compositions.

This is how "the moment in the arbour where the rain beat" and the
other concomitants of the original imagery of sexual love can be worked
up into a symbol of religious illumination. And in the same way the murder
theme with its accompanying sense of guilt travels through many stages
(e. g. the rejected mistress in "La Figlia", the Philomela myth in *The Waste
Land,* the actual murder in *Sweeney Agonistes* and the contemplated murder
in *The Family Reunion)* to acquire a deep spiritual significance. To grasp
the essential of this significance, it is not necessary to "dissect / The recurrent
image into pre-conscious terrors", for the image is no longer private, but
general.

Eliot's poetry rarely tells us directly what the poet thinks or feels.
Considering his themes, it relies to an unusually great extent on imagery
and symbols.

To sum up our impressions, we may say that this imagery, and these
symbols are closely concerned with thought and attitude, with suggesting
and stating spiritual truths.

On the other hand, when an image becomes a symbol, it is simplified
and reduced to bare outlines. Details and appurtenances of the particular
object or event are shorn away, and usually only something that resembles
a geometrical figure remains, as in heraldic flowers or animals. But this
again means that the formal element becomes prominent. A symbol, one
might say, is a point at which pure form (or beauty) and concentrated
meaning strive to come to terms. So that the more the poet relies on
symbolism, the more formal, as well as meaningful, does his expression
become. Eliot's rose garden, more often than not, is nothing like the
rambling area that surrounds an English cottage, but "The single Rose / Is
now the Garden". Thus Dante's supreme vision of the blessed was of one
vast white rose, whose petals they formed. The pattern is simple and very
formal, but it is replete with meaning. In fact there is hardly a symbol
more full of meaning than that of the rose. In it there is the transition
from eroticism to piety, from the *Roman de la Rose* to the *Paradiso,* "from
Beatrice living to Beatrice dead, rising to the Cult of the Virgin". There is
the idea of an ordered gathering around a still centre. And if one cares to

---

[1] Spender: "The Crisis of Symbols", *Penguin New Wr.* 19.

meditate on the symbol, its connotations and associations could be multiplied almost indefinitely.

But always, the more stylised the symbol, the richer its potential meaning. The more symbolic the poetry, the more abundant its communication.

The Wider Synthesis.

In texture, rhyme and rhythm, in structure, in diction, imagery and symbols, Eliot unites form and matter in an intimate union which seems to give almost equal prominence to both. A conscious purpose may quite well have played some part in securing this balance. If I can judge of these things, it seems to me that one can deliberately transport oneself into a special state of mind, or mood, which (independently of one's further volition and conscious effort) determines and harmonises such things as texture, rhythm, vocabulary, images and thoughts (and of course there are no definite boundaries, only a gradation, between these elements). The mind turns itself into a kind of filter or sieve and applies itself to the whole field of emotion and sensation experienced by the personality, letting through those of a special order. Thus, in a sense, it is the mood which determines everything in art. It corresponds to the purpose in science or philosophy. The greatest poetry, I suppose, is created when the mood comes spontaneously. But I imagine that much very good poetry has been composed in a mood deliberately induced. And in so far as Eliot prepares his mind consciously for poetic composition, he doubtlessly makes room both for formal and semantic considerations. But let him speak for himself:

What matters — — is the whole poem — —. The music of a word is, so to speak, at a point of intersection: it arises from its relation first to the words immediately preceding and following it, and indefinitely to the rest of its context; and from another relation, that of its immediate meaning in that context to all the other meanings which it has had in other contexts, to its greater or less wealth of association. — — — a "musical poem" is a poem which has a musical pattern of sound and a musical pattern of the secondary meanings of the words which compose it, and — — these two patterns are indissoluble and one. — — the sound of a poem is as much an abstraction from the poem as is the sense.[1]

And here is Edith Sitwell's testimony:

In the year 1917, with the publication of Mr. Eliot's first volume, "Prufrock and Other Observations", began what may fairly be described as a new reign in poetry. The importance of the event cannot be exaggerated. The power of English poetry had been much weakened by such poets as Matthew Arnold and Dr. Bridges, who were interested equally in matter and in manner, but who had not regarded these as an indivisible entity, treating them, instead, as railway lines, running side by side for a considerable

---

[1] MUS pp. 17 ff.

time, but bearing a different set of trains bound for different junctions. In other words, applicable both to the language and metre of these poems, that language, those metres, reproduced a certain effect of relationship, and a recognizable imitation of the theme, but did not give us the reality. — — —
With Mr. Eliot we were restored to a living world in poetry.[1]

To Gourmont, Hulme and their followers style was everything. But here was a poet who could give everything to style (in spite of Mr. Yvor Winters's opinion) and yet have something over for content. This extra something laid the foundation of Eliot's greatness.

Eliot's synthesis is wider than the synthesis of ideas which we demonstrated in the previous chapter. It also includes various formal elements, which in turn are integrated among themselves. There is a kind of synaesthesia of matter and manner, as if his mental images "glowed into words". Eliot himself, speaking of Milton's "rhetorical style", complains of the dislocation that "takes place, through the hypertrophy of the auditory imagination at the expense of the visual and tactile, so that the inner meaning is separated from the surface, and tends to become something occult, or at least without effect upon the reader until fully understood". He thinks sense and sound can be appreciated at once in Shakespeare and Dante, but "there seems to be a division, in Milton, between the philosopher and theologian and the poet".[2]

Sometimes one feels the same division in Eliot. The incantatory passages are an example. And the systematic way in which the different sensations are evoked in sections of *Murder in the Cathedral* and the *Quartets* are another. The consistent appeal to the sense of smell in *Prufrock* and to the musical sense in the 1920 *Poems* are further indications of deliberate workmanship aiming at technical effects. The way in which the key experiences are camouflaged, often grotesquely, shows a conscious manipulation aiming at effects of surprise rather than of illumination. And frequently different images are fused regardless of their meaning, for the sake of the formal impact alone.

But there are also many things that indicate the supremacy of the ideal elements. Here I will only mention the poet's rejection of earthly beauty in *Ash-Wednesday*, section VI. This hard renunciation is not necessary or even desirable for any purely poetic reasons. It would have been poetic if it had been made tragic, or if one had the sense of martyrdom. As it is, the vision of earthly bliss is dismissed as mere illusion, as dreams come through the "ivory gates": How could the poet have had the heart to make such a renunciation unless his heart and his eyes were really set on a higher vision, "the unread vision in the higher dream"? Here the purpose, the meaning, is paramount.

---

[1] *Aspects of Mod. Poetry*, p. 99.   [2] "Note on Verse of J. M.", *Essays & Studies*, p. 38.

On the whole, however, it is the synthesis that counts.

The synthesis comprises aestheticism and Christianity. In effecting this junction between metaphysical faith and devotion to formal beauty, Symbolism was no doubt instrumental. It chimed with so many of Eliot's philosophical conceptions and it also directed his artistic endeavours. Symbolism may be said to be the link between his art and his life, or rather the channel by which his beliefs flowed into his poetry and his poetry into his beliefs. And thereby not only aestheticism and Christianity were affected, but his whole mind as one comprehensive entity. "The true claim of Baudelaire as an artist", he says, "is not that he found a superficial form, but that he was searching for a form of life".[1] Eliot, too, has been searching for a form of life, and for a form of poetry, and the effort has been the same.

He is an integral poet. This may seem a foregone conclusion, and, anyway, a commonplace. But it is one of the most momentous things about him. What does it mean? It may mean that form and sense unite in his poetry without either surrendering the least part of its sovereignty. But such a welding of ideal form with ideal content is rare in the best of cases, and I think it is rare in this case.

Usually the form and content of poetry are arrived at by a compromise in which each gives up something for the sake of the other. Each tends ideally to be absolute, yet neither can be anything at all without the other. It is in practice a question of relative importance.

Now we suggested (p. 55) that form and matter, where poetry was concerned, might perhaps be regarded as different categories from what we ordinarily understand by these things. If this distinction were possible, it might also be possible to arrive at an integral view of form and matter in which neither is seen to lose anything. But on reflection it seems doubtful whether this road is practicable. Ideally one may imagine a type of speech in which the opposition between form and matter is removed, so that *what* one wishes to say can always be said in the *way* one wishes to say it, which generally means with the maximum of power and beauty. In practice, however, the opposition cannot be made to disappear. Therefore in everyday communication we usually give precedence to the matter, whilst in poetry the form is commonly considered first, or a sort of balance is obtained between the two factors by letting now the form predominate and now the contents.

Yet it is a common experience that the more one attends to questions of style, the more frequently and easily does one produce a happy union between formal and conceptual elements. To take only the English language, it is so rich in possibilities of expression, that somewhere in its recesses one may always expect to find *the* word, *the* phrase, *the* sentence which exactly renders the meaning one wishes to communicate and at the same time gives

---

[1] "Baudelaire", SE p. 386.

the maximum aesthetic satisfaction. It only has to be searched for perseveringly enough. An integration is obtainable by talent and hard work. There is no "open Sesame", and there are no special intrinsic facilities for the poet. The integration of form and matter cannot be found as a general principle, but has to be found in each detail of speech. But poets, we suppose, are exceptionally sensitive both to what it is they wish to say, and to the nuances of language, and so they have a purely personal advantage in their search for *le mot juste*. To them, too, by accident or after protracted toil, the happy expression must come as a discovery. And if they persevere, it will set its stamp on their entire production.

As the ideal measure of what the poet can achieve in the way of integrating sense and form, stands the perfect symbol, the meeting-ground, as we saw, of the fullest meaning with the most formalised expression. But of course the poet may wish to particularise his meaning more than the symbol allows him to do; in which case he will find the hardest, driest, narrowest word that suits his purpose; and that also will be a happy find.

In calling Eliot an integral poet, I do not mean that he has performed miracles in fusing sense and sound. But I mean that he has balanced the various elements of his poetry better than most writers bother to do. To a great extent he is content with compensating for particularly formal, "poetical" words, lines and sections of his poems by means of alternating "prosy" parts. Deliberate parody would scarcely provide a clearer example than the stanzas of the second section of "East Coker". But he celebrates his greatest triumphs in the memorable expressions which in themselves fuse the perfection both of matter and manner. They are everywhere in his poetry, and they also occur in his prose. No wonder he believes in hard work, for such things cannot be achieved merely by talent.

It is one thing to find the best expression for what one has to say. It is quite a different thing to pretend that what one has said is what one originally meant. When an idea has been put into poetry, it appeals to the belief of the poet as well as to that of the reader. Obviously Eliot, as he says himself, has written many lines simply because they sounded well. But I cannot see that any of the important ideas in his poetry owe anything to this kind of composition. They are too persistent as themes to be so lightly explained away.

Because what he says has meaning to him, he means what he says. But it is tempting to a reader to exaggerate the importance of ideas and attitudes; the most purely formal elements (texture, rhyme, rhythm) are so unobtrusive and the satire or the devotion seems so obvious. Besides, the formal qualities which caused surprise when the poems were first published have become more customary now, and are often taken for granted. We should not be in agreement with Eliot, however, if we disregarded his pre-occupation with form. He is undoubtedly thinking of himself in his essay on Kipling, where he declares that "for some other poets — the poem may begin to shape itself in fragments of musical rhythm, and its structure will first appear in terms of something analogous to musical form; and such poets find it expedient to occupy their conscious mind with the craftsman's problems, leaving the deeper meaning to emerge, if there, from a lower level".

Of course, the thoughts which "emerge from a lower level", and with which the poet need not consciously concern himself, may seem important to the reader *qua* thoughts, precisely because they come to him clothed in a poetic form, and because he must pay attention to them in order to appropriate them. What the poet gives unconsciously, the reader must receive consciously. So the relation between form and content can never be the same to the reader as to the poet. This is why the poet may appear as an "irresponsible propagandist", as Mr. Belgion calls him. But a little training in the appreciation of poetic form will help one to obviate the danger of contenting oneself with understanding the contents. It may also help one to estimate the importance of Eliot's formal work if one remembers that in the beginning his task was largely negative, consisting in a reaction against conventional manners which did not leave him his full opportunities to develop positive qualities of style. A further point which should be borne in mind is the poet's treatment of ideas in the manner of musical themes.

As a near enough truth we may conclude that even when the formal elements of poetry receive their due attention it is possible also to satisfy the demands of religious orthodoxy and of faithfulness to personal religious experience. In Eliot's case it is the personal experience that counts most. His poems from *Ash-Wednesday* onwards are not typically "Christian poetry". They would nevertheless comply with a Christian aesthetic of the kind we have indicated.

Eliot has availed himself of the legitimate autonomy of art. His subject-matter is not directly controlled by his creed. But on the other hand it has a general Christian bias. It fills the mind with appropriate contents which are energised by the beauty of a carefully evolved form; thus thought is activised in its aspiration towards the highest things. Enjoyment is edification.

IX.

Final Remarks.

On the nature and significance of Eliot's poetry.

"Britain is the bridge between Latin culture and Germanic culture in both of which she shares", wrote Eliot in a Commentary in 1928. He added that Britain, because of the Empire, was also "the connection between Europe and the rest of the world".[1] And almost twenty years later, in his "Reflections on the Unity of European Culture", he declared that "the

---

[1] CRICOM, March 1928.

variety of the elements of which English is made up" makes it of all languages the richest for poetry.[1] These pronouncements help to explain the comprehensiveness of tradition, both philosophical and linguistic, that we find in his work. He is steeped in the English heritage on the one hand, and on the other hand he acknowledges his debt to such remote literatures as those of ancient India and China.[2] His works have such various affiliations that to many people they are a puzzle for that reason, and critics, fixing their attention on only this or that aspect, may describe him in diametrically different ways. For he adheres to his own precept, enunciated in "Tradition and the Individual Talent" long ago, that a poet must write "not merely with his own generation in his bones, but with a feeling that the whole of the literature of Europe from Homer and within it the whole of the literature of his own country has a simultaneous existence and composes a simultaneous order". Just as the synthesis of many philosophies is typical of the general outlook evinced in his poetry, so the combination of many traditions is typical of his position as a whole, in criticism and in poetry, in technique, in feeling and in ideas.

The Elizabethan inheritance, itself a composite affair, is conspicuous in his work. Its thefts and borrowings, echoes and re-echoes, its baroque phrasing penetrated by thrusts of startling simplicity, its subtlety of sensual and emotional effect, its feeling for the horrible and grotesque, even the perverse, its metaphysical curiosity, are all present in Eliot. From Webster, Chapman and Drummond, by way of Donne, Marvell and Browning, there is an unbroken line to the contemporary poet. Nor has Eliot remained unaffected by the poets of this succession or of collateral lines whom he finds less congenial: Spenser, Shelley, Tennyson, Rossetti, Swinburne. To point to specific debts to all of these poets would be simple but supererogatory.

The French Symbolist succession, which may be said to start with Baudelaire, is related to this English line. And it would not be out of place to mention the New England tradition, especially the novelists Hawthorne, Melville and Henry James, in the same breath, for there are distinct similarities. The Symbolist movement was in part a reaction against naturalism, and by its belief in a transcendent reality it had strong affinities with Christian and philosophical idealism, though its connection with neo-thomism is a later phenomenon and to a great extent due to Eliot.

A line of religious and mystical poetry cuts across national and denominational boundaries, and connects Dante with Herbert, Milton and Blake. Of these Dante has exerted incomparably the greatest influence on Eliot's poetry, from first to last. We should also mention St. John of the Cross, Pascal, and other great men and women of faith and illumination, whose prose writings have appealed strongly to many modern poets.

---

[1] NDC p. 111. [2] Cf. NDC p. 113.

Right faith is associated in Eliot's mind with Toryism and classicism, and the combination of these elements seems to him to represent the summit of what the cultured mind should aspire to. From Homer and Virgil and their countrymen comes a legacy of maturity and poise, from the Old and New Testaments a sense of the infinite, which meet in the theology of St. Thomas, of Hooker and Andrewes, in the poetry of Dryden and the criticism of Johnson. Newman and Chesterton continue the catholic tradition, Flaubert and Valéry the classical tradition. Arnold's influence on Eliot has obviously been immense, in spite of a certain antagonism to Arnold in the essays. Mr. Winters also suggests the importance of Henry Adams. Adams, he says, worked out "the entire theory of modern society and its relationship to the society of the Middle Ages, upon which Eliot's critical theory rests".[1] Eliot himself salutes the ideas of Hulme, whom he regarded (writing in 1924) as "the forerunner of a new attitude of mind, which should be the twentieth century mind, if the twentieth century is to have a mind of its own. Hulme", he said, "is classical, reactionary, and revolutionary; he is the antipodes of the eclectic, tolerant, and democratic mind of the end of last century." Hulme's closest affinities he found to be in France, with Charles Maurras, Albert Sorel and Pierre Lasserre.[2] A nearly-related critic, however, who greatly affected the course of the poet's development, was Irving Babbitt.

Not all of these people (Arnold and Babbitt are notable examples) satisfied Eliot's demands for orthodoxy and classicism in every way. But they possessed a general culture and a cultural equilibrium which he regarded as supreme values. It is clear that he himself has laboured to build up for himself, with the aid of his predecessors, a general and consistent cultural position from which to survey the various fields of human life. And, further, it seems clear that he wishes his poetry to be informed by his cultural views, and to form a harmonious, if independent, part of his main philosophical entrenchments.

A tradition that runs counter to the religious, if not to the classical strain of his poetry is that of worldly-wise scepticism and disrespectful satire. Richard Aldington calls it "the secular tradition of 'poètes contumaces' or 'poètes libertins', which runs from the poets of to-day to Laforgue and Verlaine, to Rimbaud and Corbière, to Aloysius Bertrand, to Saint-Amant, to Théophile, back to Villon, and beyond him to a shadowy host of mediaeval 'pinces-sans-rire', 'goliards' and satiric 'goguenards', whose sharp tongues spared neither the Church nor the rich nor the pretty ladies".[3] We find a good deal of this in James Joyce, and we are not surprised to find the author of "Mr. Eliot's Sunday Morning Service" expressing the liveliest admiration for the author of *Ulysses*.

---

[1] SELCR p. 110.   [2] CRICOM, April 1924.   [3] SELCR p. 7.

In philosophy Eliot exhibits such varied ancestry that it is easiest to define him by negatives. He dislikes Utilitarianism, Pragmatism, Behaviourism and the New Realism, as well as secular Humanism, his inclination being against the schools of thought which tend to emphasise the practical and contingent. His tastes in philosophy, as in literature, are definitely classical. But he has not escaped the impress of individualistic thought, such as that of Schleiermacher and Emerson.

Poetry does not have to worry about contradictions. In fact, they almost cease to exist as soon as they are embodied in poetry. Eliot reconciles very many. And whether an actual compromise takes place or a balance of opposites is established, the effect is usually that of moderation, of the avoidance of extremes, of what is so very characteristic of Eliot both as a critic and as a poet: the *via media*.

"During the past twenty years the chief or average complaint against the almost reverend Eliot has been that he exaggerated his moderations".[1] The words are Ezra Pound's, and were written in 1937. They may not be quite true as a statement of average criticism, but they do put something of the essential Eliot in a nutshell. It was no accident that made him choose the *via media* of the Church of England [2] and a political Toryism that was neither conservative nor liberal; that brought him to England rather than to France, and to a classicism that was almost absorbed into modern romanticism. It was not for nothing that he applied for guidance to the philosophers of the golden mean, Aristotle and Buddha, or that he wrote in praise of Machiavelli: "For Machiavelli is a doctor of the mean, and the mean is always insupportable to partisans of the extreme".[3] In another connection he declared that "there must always be a middle way, though sometimes a devious way when natural obstacles have to be circumvented; and this middle way will, I think, be found to be the way of orthodoxy; a way of mediation, but never, in those matters which permanently matter, a way of compromise".[4]

Thus the middle way represents no mere pruning and abandonment of extreme or absolute ideas. Eliot "n'abandonne rien en route". He revolted (e. g. in "Tradition and the Individual Talent") against the individualism of the Imagists, but did not drop it; instead he brought it, by a kind of transcendence, into a wider whole. Both the personal and the objective were to count in poetry: the personal as brute matter, the objective as the finished product. And similarly his Puritanism, his Unitarianism, his Absolute Idealism remained very actively with him to mingle with his Catholicism.

---

[1] *Polite Essays*, p. 98.   [2] "the bastard, schismatic and provincial if genteel kind of Catholicism that, for the time being, at any rate, he has, somewhat New Englishly stopped at"! (McGreevy).   [3] *For Lancelot Andrewes* p. 63.   [4] EAM p. 134.

For that reason he was first outlawed by the orthodox, then set beyond the pale by the unorthodox, and now perhaps he is beginning to be suspected by the orthodox again. Richard Lea is not the only critic to find less Christianity in the *Four Quartets* than in *Murder in the Cathedral*. The trouble with Eliot is not his own extremes, for in his early phase there was much Christianity mingled with his scepticism, and in his later phase there is much scepticism and unorthodoxy mingled with his Christianity. The trouble is the extremes of the belligerents who surround him. Eliot, in fact, has proved to be, what he admired Hulme for not being, eclectic and tolerant.

As to the literary problems that have chiefly concerned us in this book, these, too, are solved in Eliot's typical mediating fashion. In theory as well as in practice, he tries to reconcile the demands of thought with the demands of form. The following three passages from his criticism sum up his views on this point very clearly:

I do not suppose that there ever has been, or ever will be, a critic of any art, whose appreciation was a separate faculty, quite judicious and wholly isolated from his other interests and his private passions: if there was, is or will be, he was, is or will be a bore with nothing at all to say. And yet, on the other hand, there is no worse bore, and no more futile critic, than the one who renounces all objective standards. in order to recount his own reactions.[1]

My point of view is that the legitimate motives of the poet, and also the legitimate responses of the reader, vary very widely, but that there is a possible order in the variations. In my series let us put Mr. Belgion at one end of the scale and Mr. Richards at the other. The one extreme is to like poetry merely for what it has to say — — — The other extreme is to like the poetry because the poet has manipulated his material into perfect art. — — Between these extremes occurs a continuous range of appreciations, each of which has its limited validity.[2]

— — we must avoid being seduced into one or the other of two extreme opinions. The first is that it is simply the value of the *ideas* expressed in a poem which gives the value to the poetry; or that it is the *truth* of his view of life — by which we ordinarily mean its congruity with our own view — that matters. The other is, that the ideas, the beliefs of the poet do not matter at all; that they are rather like some alloy, necessary for the poet in order to manipulate his true material, which is refined out of the poetry in the course of time.[3]

The moral and educational value of poetry is regarded as positive but limited. In Eliot's words, "between the motive which Rivière attributed to Molière and Racine [distraire les honnêtes gens] and the motive of Matthew Arnold bearing on shoulders immense what he thought to be the orb of the poet's fate, there is a serious *via media*".[4]

---

[1] PP p. 32.   [2] PP p. 33.   [3] SFP.   [4] UPC p. 137.

In poetic form and imagery Eliot avoids all kinds of overloading, unless he is out for very special effects. Generally he finds a middle way between intellectualism and lyricism, or he balances the two in alternate lines and stanzas. The difficult and involved is continually set off by the simple and translucent, a fact which immediately emerges if his poetry is compared with the far opaquer medium of W. H. Auden. And Eliot's symbolism is supported and made accessible by naturalistic imagery, as a comparison with Yeats will bring out.

Eliot is not the arch-intellectualist in poetry that many people think. But, of course, his intellectual habits are mirrored in his poetry, so that the latter presents the *feelings* of one accustomed to reflection. He may have had good reasons for the anti-emotionalism expressed in "Tradition and the Individual Talent", but it is impossible to refine emotion out of poetry altogether; and this Eliot has recognised, for he has told us repeatedly of late that his poetry expresses what it *feels* like to believe in something.

We may reasonably ask in what lies the greatest beauty of poetry in general and of Eliot's poetry in particular. Are not the most beautiful passages of Eliot's work the emotional ones, and the intellectual sections rather like intervening prose commentaries? And is his poetry "poetic" in the same measure as it is "traditional"? That this may be so seems to be testified by the admiration to which many critics are moved by the musical evocativeness of "Marina" or the poignant emotions of "Journey of the Magi", or the lavish, Pre-Raphaelite picturesqueness of *Ash-Wednesday*. It might even be asked whether, for real beauty, it is not necessary to use images from nature, like Eliot's orchards and thrushes and New England coastline. Are not his streets and smoke and fog made poetically beautiful, as far as they *are* poetically beautiful, by being compared with natural objects and living beings: "muttering retreats", cats, the ocean? Spender says that his aeroplane is "more beautiful and soft than any moth";[1] yet it is precisely the image of the moth that lends it its beauty. Beauty, like humour, feeds on comparison.

It is true that poetry which seems to vibrate with emotion, and poetry which uses natural imagery or picturesque substitutes for it moves us more immediately with a sense of beauty than soberer kinds of poetry. "La Figlia" moves us with a sense of beauty, whilst "Sweeney Erect" moves us primarily with a sense of the ludicrous. If beauty is the soul of poetry and wit-writing another thing altogether, then, one might say, "La Figlia" is poetry and "Sweeney" or "A Cooking Egg" is comic verse. But that is not to say that the poetry which stirs our emotions most deeply embodies the deepest or most original feelings of the poet. "La Figlia" may contain much personal matter, but it certainly contains much pasticcio, ranging from Drummond's "Madrigal" to Rossetti's "Blessed Damozel" and Laforgue's

---

[1] "Landscape near an Aerodrome".

"Pétition" and "Sur une défunte". Even the prosiest parts of "Gerontion", on the other hand, may spring from very intense feelings indeed. It is all a matter of how we read. If we are capable of being moved by the same things as the poet, we shall find that the outward shows may be least themselves; and that even the grotesque and ribald may hide a pathos that gives it poetic dignity. Eliot's cat poems are no more than comic verse, for they are void of pathos. But everything that he has submitted as poetry has a good right to that name. And this right is not impaired by his sparing use of "beautiful" effects, because this is only one of his ways of showing moderation. We are not required to call ugliness beautiful; but we are required "to see beneath both beauty and ugliness; to see the boredom, and the horror, and the glory". These things Eliot can make us see, and there is an amazing power in the imagery, the associations and the sequences by which he makes them visible to us.

Because of the balance of his effects, it is necessary for his readers to develop a sense of counterpoint. And this must not only embrace the style, so that one obtains, for instance, a systematic accompaniment to the actual rhythm; but it must also embrace descriptions, ideas and feelings. Thus ugliness will set off beauty and both together will point to something beneath or beyond them. And the intellect and the emotions will be constantly united, realising Eliot's great ideal, the sensous apprehension of thought and the fusion of ideas with feelings.

Eliot's message to our divided age, and his importance in our spiritual situation, lie chiefly in these two things together : synthesis and compromise. These things have nothing to do with petty bourgeois timidity, and are not despicable, but wise and sane. There is a sort of fortuitous synthesis which is due to lack of critical ability, and there is a sort of compromise which is due to lack of moral fibre and moral standards. But rightly understood the two ideals can only be realised in any degree by understanding and imagination, by critical intelligence and daring passion. They need, in fact, the imagination and the daring of a poet.

"Our age is an age of moderate virtue / And of moderate vice."[1] We need no further moderation at least in virtue. But we need moderation in intellectual and materialistic aspirations, in political allegiances, in mass consciousness. The doctrine of the mean must not be applied indiscriminately. Eliot on the whole applies it rightly. In our contemporary situation, the importance of his visionary and philosophical approach to poetry must not be underestimated.

We have already discussed the difficulty of integrating present-day theories of life into a unified view of life. The difficulty is aggravated by the unprecedented chaos in our ideas of ultimate purpose and meaning,

---

[1] *Rock*, Chorus VIII.

which leaves multitudes of people without a final goal for their endeavours. This state of affairs makes the work of the poet particularly significant. Even in spite of his own protests to the contrary, he is still the *vates* to whom we look for an understanding of our position and perhaps also for spiritual guidance. And "the need for an evaluating, clarifying poetry has never been greater than it appears to be today".[1]

From the beginning of the century poets have been in search of Paradise Lost. Yeats found his way to a paradise of Art. To the young poets of the thirties this would not do, for they could not deny this life and this world as Yeats was more than half inclined to do, nor did Yeats's incantations succeed in charming them. They saw their problems from a social and political point of view. Their political fervour, however, did not last long, probably because specific political truths must sooner or later prove relative and unreliable, especially in a world of rapid changes like ours.

Eliot, the poet, faced the great problems of our time from a point of view which was at once more individualistic and self-sufficient and more general. He demonstrated the need of a metaphysical truth and sought his paradise in Revelation. When he allowed his Knights to speak in their own defence in *Murder in the Cathedral,* he gave them arguments which were unanswerable except by appeal to a higher logic. And he showed the higher logic to be justified.

As far as we can follow our leaders of thought, Freud, Einstein and their successors, we cannot help being convinced by their arguments. But they have not got the whole truth, because they cannot answer ultimate questions. And if there are truths in various fields it must be possible to combine and reconcile them. Our lives are based upon the assumption that Truth is one, and even theories of discontinuity such as Hulme's can only take their arguments from such an assumption. The task to-day is to relate modern psychology, modern anthropology and modern physics to meta-physics, ethics and art. It is a task for the philosopher, but also for the poet. And only the poet (though he may be dressed up as a philosopher) can have the assurance to announce his belief in a general and commanding truth before he has laboriously argued his way to it. Most great poets seem to be led sooner or later to religion. Even if in this they are merely obeying the needs of their art, they are obeying the needs of something which has its place in the common fabric of human life.

Eliot has not embraced the whole of modern thought by any means. But we feel that he would be capable of encompassing what he has still left out of his poetry. And as it is he has achieved a wider synthesis of thought than most other poets. His note of idealism is particularly beneficial now that the pessimistic stoicism of Bertrand Russell and similar philosophies have gained such a large following. His mysticism is highly salutary in the

---

[1] M. Roberts, Introd. to *Faber Book of Mod. Verse*, p. 9.

contemporary world. It is good that there are mystics. And let us recognise Eliot as a very minor, but a true mystic; and let us take the likely view that the path of ascetic discipline that he has chosen is the difficult path and not the way of escape. Of course it would be fatal if all should become mystics. There would be much cheap escapism. But there is no immediate danger of such a state of affairs.

Eliot's message may not be a message in the ordinary sense. It may also be misunderstood. It may be appreciated, as R. P. Blackmur appreciates it,[1] only as poetic and dramatic material, or as a useful schooling in purely historical lore. But it is nevertheless a very real message. It tells us that the distinction between physical life and death matters less than the distinction between the good life and a life that is neutral or bad; that the distinction between pain and pleasure matters less than the distinction between spiritual despair and bliss. It makes the very rigour of religion something to be desired, because it shows it to be lofty and powerful.

Even strict dogma can be made acceptable when presented poetically, because one realises that it is not scientific belief that is demanded. The old books of the Bible might very well be regarded as poetry by the Jews, and still be devoutly believed in. Many of the specific dogmas that underlie Eliot's later poetry are strict enough. But they have a grace of presentation to recommend them to our adherence. And it must be admitted that the general eclecticism and latitude of dogma, which I have pointed out before, leaves the intellect no reason to take offence at any particular teaching. As it is, Eliot castigates humanity, and humanity comes and eats out of his hand.

Is it a fault in his poetry if it does not content itself with interpreting the outlook of a generation? I think not.

His importance in our literary situation is even greater than in our spiritual situation. I do not think it is true that modern poets must be difficult, or that there is any reason why ideas connected with a complex civilisation must be expressed in complex terms. But Eliot fortunately does not practise these principles to the extent that might be feared. He has gone one better than Joyce in that he has found a way of fusing many meanings without playing pranks with spelling and grammar. But, anyway, he is more important in other respects than as a representative of difficult poetry. Mr. Michael Roberts, in his preface to *New Signatures* (1932), wrote: "The poems in this book represent a clear reaction against esoteric poetry in which it is necessary for the reader to catch each recondite allusion." And Louis MacNeice, who quotes this preface, adds: "These new poets, in fact, were boiling down Eliot's 'variety and complexity' and finding that it left them with certain comparatively clear-cut issues."[2] Thus in spite of all the imitation of Eliot's complexity of form and matter that undoubtedly has

---

[1] Cf. SELCR.   [2] MacNeice: *Mod. Poetry*, p. 15.

taken place, it was not this aspect that young poets found most stimulating,
and many of them found it a hindrance.

But Eliot has realised, in his own way, MacNeice's wish for *"impure
poetry,* that is, for poetry conditioned by the poet's life and the world around
him", adding the metaphysical element which MacNeice did not include in
his wish. "Poetry to-day", continues MacNeice, "should steer a middle
course between pure entertainment ('escape poetry') and propaganda. — —
The writer to-day should be not so much the mouthpiece of a community
(for then he will only tell it what it knows already) as its conscience, its
critical faculty, its generous instinct. — — others can tell lies more effi-
ciently; no one except the poet can give us poetic truth."[1] These conditions
Eliot has fulfilled (with the addition that I mentioned) most admirably;
and it is a literary as well as a spiritual achievement.

While allowing for the application of art for useful purposes, Eliot
has been one of the staunchest upholders of its integrity, and has thus
done it an inestimable service in an age when propaganda is seeking whom
it may devour. He has helped to save it from the indignity to which psycho-
analytic, marxist and other theories (including religious ones) might have
reduced it. He has earned the gratitude of the aestheticists, particularly
Edith Sitwell, while he has exercised a considerable ascendancy over such
integral writers as Day Lewis and Henry Treece. The latter's "Apocalypse"
is not much more than a different name for Eliot's synthesis of experience
and ideas, and his "Anarchism" differs only slightly from Eliot's Toryism.[2]

Modern poets have been greatly occupied with symbols and images,
and a good deal of critical writing on these subjects has been produced.
Symbolism and allegory as means of stating difficult thoughts in "clear
visual imagery" owe much of their popularity (which has extended even
to fiction) to Eliot's theory and practice. The break with surface realism
with which Eliot was associated and which he has more and more come to
stand for, was a break both with Georgian descriptive prettiness and late
Victorian narrative and picturesque poetry. Symbolism, as it has been
practised by Eliot (and not the "dislocation" of language or verbal conceits)
is the best means of grappling with a complex civilisation, for it gives an
amazing penetration and power to the poet's vision, and enables him to
combine concepts which ordinary language has no way of combining.

Many people would say that Eliot's greatest contribution to literature
is a modern poetic idiom. His adaptation of contemporary speech to poetic
uses gave his diction an air of sophisticated crudity at first; but it has
become more and more fluent and un-selfconscious with time. He has
generally kept clear of slang and technical jargons but otherwise he has
won recognition in poetry for the whole vocabulary of cultivated speech and
for common conversational style at its best. At the same time his careful

[1] Ibid., Preface.   [2] Cf. Treece: *How I See Apocalypse,* pp. 21, 76 and passim.

use of words and this deliberate archaisms have reminded us more forcibly than most linguists have been able to, of the urgent need for word-consciousness and precise expression. As for his metrical achievements, not many of his imitators have fully appreciated his discreet use of "free verse". But it is constantly there as an example.

It is no doubt Eliot's technique and imagery that have attracted the largest number of disciples to his poetry. Young poets, as Edmund Wilson says, "took to inhabiting exclusively barren beaches, cactus-grown deserts and dusty attics overrun with rats"[1] in imitation of the author of *The Waste Land,* and Eliot's visionary concepts often became mere technical props in the hands of his admirers. But sometimes they were more than an affectation. "No one", wrote Archibald MacLeish in 1938, "has made his language, his rhythms, more nearly a part of our own lives, our own experience [than Eliot] — so that there are streets, houses, windows, people, cities in our past which recall only his poems".[2]

In Anne Ridler's opinion, "Eliot provides the necessary standard of perfection", but for that very reason she thinks it is difficult to learn from him. "For the generations following Eliot", she declares, "it was a more voluble poet who loosened their tongues — — . It was Auden's use of stanza and stress which proved the easier for the novice to handle".[3] Auden himself, however, transmitted much of Eliot's influence indirectly;[4] and, by whatever channels it has penetrated, Eliot's manner is discernible in the work of most contemporary poets writing in English. It has not always been beneficial, but this will usually be found to be due to a lack of just estimation on the part of his imitators. Few have achieved his balance in the use of free verse. Many have found their chief inspiration in his modernistic conceits — and Auden is not entirely innocent of exaggerating effects such as these. Some, like Dylan Thomas, have gone to extremes in obscure symbolism. Others have over-reached themselves in experimenting with discontinuity in their thematic variations.

Perhaps the most generally successful (or the least frequently unsuccessful) influence of Eliot's form has been the establishment of the long-short poem of the type of *The Waste Land* or the *Quartets*. These varied, descriptive-philosophical poems have obviously meant much to Edith Sitwell. Her *Song of the Cold,* for instance, plainly owes a great deal to *The Waste Land,* as well as to St.-J. Perse's *Anabase*. (The latter poem Eliot has helped to make known to English readers by his translation of it, though of course Miss Sitwell would have known it in any case.)

Such similarities with Eliot as we find in *The Song of the Cold* and *The Shadow of Cain,* are similarities of content as well as of form. And this is all to the good. There is an intimate correspondence between matter

---

[1] AC p. 114.   [2] HA, Dec. 1938, p. 18.   [3] F3 pp. 109, 118.   [4] Cp. G. M. O'Donnell, HA, Dec. 1938, p. 18.

and manner in Eliot's poetry, as I have tried to show, and many of his imitators have probably gone astray in indiscriminately admiring his technique whilst rejecting his thought. On the other hand, though Eliot's influence has been primarily technical, the influence of his thought has been far from negligible. And this has extended far beyond the bounds of poetry. Thus Eliot has contributed powerfully to the general interest in Oriental mysticism in our time. The enormous interest in poetic technique which dominated the decade from 1912 to 1922 began to wane among poets after the latter date,[1] and their attention was turned more to ideas. It was fortunate for Eliot's growing ascendancy that he could stimulate thought as well as formal invention, and though many poets refused to follow him into the Christian camp, he may yet have been instrumental in bringing them to realise the need of a programme and a message.

But Eliot, we repeat here, is an integral poet, and the stimulus of his poetry has led to the happiest results when form and matter have been affected in conjunction. This double influence has also been considerable, and many writers have expressed their appreciation of and indebtedness to the *wholeness* of Eliot's poetry.[2] The later Edith Sitwell and the later Auden have been occupied with religious and philosophical themes which may in part have been suggested by Eliot. In his more direct following we find such poets and playwrights as Anne Ridler, Kathleen Raine, Norman Nicholson, Robert Duncan, Christopher Fry, John Betjeman, Allen Tate and Robert Lowell. Nicholson, Duncan and Fry, as well as Miss Dorothy Sayers, have benefited greatly by Eliot's revival of the religious verse drama; and judging by the notices of his latest work, *The World Turned Upside Down*, Clive Sansom seems to have been attracted to the same genre.

Most of these poets share Eliot's Christian faith. And together they surely exercise a considerable collective influence on the reading public. This makes it all the more necessary that one should pay critical attention to their conceptual assumptions, whether didacticism and edification form part of their intention or no. One thing seems certain: that Eliot, with his disciples and sympathisers, has made Christianity more acceptable than it would otherwise have been to the modern mind and especially to the intelligentsia. This they have achieved partly by a form of poetry suited to contemporary speech and contemporary life; and partly by bringing Christian ideas into poetic relation with the ethos of the age.

Eliot has greatly stimulated Christian and mystic poetry. And though, as I said, his influence has hitherto been mainly technical, a time may quite conceivably come when not his technical but his ideological influence will be supreme. The less new and surprising his technique appears to his readers — and in all probability it will soon seem perfectly conventional — the more will people look for his ideas. In the same way it was Words-

---

[1] Cp. Malcolm Cowley, SELCR p. 32.   [2] Cf. HA, Dec. 1938, SELCR, etc.

worth's ideas rather than his style which came to be directly significant to his readers after the first decade or two of the last century. If the poetry of the future makes a convention of Eliot's form, his readers of the future will probably judge him by his contents.

This is probable for another reason besides. The arts to-day tend to separate themselves from direct enjoyment. The kind of paintings which we hang in our homes are the ones we enjoy spontaneously, whilst what we generally understand by "art", the paintings exhibited in galleries, seem to be of a different kind. The kinds of poems that we enjoy spontaneously are poems for festive occasions, songs, poems of homage, poems that touch us intimately in our private particularities and those of our friends and relations; whilst the poems that are printed and published in books frequently have no such immediate appeal. In freeing itself from decorative or festive or commemorative usefulness art seems paradoxically to be freeing itself also from pure enjoyment, i. e. from existing as far as possible for its own sake. Instead it offers itself up for *study,* and for enjoyment in, or subsequent on, critical contemplation. In other words, the arts to-day, especially poetry, are, if not a branch of philosophy, at least related to philosophy. It only remains for us to return to the view of the ancients, who were always ready to bracket poetry and philosophy. And the work of the most representative poet of to-day would be no obstacle to our doing so.

Bibliography.

It would need a separate volume to list all of Eliot's published writings, so for most of his uncollected poems and articles I must refer the reader to Mr. Donald C. Gallup's invaluable *Bibliographical Check-List of the Writings of T.S.Eliot*, New Haven, 1947. This *Check-List* contains full bibliographical information on its subject down to the beginning of 1947. In my footnotes I have merely named the books or periodicals to which Eliot has contributed, without giving details of them. Such details will be found in Mr. Gallup's work.

The writings which have appeared in collected volumes I have usually quoted from those volumes.

In the body of my text, as well as in the notes, I have tried to adhere to the principle of citing the titles of volumes, periodicals etc. in italics and those of writings not published separately in inverted commas.

The best list of critical writings on T. S. Eliot that has come to my notice is the one appended to Mr. Leonard Unger's: *A Selected Critique*, New York, 1948. Mr. Unger's book is itself a comprehensive and varied collection of critical essays by a great number of authorities. Many of the essays contained in this book and in similar collections I have not listed separately; but I have of course referred to the individual authors in my footnotes.

In general, I have not listed fiction, drama and poetry apart from Eliot's. But it is well known that some familiarity with Dante, Webster, Donne, Laforgue, Pound, Waley and many others is very relevant to a study of Eliot's poetry.

Dates in brackets are those of first publication.

Eliot's works in the editions consulted:

Ezra Pound | His Metric and Poetry, New York, 1917.
The Sacred Wood, 2nd ed., London, 1928 (1920).
For Lancelot Andrewes, London, 1928.
Ezra Pound | Selected Poems, London, 1928.
Selected Essays, London, 1946 (1932).
John Dryden | The Poet | The Dramatist | The Critic, New York, 1932.
The Use of Poetry and the Use of Criticism, London, 1945 (1933).
After Strange Gods, London, 1934.
Selected Poems by Marianne Moore, New York, 1935.
Essays Ancient and Modern, London, 1945 (1936).
The Idea of a Christian Society, London, 1942 (1939).
A Choice of Kipling's Verse, London, 1946 (1941).
The Music of Poetry, Glasgow, 1942.
The Classics and the Man of Letters, London, 1942.
Introducing James Joyce, London, 1945 (1942).
Reunion by Destruction, London, 1943.
What is a Classic? London, 1945.
Catholicity (a report to the Archbishop of Canterbury by Eliot and others), London, 1947.

On Poetry, Concord, 1947.
Milton, London, 1948 (1947).
Notes towards the Definition of Culture, London, 1948.

Anabasis / a Poem by St.-J. Perse (transl. by Eliot), London, 1930.
The Rock, London, 1934.
Murder in the Cathedral, London, 1945 (1935).
Collected Poems 1909—1935, London, 1937 (1936).
The Family Reunion, London, 1939.
Old Possum's Book of Practical Cats, London, 1939.
Four Quartets, London, 1946 (1943).

Books and essays on Eliot:

Grudin, Louis: *Mr. Eliot among the Nightingales,* Paris, 1932.
Häusermann, H. W.: *L'Oeuvre poétique de T. S. Eliot,* Genève, 1939.
Lea, Richard: Review of *Four Quartets, Adelphi,* July/Sept. 1945.
Matthiessen, F. O.: *The Achievement of T. S. Eliot,* 2nd ed., New York, 1947.
McGreevy, T.: *T. S. Eliot. A Study.* London, 1931.
Moore, Dom Sebastian: "East Coker: The Place and the Poem", *Focus Two* (ed.
   B. Rajan and A. Pearse), London, 1946.
Nicholson, N.: "T. S. Eliot", *Writers of To-day* (ed. D. Val Baker), London, 1946.
Oras, Ants: "The Critical Ideas of T. S. Eliot", *Acta et commentationes Universitatis
   Tartuensis,* 1932.
Preston, R.: *"Four Quartets" Rehearsed,* London, 1946.
Sansom, Clive: *The Poetry of T. S. Eliot,* Oxford, 1947. .
Stephenson, E. M.: *T. S. Eliot and the Lay Reader,* London, 1946.
Williamson, G.: *The Talent of T. S. Eliot,* Seattle, 1929.
Williamson, H. R.: *The Poetry of T. S. Eliot,* London, 1932.
Wilson, Frank: *Six Essays on the Development of T. S. Eliot,* London, 1948.
March, R., and Tambimuttu (ed.): *T. S. Eliot,* London, 1948.
Rajan, B. (ed.): *T. S. Eliot / A Study of His Writings by Several Hands,* London,
   1947.
Unger, Leonard (ed.): *A Selected Critique,* New York, 1948.

Literary history and criticism:

Sidney, Sir Philip: *Defence of Poesie.*
Dryden, John: *Essay of Dramatic Poesy.*
Coleridge, S. T.: *Biographia Literaria.*
Arnold, Matthew: *Essays in Criticism, The Works of Matthew Arnold,* London, 1903,
   Vols. III—IV.

Foerster, N.: *American Criticism,* Boston, 1928.
Ransom, J. C.: *The New Criticism,* Norfolk, 1941.

Baker, D. Val: *Little Reviews 1914—1943,* London, 1943.
Brooks, V. W.: *New England: Indian Summer,* Cleveland 1946.
Evans, B. Ifor: *English Literature between the Wars,* London, 1948.
Grierson, H. J. C., and J. C. Smith: *A Critical History of English Poetry,* London, 1947.
Lanson, G., et P. Tuffrau: *Manuel illustré d'histoire de la littérature française,* Paris,
   1931.
Routh, H. V.: *English Literature and Ideas in the Twentieth Century,* London, 1948
   (1946).
Scarfe, Francis: *Auden and After,* London, 1947 (1942).

Berger, P.: *William Blake. Mysticisme et poésie,* Paris, 1907.
Bowra, C. M.: *The Heritage of Symbolism,* London, 1947 (1942).
— *The Background of Modern Poetry,* Oxford, 1946.
Michaud, Guy: *Message poétique du symbolisme,* I—III, Paris, 1947.
Quennell, P.: *Baudelaire and the Symbolists,* London, 1929.
Symons, Arthur: *The Symbolist Movement in Literature,* London, 1908 (1899).
Taupin, René: *L'Influence du symbolisme français sur la poésie américaine,* Paris, 1929.

Daiches, David: *Poetry and the Modern World,* Chicago, 1940.
— *Literature and Society,* London, 1938.
Dobrée, B.: *The Lamp and the Lute,* Oxford, 1929.
Leavis, F. R.: *New Bearings in English Poetry,* London, 1942 (1932).
Nicholson, N.: *Man and Literature,* London, 1945 (1943).
Wilson, Edmund: *Axel's Castle,* New York, 1931.

Bailey, Ruth: *A Dialogue on Modern Poetry,* Oxford, 1939.
Bradbrook, M. C.: "The Liturgical Tradition in English Verse", *Theology,* Jan. 1942.
Epstein, Jean: *La Poésie d'aujourd'hui,* Paris, 1921.
Gibbon, J. M.: *Magic of Melody,* London, 1933.
Graves, Robert: *Contemporary Techniques of Poetry,* London, 1925.
Housman, A. E.: *The Name and Nature of Poetry,* Cambridge, 1945 (1933).
Lewis, C. Day: *A Hope for Poetry,* Oxford, 1945 (1934).
— *The Poetic Image,* London, 1948 (1947).
MacNeice, Louis: *Modern Poetry,* Oxford, 1938.
Morgan, Charles: "Creative Imagination", *The Queen's Book of the Red Cross,* London, 1939.
Peacock, R.: *The Poet in the Theatre,* London, 1946.
Pound, Ezra: "Vorticism", *Fortnightly Review,* Sept. 1, 1914.
Read, Herbert: *Form in Modern Poetry,* London, 1932.
Roberts, Michael: Introduction to *The Faber Book of Modern Verse* (Roberts ed.), London, 1947 (1936).
Sitwell, Edith: *Aspects of Modern Poetry,* London, 1934.
— *A Poet's Notebook,* London, 1944.
Spender, S.: "The Crisis of Symbols", *The Penguin New Writing,* no. 19, 1944.
Treece, Henry: *How I See Apocalypse,* London, 1946.
Williams, Charles: *Poetry at Present,* Oxford, 1930.

General criticism:

Belgion, M.: *Our Present Philosophy of Life,* London, 1929.
— *The Human Parrot and Other Essays,* Oxford, 1931.
Benda, Julien: *Belphégor,* Paris, 1924 (1919).
— *La Trahison des clercs,* Paris, 1926.
Forster, E. M.: *Life and Letters,* London, 1929.
Hulme, T. E.: *Speculations,* London, 1924.
Huxley, Aldous: *On the Margin,* London, 1948 (1923).
Knickerbocker, W. S. (ed.): *Twentieth Century English,* New York, 1946.
Murry J. M.: *Aspects of Literature,* London, 1920.
— *The Problem of Style,* Oxford, 1922.
— *Countries of the Mind,* II, Oxford, 1931.
— *The Price of Leadership,* London, 1939.
Pound, Ezra: *Polite Essays,* London, 1937.
Sayers, Dorothy: *Unpopular Opinions,* London, 1946.

Philosophy, aesthetics, theology:

Aristotle: *The Works of* — (W. D. Ross, ed.), Vol. III, *De anima*, Oxford, 1931,
Vol. VIII, *Metaphysica* Oxford, 1908.
Lucretius: *De rerum natura*. Transl. W. H. D. Rouse, London, 1928 (1924).
Kierkegaard, S.: Samlede Værker (Drachmann, Heiberg, Lange edd.), Copenhagen,
1920. Vol. II, *Enten-Eller*. Vol. XI, *Sygdommen til Døden*. Vol. XIII,
Om min Forfatter-Virksomhed.
Meinong, A.: *Abhandlungen zur Erkenntnistheorie und Gegenstandstheorie*, Leipzig,
1913.
Bradley, F. H.: *Appearance and Reality*, 2nd ed., London, 1906.
— *The Principles of Logic*, 2nd ed., Oxford, 1922.
— *Ethical Studies*.
Santayana, G.: *The Philosophy of* — (I. Edman ed.), New York, 1936.
Wright, W. K.: *A History of Modern Philosophy*, New York, 1941.

Arnold, Matthew: *The Works of* — Vol. VII, *Literature and Dogma*, London, 1903.
Brémond, Henri: *Prière et poésie*, Paris, 1926.
— *La Poésie pure*, Paris, 1926.
Croce, Benedetto: *Grundriss der Ästhetik*, Aut. deutsche Ausgabe von Theodor Poppe,
Leipzig, 1913.
Heppenstall, R.: "Poetry and *Existenz*", *Humanitas*, Winter 1948.
MacGregor, G.: *Aesthetic Experience in Religion*, London.
Maritain, J.: *Art et scolastique*, 3rd ed., Paris, 1935.
— *Réponse à Jean Cocteau*, Paris, 1926.
— *Frontières de la poésie*, Paris, 1935.
— *Humanisme intégral*, new ed., Paris, 1947.
Maritain, J., et Raïssa: *Situation de la poésie*, Paris, 1938.
Ording, Hans: *Estetikk og kristendom*, Oslo, 1929.
Richards, I. A.: *Principles of Literary Criticism*, 2nd ed., London, 1926.
— *Practical Criticism*, London, 1929.
— *Science and Poetry*, London, 1935 (1926).
— *Mencius on the Mind*, London, 1932.
Valéry, P.: *Poésie et pensée abstraite*, Oxford, 1939.

Hyde, Lawrence: *The Prospects of Humanism*, London, 1931.
Russell, B.: *What I Believe*, London, 1925.
Knight, G. Wilson: *The Christian Renaissance*, Toronto, 1933.
Kaye-Smith, S.: *Anglo-Catholicism*, London, 1925.
Oldham, J. H., etc.: *The Church Looks Ahead*, London, 1941.
Doctrine in the Church of England. The Report of the Commission on Christian Doctrine
Appointed by the Archbishops of Canterbury and York in 1922. London, 1938.

Deussen, Paul: *Sechzig Upanishad's des Veda*, Leipzig, 1897.
Prabhavananda and Isherwood (transl.): *Bhagavad-Gita*, London, 1947.
Warren, H. C.: *Buddhism in Translations*, Cambridge, Mass., 1896.
Augustine, Saint: *Confessions*. Transl. E. B. Pusey, London, 1945.
Ballou, R. O.: *World Bible*, New York, 1944.
Huxley, Aldous: *The Perennial Philosophy*, London, 1946.

Frazer, Sir James: *The Golden Bough*, IV, London, 1907.
Weston, Jessie: *From Ritual to Romance*, New York, 1941 (1920).
Cailliet, E., et J.-A. Bédé: *Le Symbolisme et l'âme primitive*, Paris, 1932.

Key to Abbreviations.

A&R   : F. H. Bradley: *Appearance and Reality*.
AC   : Edmund Wilson: *Axel's Castle*.
AeS   : Jacques Maritain: *Art et scolastique*.
ASG   : Eliot: *After Strange Gods*.
ATSE   : F. O. Matthiessen: *The Achievement of T. S. Eliot*.
BN   : Eliot: "Burnt Norton".
CRI   : *The Criterion* (Eliot ed.).
CRICOM   : Eliot: Commentary in *The Criterion*.
DS   : Eliot: "The Dry Salvages".
EAM   : Eliot: *Essays Ancient and Modern*.
EC   : Eliot: "East Coker".
FR   : Eliot: *The Family Reunion*.
F3   : *Focus Three*. B. Rajan (ed.): *T. S. Eliot. A Study of His Writings by Several Hands*.
GITA   : *Bhagavad-Gita*, transl. by Prabhavananda and Isherwood.
HA   : *The Harvard Advocate*.
HM   : Eliot: *The Hollow Men*.
LG   : Eliot: "Little Gidding".
LIS   : *The Listener*.
MC   : Eliot: *Murder in the Cathedral*.
MP   : Eliot: "The Metaphysical Poets".
MUS   : Eliot: *The Music of Poetry*.
NDC   : Eliot: *Notes towards the Definition of Culture*.
NEW   : *The New English Weekly*.
NPB   : Eliot: "A Note on Poetry and Belief", *The Enemy*, Jan. 1927.
PP   : Eliot: "Poetry and Propaganda", W. D. Zabel (ed.): *Literary Opinion in America*, New York, 1937.
RAN   : J. C. Ransom: *The New Criticism*.
SE   : Eliot: *Selected Essays*.
SELCR   : Leonard Unger (ed.): *A Selected Critique*.
SFP   : Eliot: "The Social Function of Poetry", *Adelphi*, July/Sept. 1945.
SW   : Eliot: *The Sacred Wood*.
TIT   : Eliot: "Tradition and the Individual Talent".
TLS   : *The Times Literary Supplement*.
UPC   : Eliot: *The Use of Poetry and the Use of Criticism*.
WL   : Eliot: *The Waste Land*.
4Q   : Eliot: *Four Quartets*.
4QR   : R. Preston: *"Four Quartets" Rehearsed*.

There are a few more conservative abbreviations in the footnotes which should need no explanation. Where no author is given in the footnotes, either Eliot is meant, or an author mentioned in the text.

Printed November 1949.